Defending the West

By the same author

FIRST JOURNEY Published 1964 by
William Heinemann (London)
and by Random House (New York)

THE SIX DAY WAR (written jointly with author's father,
Randolph S. Churchill)
Published 1967 by William Heinemann
(London) and by Houghton Mifflin
(Boston)

DEFENDING
THE WEST

WINSTON S. CHURCHILL

ARLINGTON HOUSE/PUBLISHERS
Westport, Connecticut

First published in Great Britain in 1981
by Maurice Temple-Smith Ltd.
Gloucester Mansions, Cambridge Circus,
Charing Cross Road, London WC2 8 HH

Library of Congress Cataloging in Publication Data

Churchill, Winston S. (Winston Spencer), 1940-
    The defense of the West.
    1. World politics—1945-   2. Balance of
power. I. Title.
D843.C56   327.1′12   81-3531
ISBN 0-8700-522-7   AACR2

Photoset by Robcroft Ltd., London.
Production services by Cobb-Dunlop, Inc. (U.S.A.)
Manufactured in the United States of America
by the Maple-Vail Company.

9 8 7 6 5 4 3 2

Contents

Preface

PART ONE: AMERICA SUPREME
1   Victory Betrayed   17
2   Supremacy Lost   26

PART TWO: THE SOVIET CHALLENGE
3   The Detente Offensive   39
4   The Soviet War Machine   57

PART THREE: THE WEST VULNERABLE
5   America Threatened   73
6   Crisis in Europe   87
7   Britain: The Unsinkable Carrier?   102

PART FOUR: THE GLOBAL THREAT
8   Admiral Gorshkov's Navy   123
9   The Soviet Master Plan   137
10   The Energy Treasure-House   148
11   Afghanistan and After   162
12   Africa Invaded   173
13   China: The Waking Giant   190

PART FIVE: TOWARDS THE CATACLYSM
14   Deterrence and Subversion   203
15   The Soviet Empire Quakes   224
16   A Strategy for Freedom   236

Maps

The Rape of Europe 1945-48   22
The Balance of Conventional Forces in Central Europe 1980   93
The Soviet Empire 1980   141
Worldwide Oil Flow 1979   142

Figures

1 US and Soviet strategic launchers 1965-80   27
2 US and Soviet submarine-launched ballistic missiles 1965-80   47
3 US and Soviet inter-continental ballistic missiles 1965-80   48
4 US and Soviet armed forces manpower 1965-80   63
5 US and Soviet strategic warheads 1966-86   77
6 Soviet tanks in Eastern Europe and Western Military   98
     Districts of the USSR 1970-80
7 UK: expenditure on defence and social security 1955-80   115
8 US: expenditure on defence and social services 1960-77   116

Tables

1 US and Soviet major surface ships and submarines 1965-80   133
2 US/Soviet naval balance 1965-80   134
3 Percentages of world reserves of selected minerals in the   178/9
     USSR and Africa south of the equator

Photographs

Backfire bomber   90
Soviet Delta III submarine   125
Tomahawk cruise missile   205
Trident I missile   206

To

Minnie

At this day
When a Tartarean darkness overspreads
The groaning nations; when the impious rule,
By will or by established ordinance,
Their own dire agents, and constrain the good
To acts which they abhor; though I bewail
This triumph, yet the pity of my heart
Prevents me not from owning, that the law,
By which mankind now suffers, is most just.
For by superior energies; more strict
Affiance with each other; faith more firm
In their unhallowed principles; the bad
Have fairly earned a victory o'er the weak,
The vacillating, inconsistent good.

The Excursion, William Wordsworth

I am indebted to Her Majesty Queen Elizabeth
the Queen Mother for the lines of Wordsworth
reproduced above. On 18 March 1940,
Her Majesty transcribed these words on notepaper
from the Royal Lodge, Windsor, and sent them to
Winston Churchill, at the time First Lord of the
Admiralty and six weeks later to be Prime Minister.
This letter, which is now framed and enjoys pride
of place among family memorabilia at my Sussex
home, bears a note written in Her Majesty's hand:
'I suppose written when Europe was terrified of
Napoleon?'

Acknowledgements

First and foremost I wish to express my thanks to Her Majesty Queen Elizabeth, the Queen Mother for so graciously granting me permission to publish the words of William Wordsworth reproduced on Page viii, together with Her Majesty's own hand-written comment.

I am especially indebted to my Personal secretary Mrs Barbara Ryan and my House of Commons secretary Mrs Gillian Chruscikowska whose assistance in the typing and preparation of this book has been invaluable. I am also most grateful for the assistance of Mrs Barbara Miles in the preparation of the typescript and graphs for the publishers.

My special thanks are due to Dr J. B. Poole and his staff in the Scientific Section of the House of Commons Library for their unfailing courtesy and helpfulness in the provision of factual data and statistics. I wish further to express my appreciation of the great assistance of Mr Roger Hertz of Denver, Colorado in the research for this work and the preparation of data for the graphs and table included in it. My thanks are also due to Major Bob Elliot and his colleagues at the International Institute for Strategic Studies in London for their kindness in furnishing statistical data, relating to the East-West balance of military power.

It would be remiss of me if I did not express my special thanks to my English publisher Mr Maurice Temple Smith for his original proposal that I should write a book on this theme which happily coincided with my own wish to place before the public the gravity of the situation confronting the Western democracies today.

Finally and most of all I am indebted to my wife Minnie for the very great encouragement that she has given me in the preparation of this work in which, as with my previous books, she has assisted in the typing as well as in the provision of most valuable advice and criticism; also to my children Randolph, Jennie and Marina who, together with their younger brother Jack doing his best to be helpful, spent long hours collating photocopies of the typescript for the publishers and marking corrections.

Winston S. Churchill

*'Trust us, Comrades, for by 1985, as a
consequence of what we are now achieving with 'Detente',
we will have achieved most of our objectives in Western
Europe. . . . And the shift in the correlation of forces
will be such that, come 1985, we will be able to exert
our will wherever we need to.'*

Leonid Brezhnev, addressing Warsaw Pact heads of
government meeting in 1973

PREFACE

Already two generations have come of age who either never knew or, like myself born as a 'Blitz Baby' in wartime London, have only the haziest childhood recollections of the Second World War. Of all the generations this century, ours have been the first that have not had to face the supreme ordeal of world war, though it is a blessing for which few of us spare so much as a passing thought as we rush through our daily lives. Were we to pause a moment for reflection, we could not fail to recognise that everything we do, however important it might appear in the instant, would cease to have any relevance or meaning should the peace and freedom that form the cornerstones of our lives be imperilled. If either one were to be lost all our hopes for the future and our children's future would turn to ashes.

For a quarter of a century after the end of the war in Europe, the peoples of the Western democracies lived secure under the protection of the United States, which enjoyed at first a monopoly then, for many years, supremacy in nuclear weapons. Brush-fire wars might rage in Africa, Asia or the Middle East, occasionally reaching the level of a major, albeit localised, conventional war as in Korea or Vietnam, but throughout the intervening period the idea that the Western world itself might ever again be involved in a serious war – a Third World War that would engulf and potentially destroy us all – was so remote as to seem absurd except in a brief moment of crisis triggered by the Cuban missile crisis of 1962. If there was any serious danger it arose, in the judgment of many, more from the likelihood of military bungling (Western, of course), as epitomised by the fictional Dr Strangelove, that would unleash a nuclear holocaust by incompetence, than from any possibility of a deliberate attack by a power bent on world domination.

How far we have come from those halcyon days! It is of course true that the Soviet Union has, since the end of the Second World War, enjoyed a vast preponderance over the West in conventional military power. Until now, however, this has been offset by the overwhelming supremacy of the United States in the strategic and theatre-nuclear field. But today the Soviet Union has established a decisive advantage in these fields too and has become the most formidable military power the world has ever seen.

With this new-found might has come a new brazenness and arrogance in the Soviet Union's relations with the West and in its dealings with the independent nations of the Third World. For those who still clung to fond illusions as to the true nature and intentions of those enthroned in the Kremlin, the Soviet invasion of Afghanistan over Christmas 1979 and the subsequent brutal occupation of that unfortunate country proved a rude awakening. Too many – not only individuals but governments as well – have since resumed their slumbers, following words of reassurance from the Soviet leadership about as substantial as those given by Adolf Hitler forty years before as, one after another, the Rhineland, Austria, Czechoslovakia and Poland were swallowed up by Nazi Germany. However, in spite of insistent official reassurances that 'Detente is still alive' and that, at all events, the Western allies remain militarily strong, among ordinary people throughout the Western democracies there is a deep and growing sense of unease, even anxiety. For the first time in my lifetime, millions of people who hitherto have had a carefree attitude towards the world are asking themselves: 'Could it happen again? Could there be another world war which, in the nuclear age, might lead to the ultimate catastrophe, the ending of human life on this planet?'

It is worrying that such a question should be asked at all. It is even more disturbing that, up to the time of writing, the Western world has been devoid of the strong, resolute leadership that alone might allay these all too well-founded fears. In recent years the West, attributing to others its own spirit of goodwill, has been sliding fecklessly but remorselessly towards the cataclysm. Even now it is not too late for mankind to pull back from the brink, but only if, by a supreme effort of moral revival, the Western democracies are able to demonstrate resolve and unity in the face of the growing Soviet menace to freedom and world peace.

Winston S. Churchill
20 January 1981

Part I

AMERICA SUPREME

Chapter One

VICTORY BETRAYED

In the hour of victory as the last survivors of the Nazi concentration camps were being liberated, at the end of the Second World War, there was an assumption in the West, whose peoples had endured, suffered and sacrificed so much, that they had won freedom, not for themselves alone, but for all mankind. Alas, it was not to be. At the very moment of triumph, the wartime alliance of Britain, the United States and the Soviet Union was betrayed.

Following the liberation of Italy, France and the Low Countries, the British and American Allied Forces advanced into Germany from the west. Meanwhile the Soviet Red Army occupied all of Eastern and most of Central Europe. The Russian troops, who came in the guise of liberators to free the oppressed millions from the Nazi scourge, had in reality come as invaders and enslavers themselves.

The tragedy that befell the peoples of Eastern Europe, not least the Polish nation in whose defence Britain had drawn the sword against Nazi Germany in September 1939, can be directly traced to the decisions reached by the Great Powers – Britain, the United States and the Soviet Union – in those fateful days of early February 1945 when Churchill, Roosevelt and Stalin met at Yalta, in the Crimea of the Soviet

Union, to plan the aftermath of victory. It was the last time that the three great war leaders were to meet, for within two months President Roosevelt was to die. Already at Yalta the President's frailty was noticeable and Churchill remarked in his war memoirs: 'His face had an air of transparency, an air of purification and often there was a far-away look in his eyes.'

As the hour of victory approached, the problems of peace loomed greater and more intractable than the problems of war. The President's tenuous grip on life weakened the bargaining position of the two Western Allies at a crucial moment when Stalin's Red Army had already 'liberated' vast tracts of Eastern Europe, including Poland.

At the very first meeting, Roosevelt announced that once the war was won, the United States would be unwilling to keep a large army in Europe and that any American occupation would therefore be limited to two years. Churchill was alarmed and recorded in his war memoirs: 'Formidable questions rose in my mind. If the Americans left Europe, Britain would have to occupy single-handed the entire Western portion of Germany. Such a task would be far beyond our strength.' It cannot be doubted that this proclaimed weakness in the Western position was welcome news to Marshal Stalin.

However, the critical weakness of the Yalta agreement arose less from the terms of the agreement itself, than from the fact that it depended entirely on the good faith of the Russians, when they pledged their full support for the right of the peoples of Eastern Europe to self-determination and national independence. Special attention was devoted to the case of Poland, which was discussed at length throughout the conference. Stalin was insistent that the Communist Lublin Committee, installed by the Red Army as it had driven the Nazis westward through Poland in recent months, be recognised by the other Allies as the government of Poland. Churchill and Roosevelt, however, supported the claims of the Polish Government-in-exile which had been established in London at the beginning of the war and which commanded the loyalty of the 150,000 Polish soldiers who were fighting alongside the Allies on the Western front. But with the Red Army in control of Poland, the two Western leaders were not in a strong bargaining position and had no choice but to accept, albeit with misgivings, Stalin's undertaking that the Lublin Committee would be expanded to incorporate 'democratic' elements, drawn from all parties including Poles abroad, and his promise that free elections, based on universal suffrage, would be held in Poland 'within one month' to elect an independent and democratic Polish government.

With the benefit of hindsight it is difficult to understand how the British and American leaders could have allowed the fate of the more than 100 million people of Eastern Europe to depend on the word of the Russian dictator. The Lublin Committee was never 'democratised' to form the promised Provisional Polish Government and no free elections were ever held. Bearing in mind not only the, then unconfirmed, reports of the massacre of over 14,000 Polish soldiers by the Russian NKVD, the even more notorious forerunner of the KGB, in the forests of Katyn in 1940 and, above all, Stalin's brutal and cynical betrayal of the non-Communist Polish resistance to the Nazis in the summer of 1944, the warning signs should have been clear. At that time, after a remarkable advance of 250 miles in five weeks, in which they annihilated no fewer than twenty-five German divisions, the Soviet Red Army had reached and crossed the river Vistula immediately to the east of Warsaw. Following repeated calls by Radio Moscow for all anti-Nazi forces in Warsaw to rise against the Germans who continued to hold the city, General Bor-Komorowski, the Commander of the Polish Underground Army, had given the order for a general uprising on 1 August 1944.

The tale of the martyrdom of Warsaw is one of heroism and of betrayal on a grand scale. Forty thousand non-Communist Polish resistance fighters, with reserves of food and ammunition for only seven to ten days' fighting and armed with nothing heavier than rifles, took on five Nazi divisions including the crack Hermann Goering Division, hastily rushed in from Italy, as well as two SS divisions. The Russians not only made no attempt to continue their advance towards Warsaw or to support the Polish resistance with supplies of food and ammunition, but even categorically refused permission for British and American aircraft to land and refuel at Soviet fields, which alone would have enabled them to make supply drops on Warsaw, which otherwise was beyond their range. Churchill was so appalled that he even considered interrupting British convoys carrying war materials to the Soviet Union. Roosevelt, however, was adamant. He was not prepared to force the issue with the Russians.

In consequence, after two months of heroic resistance in the shattered ruins of Warsaw and of hand-to-hand fighting in the sewers beneath the city streets, the Nazis regained control of the city. Some 15,000 men and women of the Polish Underground Army had been killed and nearly 20,000 civilians of a population approaching one million had been massacred. No doubt Stalin had in mind that by assisting the Nazis to exterminate the non-Communist Polish resistance it would be easier for the Soviet Union subsequently to impose the pro-Moscow puppet Lublin Committee on Poland.

In the light of this brazen betrayal of Polish nationalist forces by the Russians only six months before, it is difficult to understand how Churchill and Roosevelt can have trusted anything the Soviet dictator promised, especially in relation to Poland. However, though it is easy to pinpoint the faults and weaknesses inherent in the Yalta agreement, it is hard to see how the interests of the peoples of Eastern Europe could have been safeguarded, given the strength of the dictum that 'Possession is nine-tenths of the Law.' The Soviet Red Army already had physical control of most of Eastern Europe.

Certainly Churchill never entertained any illusions about either the nature of Soviet Communism or the intent of its protagonists in the Kremlin – indeed it was something of which he was acutely aware and which troubled him deeply. Harold Macmillan the former British Prime Minister, has told me how one evening in Cairo, where Churchill had stopped off for preliminary discussions with President Roosevelt prior to their meeting with Marshal Stalin in Tehran in November 1943, he had accompanied the Prime Minister back to his villa beside the pyramids after a long day of discussions with the American President.

The hour was late [Macmillan recalls] but the Prime

Minister bade me sit down and join him in a glass of brandy. He brooded for a while and his thoughts appeared to be far away. Suddenly his eyes focused sharply on me and he addressed me in these words: 'Cromwell was a great man, wasn't he?' – 'Yes indeed, Prime Minister,' I replied, not quite sure where his train of thought would lead him. Then, after a pause he rejoined: 'But, obsessed with the power of Spain, he failed to observe the rise of France.' There was a further silence before he added with poignancy: 'Do you think they will say that of me?'

Already by 1942 – in fact as soon as the United States had entered the conflict – Churchill knew that it was only a matter of time before Hitler was defeated. While there may have been many who fell victim to Western wartime propaganda portraying Stalin as a defender of the cause of freedom and the popular leader of the Russian people, Churchill was the first to recognise that Soviet Russia could not be trusted, although in the heat of the battle, while ever conscious of the Soviet dictator's great crimes, he came to respect him as a war leader and even, at a personal level, to develop a certain affection towards his comrade-in-arms. But even then he saw more clearly than any other the mortal threat that the Soviet state would pose to the nations of Europe once the defeat of Hitler was accomplished.

Britain and the United States could undoubtedly have presented a more forceful and united position to the Soviets at Yalta, and especially in the weeks immediately following the conference when it was becoming clear that Stalin was doing nothing to fulfill his side of the bargain. The telegrams that passed between the Prime Minister and the President in March and early April show that Churchill was anxious to bring greater pressure to bear but the American Government did not believe this to be practicable. This lack of resolve was, no doubt, a reflection of Roosevelt's failing strength. His illness could not have come at a more inopportune moment for the fortunes of the peoples of Eastern Europe. With the death of

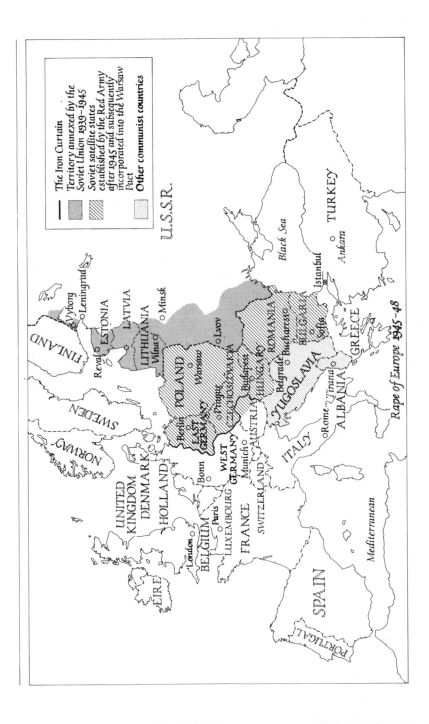

The Iron Curtain

Territory annexed by the Soviet Union 1939–1945

Soviet satellite states established by the Red Army after 1945 and subsequently incorporated into the Warsaw Pact

Other communist countries

U.S.S.R.

NORWAY

SWEDEN

FINLAND

Vyborg

Leningrad

ESTONIA

Reval

LATVIA

LITHUANIA

Vilna

Minsk

Lvov

POLAND

Warsaw

EAST GERMANY

Berlin

Prague

CZECHOSLOVAKIA

Budapest

HUNGARY

ROMANIA

Bucharest

BULGARIA

Sofia

Belgrade

YUGOSLAVIA

Istanbul

Ankara

TURKEY

GREECE

ALBANIA

Tirana

Rome

ITALY

Black Sea

UNITED KINGDOM

DENMARK

HOLLAND

London

BELGIUM

LUXEMBOURG

Paris

FRANCE

SWITZERLAND

AUSTRIA

Munich

WEST GERMANY

Bonn

EIRE

SPAIN

PORTUGAL

Mediterranean

Rape of Europe 1945–48

Roosevelt on 12 April and the dismissal from office of Churchill three months later in the general election of 5 July 1945, in the very hour of victory, the Western Allies were deprived of the two great leaders who had guided their destinies through the long ordeal of war to ultimate victory. With them passed much of the authority and respect, forged in the furnace of war, in their dealings with Stalin, an authority that Harry Truman and Clement Attlee could never regain.

More than thirty-five years after the end of the war in Europe, some 150 million peoples of once proud, independent states – Poland, Czechoslovakia, Hungary, Romania, Bulgaria, Latvia, Estonia, Lithuania and nearly half of Germany – remain within the Soviet colonial empire. Under the police-state rule of Communist puppet governments, which enjoy a strictly limited autonomy from Moscow and are backed in the case of all the countries incorporated within the Warsaw Pact, with the exception of Romania alone, by the physical presence on their soil of Soviet troops, the nations of Eastern Europe continue to be denied the right to freedom and self-determination.

Every attempt on the part of these subject nations to embark on an independent course has been met – as in the case of Hungary in 1956 and Czechoslovakia in 1968 – with the most ruthless repression by Soviet troops and armour. For many, as in the case of the Czechoslovaks, seven years of Nazi occupation have been followed by more than thirty-five years of Soviet occupation. In Czechoslovakia alone there are today no fewer than five Soviet divisions with more troops than Britain's entire Rhine Army and twice as many tanks. It is evident that they are not there in any sense as a defensive force, but as an army of occupation.

Looking at Eastern Europe today it is possible to gain some idea of what might have been the fate of Western Europe but for the might and protection of the United States and the birth of NATO.

The end of the war found Western Europe devastated and in ruins. The victorious British and Americans were exhausted and war-weary. By 1946 demobilisation was already in full swing in the West as armies, navies and air forces were slashed to but a fraction of their wartime strength, and the warriors, after six long years of testing in the crucible of war, set about re-adapting to civilian life. But it was not so in the case of the Soviet Union which maintained its forces largely intact. Thus, as half of Europe was being swallowed up and incorporated within an enlarged Soviet empire, the rest lay smouldering in ruins, devastated, defenceless and imperilled.

Churchill, out of office since the general election of July 1945, was acutely conscious that nothing stood between the Red Army and the Channel ports, and that all of Europe, not only the East, was menaced by Communist subversion master-minded in Moscow if not by actual invasion. He saw that the United States alone, with her new-found monopoly of nuclear power, possessed the key to the maintenance of freedom in Western Europe and that her might was such that she was in a position to safeguard it without so much as firing a shot.

It was under these circumstances that the former Prime Minister made his pilgrimage to Fulton, Missouri, in the American Mid-West in the spring of 1946. There on 5 March, at the feet of President Truman, who had travelled over 1,000 miles to be present for the occasion, he delivered his now-famous 'Iron Curtain' speech in which he warned that:

> From Stettin in the Baltic to Trieste in the Adriatic, an Iron Curtain has descended across the Continent. Behind that line lie all the capitals of the ancient states of Central and Eastern Europe. Warsaw, Berlin, Prague, Vienna, Budapest, Belgrade, Bucharest and Sofia, all these famous cities and the populations around them lie in what I must call the Soviet sphere. . . .

But his purpose was more than to warn. It was above all to persuade the United States not to repeat the mistake that she had made with such disastrous consequence after the First World War, when she had quit Europe and adopted a 'Fortress America' isolationism, but instead to lend the full weight of her authority and might to the protection of the Western democracies.

In three years Churchill's hope had become a reality. On 17 March 1948 the Brussels Treaty, pledging mutual assistance, was signed by Belgium, France, Luxembourg, the Netherlands and the United Kingdom.

Within weeks of the signing of the treaty, the Soviet Union blockaded Berlin. The blockade began in June 1948 and was to last 324 days; it was broken only by a massive airlift organised by the Western powers. So successful was the airlift that in the winter months of 1948/9 more supplies were flown into Berlin than had previously reached the city by rail, 2·3 million tons being flown in on 278,000 flights. At the height of the airlift the Royal Air Force had aircraft landing at RAF Gatow at the rate of one every three minutes day and night and the US Air Force had a parallel operation under way at USAF Tempelhof.

The Berlin blockade proved to be disastrously misconceived from the Soviet point of view. Evidently intended to test the commitment of the United States to a free and independent Europe, it had the immediate effect of involving the United States for the first time directly against Soviet expansionism in Europe, and undoubtedly proved a factor of great significance in the decision of the United States to accede to the North Atlantic Treaty Organisation – NATO –, which was established in Washington on 4th April 1949. The key element in this alliance, which initially included twelve and, ultimately fifteen nations, was the full participation of the United States.

Chapter Two

WESTERN SUPREMACY LOST

With the dawn of the 1980s the Soviet Union had established a decisive lead over the United States as a military power and, more specifically, it had overtaken the United States in every field of nuclear power, except in numbers of warheads alone.

In spite of more than a decade of effort by the West to achieve an effective strategic arms-control agreement, the Soviet Union had built up its nuclear arsenal from a position of inferiority to the point where, by 1980, it had over 40 per cent more strategic missiles than the United States.* Today, not only do Soviet missiles heavily outnumber the Americans', but they have a far heavier throw-weight or payload and, in consequence, warheads of far greater destructive capacity. The Soviets' SS-18 heavy missile with a throw-weight ten times greater than that of the US Minuteman has a 25-megaton warhead, fifty times the power of the latest Minuteman III (0·5MT),* and a staggering two thousand times the destructive power of the Hiroshima bomb (0·013MT).

With the accuracy of the newer Soviet missiles demonstrated to be the order of 300 yards and close to rivalling the accuracy of

* Source: *The Military Balance 1980/81*, published by the International Institute for Strategic Studies, London.

Fig 1 United States and Soviet strategic launchers (ICBMs and SLBMs) 1965–80

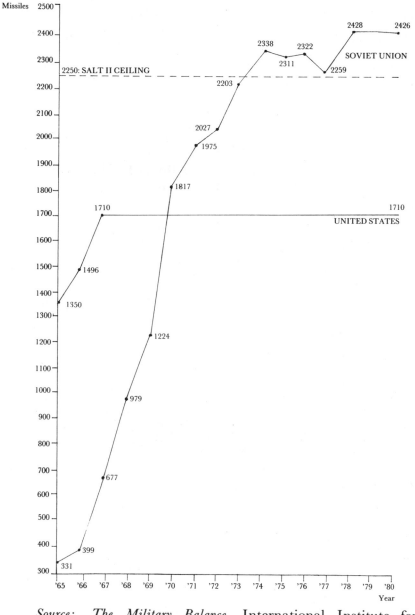

Source: *The Military Balance*, International Institute for Strategic Studies, London.

American missiles, it is only in numbers of warheads that the
United States, with an estimated 9,200*, retain a lead over the
Soviet Union, which already has close to 7,000 and is closing
the gap fast, as new multiple or MIRVed (multiple independently targetable re-entry vehicle) warheads replace the older
single warheads. On present trends the Soviet Union will overtake the United States even in this field by the mid-eighties.

This dramatic change, which has crept up on the Western
world almost unnoticed as a thief in the night, threatens to
undermine the whole basis of stability between East and West.
The Balance of Terror – the foundation of the two generations
of peace the world has enjoyed since the end of the Second
World War – is shifting decisively at the present time, with all
the dangers attendant on so momentous an event in a field
crucial to the fate of mankind. The consequences this shift will
hold for the relationship between the United States and the
Soviet Union, and its effect on the future of the Western allies,
as well as on the smaller nations of the world, have yet to be
fathomed. But it is certain that they will be far-reaching in the
extreme. A new assertiveness can already be detected in the
Soviet Union's behaviour towards other countries.

It had only been thirty-five years before that the nuclear age
had been born with the explosion, on 16 July 1945, of the first
atomic bomb at Alamogorda in the barren wastelands of
America's New Mexico desert. President Truman had
informed Churchill (who had ceased to be Prime Minister
following the British general election of July that year) of the
United States' dramatic breakthrough, with the cryptic signal:
BABIES SATISFACTORILY BORN (Winston S. Churchill, *The Second
World War, vol.VI.*, p.553). Had he been able to comprehend the
full horror of the new technology and the effect that it was so
shortly to have, especially on the young and those yet to be
born, it is unlikely that the President would have used so
unfortunate a metaphor in his telegram.

Barely three weeks later, on 6 August 1945, the morning
bustle of what promised to be a clear summer's day in the

* Source: *The Military Balance 1980/81*, published by the International
Institute for Strategic Studies, London.

Japanese coastal city of Hiroshima, a major shipbuilding and industrial centre, was scarcely disturbed by the drone high overhead of a lone American B-29 bomber. Its presence caused no immediate excitement or panic for several such aircraft had passed innocuously overhead in previous days on photo-reconnaissance missions. Suddenly a large object could be seen dropping from the belly of the aircraft. Long moments passed. The time was 8.15 a.m. All at once there was a flash of light brighter than any seen on earth before. In the same instant an intense, searing heat scorched all exposed to the light. Moments later a great fireball appeared over the city attaining a temperature of several million degrees centigrade and incinerating a vast area. This was followed almost immediately by the shockwave from the blast, which flattened the city, destroying 76,000 buildings up to five miles from the bomb's epicentre, and reducing them to a mass of smouldering rubble. In the course of the next hour a huge dark cloud, in a sinister and never-before-seen mushroom shape, billowed up to the stratosphere and hung menacingly over the city and its surrounding hills.

When in 1978, as part of a British parliamentary delegation to Japan, I visited Hiroshima I was informed that an estimated 125,000 human beings had died in the attack and in the days immediately following, from the blast, from burns or from nuclear radiation. But, in many ways, most horrific of all has been the death of an approximately equal number of people in the intervening years from leukaemia, cancer and other radiologically induced diseases that have caused tumours, gross deformities and a slow, lingering death. Today in a park, in the heart of the prosperous modern city that has been rebuilt from the ashes, stands the statue of a twelve-year-old girl – born shortly before the bomb and who died on her twelfth birthday – the silent representative of countless thousands of children whose lives were stricken and cut short by the explosion.

The decision of President Truman to authorise the dropping of the atom bomb on Hiroshima had been prompted by the failure of the Japanese Imperial Government to respond to the ultimatum issued on 26 July by the leaders of the Allied powers – the United States, Great Britain and the Soviet Union – meeting in conference at Potsdam, East Germany. When, three days after the Hioshima explosion, the Japanese Government had still not replied, the United States dropped a second bomb, this time on Nagasaki, where a further 100,000 were to die. The very next day Radio Tokyo announced that the Japanese Government was ready to accept the Allies' terms and on 14 August Japan surrendered unconditionally. The justification, at the time, for using the atom bomb rested in the Allies' conviction that without it the defeat of Japan would take at least a further year and cost upwards of a million Allied lives, a toll which, after six long years of costly sacrifice by Britain and three by America, the Allies were not prepared to contemplate. In retrospect, there can be little doubt that had it not been for the sacrifice of Hioshima and Nagasaki, demonstrating to the world the stark terror of the nuclear age, nuclear weapons would have been used in the years that have since intervened, possibly on a much larger scale and with far greater loss of life. It is difficult enough for the human mind to comprehend the power of a 25-megaton weapon but, given what we know of the physical devastation and human suffering caused by the first two nuclear weapons to be dropped in anger, we may at least gain some remote comprehension of what devastation might be wreaked by one two thousand times more powerful.

At that point the United States possessed a monopoly of nuclear power. The consequences for the whole world had Hitler's Germany or Stalin's Russia been the first to achieve the nuclear breakthrough do not even bear contemplation. Thereafter for a quarter of a century, the United States was to enjoy an unchallenged supremacy in the nuclear field, bestriding the world as a military colossus. The acquisition of this unique strength had the effect both of reassuring America's friends, who were able to shelter under her ample shield, and of intimidating any potential enemy. Above all, it invested the United States with an assurance and self-confidence that decisively coloured her outlook towards the rest of the world.

Churchill from the start saw clearly not only the true importance of the United States' bomb but, gifted with the prescience of a prophet before his time, he had a vivid awareness of the dangers it portended for the future. Addressing the Conservative Party Annual Conference in Llandudno on 9 October 1948 he declared bluntly to the people of Britain and of the world: 'I hope you will give full consideration to my words. I have not always been wrong. Nothing stands between Europe today and complete subjugation to Communist tyranny but the atomic bomb in American possession.' He went on to pose the rhetorical question:

> What will happen when they [the Soviets] get the atomic bomb themselves and have accumulated a large store? . . . No one in his sense can believe that we have a limitless period of time before us. We ought to bring matters to a head and make a final settlement. We ought not to go jogging along improvident, incompetent, waiting for something to turn up, by which I mean waiting for something bad for us to turn up. The Western nations will be far more likely to reach a lasting settlement, without bloodshed, if they formulate their just demands while they have the atomic power and before the Russian Communists have got it too.
> (Winston S. Churchill, *Europe United*, Cassell, London 1950, p.407)

Churchill's words of warning about the danger of allowing the Soviet Union to acquire nuclear weapons went as unheeded as his prewar warnings of the danger of Nazi rearmament. The Balance of Terror, under which mankind lives today and which is now in danger of getting out of balance, is the consequence. For just under a year later, on 23 September 1949, the Soviet Union exploded its own atomic bomb.

Although America's nuclear monopoly was broken and Britain and France soon afterwards joined the ranks of nuclear powers, the United States was to retain overwhelming supremacy in this field until at least the mid-seventies. The knowledge of this reality and its recognition by America's friends and foes alike endowed her with an ethos of strength and caused her to walk tall in the world. The presidencies of Truman, Eisenhower and Kennedy all provided a reflection of that strength, which was vividly demonstrated in the case of Truman by the United States' strong reaction to Soviet pressure both in respect of the Berlin blockade and the Korean War. Truman rightly saw both those actions as attempts by the Soviet Union to test the unity and resolve of the Western powers.

Barely a year after the Soviet abandonment of their blockade of Berlin – a tacit tribute to the success of the allied airlift – the Kremlin decided to test the Western allies' strength of purpose in another quarter of the globe. On 25 June 1950 North Korea, which was under the direct control of the Soviet Union, attacked South Korea. President Truman, learning of the attack the same day at his home in Independence, Missouri, reacted with decision and resolve. He recorded in his memoirs:

> The Republic of Korea needed help at once if it was not to be overrun. . . . I told my advisers that what was developing in Korea seemed to me like a repetition on a larger scale of what had happened in Berlin. The Reds were probing for weaknesses in our armour; we had to meet their thrust without getting embroiled in a world-wide war. I directed the Secretary of Defense to call General MacArthur on the scrambler phone and to tell him in person what my instructions were. He was to use air and naval forces to support the Republic of Korea with air and naval elements of his command but only South of the 38th parallel. He was also instructed to despatch the Seventh Fleet to the Formosa Strait.
> (H.S. Truman, *The Truman Memoirs: Years of Trial and Hope*,
> Doubleday, New York 1956, vol. . . p.337)

At an emergency meeting of the United Nations Security Council the very day after the attack, a resolution was approved condemning North Korean action and demanding the immediate withdrawal of their forces. The Security Council further called on all members of the United Nations to render every assistance in the execution of this resolution. Thus began the Korean War in which Britain, Canada, Australia and New Zealand all played an active part alongside the United States. In spite of the direct participation of Communist China on the side of North Korea, the Western allies, acting under the auspices of the United Nations, were able to inflict such punishment on the aggressors that by the spring of the following year, they had been driven back north of the 38th parallel. In July 1951 negotiations got under way with the Communists which subsequently led to the ending of hostilities on terms safeguarding the independence of South Korea.

The years that Harry Truman and General Eisenhower, who took over from him in 1953, held the presidency of the United States were years of strength and greatness for America. The Western allies might not always have seen eye to eye as was evident at the time of Nasser's seizure of the Suez Canal in 1956 and the subsequent fiasco of the Anglo–French operation to re-occupy the Canal Zone – about which the United States was neither consulted nor informed. However the Soviets had for the time being learnt their lesson and never throughout this period sought again openly to challenge the United States and her allies. Instead they confined themselves to the support of subversive Communist movements (including, among others, in Malaya, Aden and Cyprus, in each of which Britain fought successful anti-terrorist operations) and to an attempt to ride the tiger of Pan-Arab nationalism following their arms deal of 1955 with Nasser, cleverly disguised as a Czech/Egyptian agreement to allay Western concern.

Although the West felt powerless to intervene as Soviet tanks rolled into Budapest in the summer of 1956 to quell the Hungarian uprising within what had come to be regarded as the Soviet colonial empire, the world was left in no doubt of the determination of the United States elsewhere in the world. This was vividly demonstrated in 1958 when President Chamoun of the Lebanon was in danger of catching a political cold: within days, US Marines were landing on the beaches of Beirut to restore his authority.

Following in the wake of his two great and revered

predecessors, John F. Kennedy took up their theme in his inaugural address of 20 January 1961 with his clarion call to the peoples of the world:

> Let every nation know, whether it wishes us well or ill, that we shall pay any price, bear any burden, meet any hardship, support any friend, oppose any foe to assure the survival and success of liberty. This much we pledge – and more. To those old allies whose cultural and spiritual origins we share, we pledge the loyalty of faithful friends.

In his brief tenure as President of the United States – prematurely ended by the assassin's bullet in Dallas on that fateful day of 21 November 1963 – Kennedy, who at the very outset had to face the humiliating failure of the Bay of Pigs attack on Cuba, bungled by the CIA, went on in the autumn of 1962 to win his dramatic showdown with the Russians at the time of the Cuban missile crisis when they had attempted secretly to install in Cuba forty-two medium-range ballistic missiles (MRBMs) aimed at the United States. The Soviet missiles had a range of 1,100 nautical miles, bringing Washington, Dallas, Cape Canaveral, St Louis and all Strategic Air Command bases and cities in between within their radius of action (Theodore Sorensen, *Kennedy*, Hodder & Stoughton, London 1965, p.675).

In the days of tension of October 1962, during which the whole world held its breath as the two superpowers headed for a showdown that seemingly threatened to take mankind over the precipice and plunge it into the horrors of nuclear war, Kennedy played his cards with calmness and consummate deliberation. The fact that he held all the cards in no way detracts from the skill with which he played his hand, forcing the Soviets to make a humiliating climb-down, pack up their missiles and take them home.

Although it was not generally appreciated at the time, it is now clear that the balance of strategic military power remained firmly in the favour of the United States. In fact, the Soviet

Union then had no more than seventy inter-continental ballistic missiles (ICBMs). These were liquid-fuelled and took ten hours to make ready – longer than it would have taken bombers of the United States' Strategic Air Command to reach them from their forward bases and take them out on the ground (Henry Kissinger addressing a conference on 'NATO – The Next Thirty Years', Brussels, 1 September 1979).

But if Kennedy captured the imagination of millions around the globe and is remembered for his cool nerve and strong resolve over the Cuban missiles, he was also responsible for bequeathing to his successor the legacy of the US commitment in Vietnam.

In the spring of 1966, as I returned from a month's assignment reporting the war in Vietnam for *Look* magazine and the London *Sunday Express*, I passed through Washington where I consulted Mr James A. ('Scotty') Reston, the distinguished political columnist of the *New York Times*. I asked him if he could put his finger on the moment when US involvement in Vietnam, which had begun at a low level under Eisenhower as far back as 1954, became a commitment that could only be relinquished with either victory or loss of face. He reflected for a moment. Then he pronounced without equivocation:

> June 1961 – in the wake of President Kennedy's meeting with Khrushchev in Vienna. I happened to be the first newsman to see Kennedy after his meeting. He came into the room, slumped down on a sofa and hid his face in his hands, exclaiming: 'I have just had the most terrible experience of my life. That man thought that he could bully the President of the United States.' [Reston concluded:] Kennedy's immediate response was to return to Washington and increase tenfold from 1,500 to 15,000 the number of US military 'advisers' in Vietnam, to demonstrate his resolve to the Soviets. That was the moment the die was cast.

It is one of the ironies of history that the Vietnam commitment should have been made not in response to the situation in Vietnam itself, but arose from other pressures. Furthermore, though Kennedy could never have known it at the time, the Cuban missile crisis, barely a year later, was to provide the Kremlin with a demonstration of US resolve that they would not forget for a generation.

In the minds of those who still recall the exhilarating days of his presidency, Kennedy will be remembered not only for his decisive handling of the Cuban crisis, his successful conclusion of the Nuclear Test Ban Treaty with the Russians, banning all further atmospheric testing, and the tragic circumstances of his death in the prime of his vigour, but, above all, for the vision and hope that he imparted to millions far beyond the confines of the United States that the whole world could look forward to a brighter, happier future and that, meanwhile, those who were struggling against Communist subversion and aggression could depend on the United States as a friend and an ally that could be counted upon in a crisis. Despite the resolute and courageous leadership of Harry Truman and the high renown gained by General Eisenhower during the war as Supreme Allied Commander and, later, in his White House years, no holder of supreme office in the United States, either before or since, has touched the heart or captured the affection and trust of so many Europeans as Kennedy. For them, as for countless other non-Americans, he had come to be regarded as 'Our' President as well. The assassin's bullet in Dallas destroyed not merely a man but the dreams of an entire generation, which none has since been able to rekindle.

PART II

THE SOVIET
CHALLENGE

Chapter Three

THE DETENTE OFFENSIVE

The Cuban missile crisis, according to Prime Minister Harold Macmillan as he addressed the House of Commons shortly afterwards, represented 'one of the great turning points of history . . . a climactic period . . . even though its effects cannot be fully perceived now'. He added: 'Future historians looking back at 1962 may well mark this year as the time when the tide began to turn' (Theodore Sorensen, *Kennedy*, Hodder & Stoughton, London 1965, p.719).

Macmillan was more right than he could know. In retrospect the Cuban crisis may indeed be seen as the time when the tide began to turn, but, alas, not – as Macmillan evidently supposed – in the West's favour.

The confrontation of October 1962 was to have a profound effect on the policies of both superpowers, although it was to be several years before the consequences were to become fully apparent. Their reactions were opposite but complementary and were to weigh against the West in the long term. The United States, having confirmed her position of commanding strength, was to allow her power, self-confidence and resolve to become completely undermined. The Soviet Union, on the other hand, smarting from its defeat at the hands of President Kennedy, resolved to redress the weakness, both strategic and tactical, which had led to its public humiliation.

The first casualty was Premier Khrushchev himself who, two years later in October 1964, was dismissed from office with ignominy. In spite of his shoe-banging tantrums at the United Nations and his occasional bellicose threats to the West that, 'We will bury you', the smiling, joking 'Mr K.' as he was affectionately dubbed by the press, in fact took no decisive steps to build up Soviet military power, other than in seeking to redress the imbalance against the Soviet Union in strategic missiles. He gave every appearance of endeavouring, despite the corruption and inefficiencies of the Soviet system, to lead the Russian people towards a policy of butter rather than of guns. Indeed, during his years of power, the armed manpower of the Soviet Union was reduced by 1·75 million men from the more than 5 million it had stood at under Stalin.

The reaction of the United States in the wake of the Cuban missile crisis was markedly different. The American public, indeed the entire Western world, though relieved at the outcome, had been profoundly shocked at how apparently close to the brink of nuclear catastrophe the world had come. There was a general conviction that there had to be a better way of resolving the differences between East and West, other than in eyeball-to-eyeball showdowns, with each side threatening the other with nuclear destruction. It was from this determination that the first seeds of what was to be known as 'detente' were sown in the years ahead. The growing trauma for the people of America of seeing their country plunge ever deeper into the treacherous quagmire of South-East Asia was to provide fertile ground for those seeds to take root and flourish. By 1966 the US commitment in Vietnam had increased to 385,000 ground troops, a figure that was to escalate to 536,000 by 1968, when the conflict reached its peak. Meanwhile the Soviet Union, while taking care not to become directly involved with its own troops against the United States, ensured that the Viet-Cong and the North Vietnamese wanted for nothing in terms of military equipment, economic backing or diplomatic support. Indeed it was only this total commitment of a superpower providing tanks, MiG fighters, surface-to-air missiles and full logistic back-up that enabled the North Vietnamese to withstand the onslaught of United States' land, sea and air power over a ten-year period. America's enemies may have seemed to be Vietnamese peasants in black pyjamas wielding AK-47s, but the reality was that her forces were facing an extension of the Soviet war machine.

Unlike the Soviet Union, where, without either an electorate or a free press, the leadership is answerable to no one but themselves for their policies and their failures, the United States as a democracy can pursue only those policies that enjoy the support, or at least the acquiescence, of the American people.

Thus America's failure in Vietnam was as much due to the cracking of resolve within the United States itself, as it was to the stubborn resistance of the North Vietnamese and the Viet-Cong and the strong support of their Soviet ally.

Indeed US casualties from enemy action throughout the Vietnam War, even at their highest point in 1968 when they reached 14,589 (*Selected Manpower Statistics*, US Department of Defense), never attained the level of slaughter inflicted by Americans on each other on the highways of the United States where, in the same year, the death toll was 54,862 (*Vital Statistics of the United States*, US Department of Health, Education and Welfare, 1970).

The United States' growing involvement, increasing sacrifice and diminishing prospects of success, combined to polarise opinion and led to a cleavage within American society unknown since the days of the Civil War. I was present as a witness on Boston Common on Moratorium Day as more than one million Americans gathered solemnly to voice their protest – a protest re-echoed on countless university campuses and public squares throughout the United States. Here was evidence of an alienation from government policy that went far beyond the actions of a handful of draft-card burners and Left-wing political activists, among whom were numbered some Hollywood celebrities, who chose to identify themselves with the cause of Hanoi. As the tear-gas and Mace swirled around the delegates to the shambles that passed for the Democratic Convention in Chicago in 1968, and as two years later the bullets flew at Kent State University, Ohio, where four innocent students were shot dead by National Guardsmen during a demonstration to protest against US forces entering Cambodia in May 1970, the feelings of millions of otherwise sober Americans boiled over and even the confidence of traditionally rock-steady middle-America was shaken.

In February 1968 in the wake of the Viet-Cong's devastating Tet offensive, I was in New York and reported to the London *Evening News:*

> Coordinated attacks against 35 towns and cities of South Vietnam, the length and breadth of the country, struck a deep psychological blow at the United States. It made millions of Americans, already cynical and sceptical of the encouraging reports that have been sent back by their Commander-in-Chief, General William Westmoreland, and their Ambassador, Mr Ellsworth Bunker, have serious doubts whether the war could be won at all. A typical reaction to the President's verdict that last week's Viet-Cong attacks were 'a failure', came from a US Senator who declared: 'If that was a Viet-Cong failure, I'd hate to see a success'. In addition, the miles of television film and hundreds of horrifying photographs sent back daily showing the misery of the Vietnamese people and the suffering of young American soldiers, fresh from school, has gone far to shake the Americans' faith in the justice of their cause. That there is no glamour in modern warfare has never been more vividly demonstrated to a civilian population than it is to the American people day in, day out, through television and newspapers . . . . For how long can one go on destroying a country and desolating a people in order to save them? – This is the question being asked in America today.

The bitterness and strife engendered were epitomised for me in a conversation I had in the early hours of the morning with a Chicago policeman inside the Conrad Hilton Hotel which housed the delegates to the Democratic Convention which I had gone to report. Outside the hotel, dawn rose with a garish light over Grant Park where a few hundred youngsters, who had come to voice their opposition to government policy, lay on the ground, huddled together for warmth. Silhouetted against the dawn's early light, the outlines of National Guardsmen in full riot-gear and with weapons at the ready could be made out as they stood one yard apart surrounding the demonstrators on all four sides. Interspersed among the National Guardsmen, at intervals of a hundred feet, were Jeeps with machine-guns mounted on them, pointing at the forlorn and sorry bunch of unarmed protesters. Could this really be the Home of the Brave and the Land of the Free that I knew and loved? Surely it was some terrible nightmare? Inside the hotel I found myself in conversation with a policeman – a lean-faced Southerner – one of hundreds guarding the building. Referring to the rioting that had taken place around the hotel the night before (much of it caused by the unbridled brutality of Mayor Daley's police), I asked him if he could not imagine the possibility of his own son being among the demonstrators in Grant Park. His reply was brutal but summed up the intensity of feeling the whole of the Vietnam issue had aroused 'Man!' he answered in his Southern drawl, 'if any son of mine was out there with those kids, I would go and bust his head open first of all of them!'

Faced with these, for the most part, middle-class youngsters who, having enjoyed all the benefits of a privileged background and college education, appeared to be spitting on all the values dear to middle-class America to which the poor, for the most part, lower-class police aspired, the latter's reaction was nothing other than to beat, beat, beat. Among other observers of the Democratic Convention, my colleague Stephen Barber of the London *Sunday Telegraph* and I both fell victim to the flail of police 'night-sticks' and 'black-jacks' (lead coshes cased in leather) in the melee of the demonstration.

Richard Nixon succeeded to the presidency of the United States in January 1969 and, reflecting the mood of the nation, the new administration set in train the process of disengagement from Vietnam contriving to keep 'loss of face' to a minimum. Talks opened in Paris with the North Vietnamese and representatives of the Viet-Cong but, while negotiations dragged on inconclusively for many months, the Communists were hard at work consolidating their position on the ground and it was not until 27 January 1973 that a peace agreement was signed, six months after the United States' unilateral withdrawal. Dr Henry Kissinger, Nixon's National Security Adviser, sought to invoke the aid of the Soviet Union in extricating America from Indo-China by getting the Russians to lean on their Vietnamese allies to exercise restraint. Kissinger pressed for what was colloquially called 'convent time' – by which was meant that there should be a decent interval between the departure of the last GI from Vietnam and the rape by North Vietnamese forces of the first nun in a South Vietnamese convent. How successful Kissinger was in his goal may be judged from the fact that the withdrawal of US ground forces was completed by August 1972 (Roger Parkinson, *Encyclopaedia of Modern War*, Routledge & Kegan Paul, London 1977, p.174), yet nearly three years were to pass before the North Vietnamese forces and the Viet-Cong launched their final offensive leading to the fall of Saigon and the toppling of the Thieu regime in April 1975.

The Vietnam commitment and, above all, the failure of that commitment, shattered America's traditional self-confidence and brought about a decisive change in the mood of the nation that, for a generation since the Second World War, had seen itself as the champion of the cause of freedom in the face of the growing menace of totalitarian Soviet power. Now the overriding concern of the American people became the avoidance of all commitment, let alone confrontation, anywhere in the world. The United States had had enough, for the time being, of being the world's policeman. Others, it was suggested, could take on that role if they felt so strongly about it. But who? The reality was that the United States alone, as the only superpower in the Western camp, was capable of dealing with the Soviet Union on equal terms. From there it was not a big step for many Americans to persuade themselves that there were, at the end of the day, no basic differences between the two superpowers that could not be settled by dialogue and negotiation. Of course it was recognised that there were basic differences in the economic and social organisation of the two countries but, given goodwill – a key ingredient that was assumed to exist on both sides – there was a general conviction that outstanding matters between East and West might be resolved reasonably between reasonable men. Thus was born the era of detente.

The Kremlin was not slow to grasp the significance of this dramatically changed mood and did all it could to encourage it. Neither the Soviet Union's brazen invasion of Czechoslovakia, bringing to an abrupt end the Czech 'Spring' of 1968 and with it the fond illusions of the Czechoslovak peoples that they might be allowed to create 'Socialism with a Human Face', nor even the subsequent brutal repression of those courageous patriots who, with their bare hands, sought to prevent the advance of the Soviet tanks, was allowed to interrupt the growing dialogue between the two superpowers, except for the briefest period.

A new era in East-West relations began. If, for the West, the forties had been the 'Decade of Victory', the fifties the 'Decade of Supremacy' and the sixties the 'Decade of Retreat', the seventies were heralded as the 'Decade of Detente'. Not only the United States, but the West as a whole, entered into the spirit of things with enthusiasm. Talks were embarked upon aimed not only at curbing the strategic arms race between the two superpowers, but also at reducing tension in Central Europe, through significant cuts in the concentrations of tanks and manpower facing each other across the Iron Curtain border. It was hoped that by removing the possibility of a surprise attack by either side, the danger of war would be reduced. While negotiations on conventional arms reduction, known as the Mutual Balanced Force Reduction (MBFR) talks, were to involve all the Western allies, the Strategic Arms Limitation Talks (SALT) took place exclusively between the two superpowers. It was a time of uncertainty and unease for the NATO alliance and, on occasion, it even appeared to some in Europe that the United States administration placed a higher priority on its new-found relationship with the Soviet Union than on its traditional partnership with its NATO allies.

In November 1969, barely a year after the Soviet invasion of Czechoslovakia, the SALT talks began in Helsinki, leading to the signing of the SALT I agreement in Moscow on 26 May 1972. By its terms the United States and the USSR undertook that for a five-year period, strategic offensive weapons would be limited, in the case of the United States, to 710 submarine-launched ballistic missiles (SLBMs) in 44 submarines and 1,054 land-based inter-continental ballistic missiles (ICBMs). The Soviet Union, on the other hand, was to be allowed no fewer than 950 SLBMs in 62 submarines and a total of 1,410 ICBMs.

A bizarre element of the SALT I agreement, not to put too fine a point on it, was that under its terms the United States conceded that the Soviet Union should be entitled to 240 more SLBMs and 356 more ICBMs than the United States – a margin of 34 per cent in each case and far more than justified by any need to offset the temporary US advantage in multiple warheads (MIRVs) or the greater size of its ageing and increasingly vulnerable force of subsonic bombers. The SALT process was not merely a license to build – it proved a positive incentive to do so. Far from ending, or even putting a brake on, the strategic arms race – the hope of all in the West – the SALT negotiations and agreement can, in retrospect, be seen to have acted, on the contrary, as a spur. The fact that the United States added not a single missile to its strategic inventory between 1967 and 1980 did nothing to persuade the Kremlin to exercise any comparable restraint.

The naiveté of the Western governments and negotiators was matched only by the calculating cynicism of their Soviet counterparts. No sooner was the SALT I agreement signed than the Kremlin launched a test programme of an entire new generation of four ICBM systems, the SS-16, SS-17, SS-18 and SS-19 missiles. This massive strategic build-up was to give the Soviet Union initially parity and, ultimately, strategic superiority over the United States. Simultaneously they pressed ahead with the development of a mobile intermediate-range ballistic missile (IRBM), the SS-20 (identical to the inter-continental-range SS-16 but without the first-stage booster) and of the Backfire supersonic nuclear strike-bomber which, together, were to eliminate entirely NATO's advantage in strategic and theatre-nuclear weaponry in Europe. By the end of the seventies, the Soviet Union had not only overtaken the United States as a strategic nuclear power but had gained a

Fig 2 United States and Soviet submarine-launched ballistic missiles (SLBMs) 1965–80

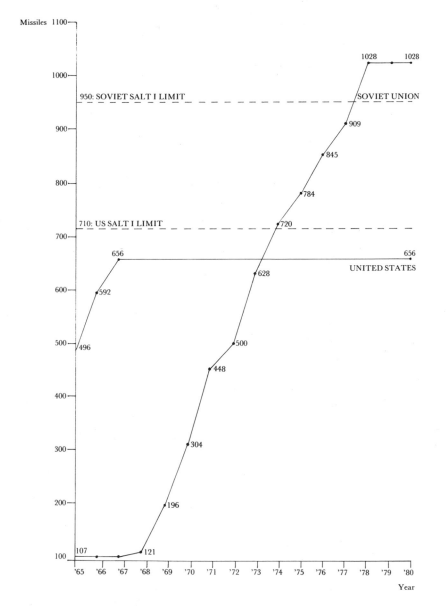

Source: The Military Balance, International Institute for Strategic Studies, London.

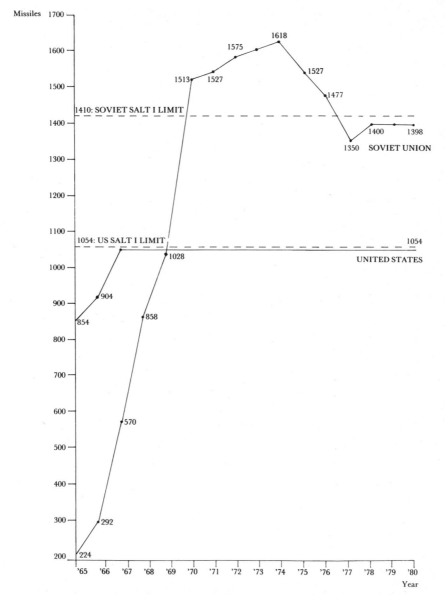

Fig 3 United States and Soviet inter-continental ballistic missiles (ICBMs) 1965–80

Source: The Military Balance, International Institute for Strategic Studies, London.

lead of more than 3·5:1 in theatre-nuclear systems in Europe.

An indication of the momentum of Soviet strategic construction is given by the International Institute for Strategic Studies in *The Military Balance 1980–1981*, which points out that:

> Replacement of a portion of the SS-11 inventory by the SS-17 also appears to have been completed. More than half the Soviet ICBM force is now less than ten years old. Within the IRBM force, the SS-4 is being replaced at a rate of *one every five days*, [author's emphasis] which is slightly more rapid than earlier deployments of one every seven days suggested. There is no indication of the fate of the missiles withdrawn, but the storage of at least a proportion of these ICBM/IRBM is considered probable.

In the same way that President Roosevelt had allowed himself to be flattered by Stalin at Yalta into believing that he could handle the Russians best on his own, pushing Churchill to one side in the negotiations, so, evidently, in his dealings with the Soviets Henry Kissinger regarded the principal allies of the United States at times more as an encumbrance than an asset.

It is not an everyday occurrence for a political figure publicly to admit the errors of his ways, though Sir Winston Churchill did have to agree that he had been forced on more than one occasion to eat his own words, which, he added impishly, 'I have on the whole found to be a most nourishing diet.' However Dr Kissinger, in a recantation as profound as Dr Spock's belated discovery of spanking being desirable in the upbringing of children, the former National Security Adviser astonished a NATO conference in Brussels on 1 September 1979 with the frankness with which he looked back on the period during which he, more than anyone else, had been responsible for the conduct of US foreign policy. He confessed:

> The amazing phenomenon about which historians will ponder is that all this [dramatic growth of Soviet strategic power since the mid-sixties] has happened without the United States attempting to make any significant effort to

rectify that state of affairs. One reason was that it was not easy to rectify. But another reason was the growth of a school of thought to which I, myself, contributed . . . which considered that strategic stability was a military asset and in which the amazing theory developed, i.e. historically amazing, that vulnerability contributed to peace and invulnerability contributed to the risk of war. . . . *It cannot have occurred often in history that it was considered an advantageous military doctrine to make your own country deliberately vulnerable* [author's emphasis].

Dr Kissinger concluded: 'Now we have reached that situation so devoutly worked for by the arms control community: we are indeed vulnerable.'

At the same time as the SALT I agreement was signed, an additional treaty was entered into limiting anti-ballistic-missile (ABM) systems in each country to two sites with one hundred defensive missiles at each. Of this agreement Kissinger reflected in his remarks in Brussels:

Against all evidence we were told that the ABM would ruin the chances of arms-control. . . . the fact was Kosygin in 1967 told President Johnson that the idea of not engaging in defence was one of the most ridiculous propositions that he had ever heard. By 1970, when we had an ABM programme – however inadequate – it was the only subject the Soviet Union was willing to discuss with us in SALT. When we gave up the B-1 [supersonic bomber] we asked the Soviets to make a reciprocal gesture. We have yet to see it. . . .

Dr Kissinger's comments are reinforced by the experience of the distinguished American diplomat Averell Harriman, Roosevelt's personal wartime envoy to Churchill and Stalin and a former US Ambassador to Moscow who, in the course of the seventies, had several lengthy meetings with President Brezhnev. Brezhnev repeatedly expressed concern to him at the intention of the United States to build the B-1 long-range supersonic bomber and made clear that if the United States decided to go ahead with the project, the Soviet Union would have no choice but to build its own equivalent. There is no doubt that it could have been a strong bargaining counter for the United States and one that might have been used to good effect in securing a reduction in the numbers of Soviet heavy missiles.

However when President Carter scrapped the B-1 he did so unilaterally, thereby ensuring that the West obtained nothing in return. Indeed there is today evidence that the Soviets are themselves going ahead with the production of a new inter-continental supersonic bomber equivalent to the B-1 and with a substantially greater range and payload than the recently deployed Soviet Backfire bomber which, unrefuelled, could strike the continental United States only on a one-way mission, recovering in Cuba.

By 1973 the detente process was in full swing, and in July of that year no fewer than thirty-five nations met in Helsinki at the start of a Conference on Security and Cooperation in Europe (CSCE). The purpose of the conference was to improve relations between the countries of NATO and the Warsaw Pact, and to agree on 'confidence building' measures. Western nations sought to insist that a major element in such measures must be a commitment by participating governments to respect the human rights of their own citizens. Bearing in mind the scant regard of the Kremlin even for the Soviet constitution, let alone the United Nations Declaration of Human Rights of which the Soviet Union is a signatory, and the fact that upwards of two million Soviet citizens languish in jails, labour camps and psychiatric hospitals for their political views, while millions of others who wish to leave the Soviet Union are denied the right to do so, the whole question of human rights was clearly a most powerful weapon, directed against the Soviet Union and its allies. When, in 1976, Jimmy Carter assumed the presidency of the United States, he indicated that in his dealings with the Soviet Union, he would insist that the Soviet Government respect the human rights of its own citizens. However, as soon as the Russians made clear that they would not tolerate any such interference, as they saw it, in their internal affairs, Carter let the matter drop and proceeded instead to devote his attentions in this field to harrying the allies of the United States that fell short of the standards of a liberal Western democracy. Among the casualties of this policy was to be the Shah of Iran, whose place was taken by men who demonstrated their commitment to human rights with an orgy of blood-letting and their regard for the conventions of international relations by taking captive the entire staff of the United States Embassy in Tehran and holding them to ransom.

Meanwhile, parallel with the SALT I and ABM negotiations, another conference opened, this time in Vienna in October 1973, for the purpose of achieving Mutual Balanced Force Reductions (MBFR) in the conventional military forces of NATO and the Warsaw Pact in Central Europe, where more than one million men face each other across the Iron Curtain border. The conference was doomed from the start by the fact that, without so much as waiting for the conference to start, the United States a few months earlier had announced the ending of the military draft, which had become one of the principal victims of the Vietnam War. It was declared that it was the intention of the United States in future to rely exclusively on all-volunteer forces – a decision that went far to undermine the bargaining position of the entire NATO alliance. The immediate effect of this decision was the demobilisation of 1·5 million men. Between 1968 and 1980 the armed forces of the United States were to fall in number from 3·5 million to barely 2 million, including women. There could be no more eloquent testimony to the commitment of the United States to the spirit as well as to the terms of detente than its decision unilaterally to slash its armed forces by more than one-third. However as Dr Kissinger has observed with the benefit of hindsight: 'I know of no instance where unilateral American restraint elicited a significant or lasting Soviet response' (*The White House Years*, Weidenfeld & Nicolson/Michael Joseph, London 1979, p.535). Nowhere is this more true than in the field of military manpower. Far from reducing their forces, which in 1968 stood at 3·2 million men – 300,000 *fewer* than those of the United States – Mr Brezhnev's contribution to the detente process was to *increase* Soviet forces by more than 400,000 to the point where by 1980, including KGB border troops and MVD security troops, they stood at 4·2 million – more than double those of the United States.

In previous years government leaders in Western countries might, with some plausibility, have been able to argue that they were largely ignorant of what a potential adversary was up to, but this can no longer be claimed as an excuse in the era of the 'Spy-in-the-Sky' satellites which give, with crystal clarity, a view of everything that happens on the surface of the earth. Both the United States and Soviet Union have several dozen such military reconnaissance satellites capable of observing not only the launch and splash-down of the other side's test missiles, but of counting each tank and aircraft as it leaves the factory or enters service with an army unit or air force squadron. The progress in the construction of each ship and submarine can be monitored from day to day. Whenever a more detailed view is required a satellite can be manoeuvred into a synchronous orbit with the earth so as to remain constantly above a given point or, alternatively, launched into an elliptical orbit in such a way as to bring it closest to the earth on each orbit at the focal point of interest. A senior NATO officer observed to me bitterly of the defence reductions being carried out in the late seventies by President Carter and Prime Minister James Callaghan: 'They have been briefed to the eyeballs on the facts of the situation, yet they continue to cut, cut and cut again.'

'Spy-in-the-Sky' satellites may be vital in providing precise detail of a potential enemy's order of battle and armaments production but, of course, can give no clue as to the intentions of those who control them. Military planners, when making their own dispositions, concern themselves above all with military capabilities, using 'worst case' analyses, rather than with intentions which are difficult to gauge and which may change overnight.

Nonetheless, a remarkable insight into the thinking and intentions of the Kremlin was afforded Western leaders when, towards the end of 1973, a British intelligence report of high reliability, in the form of a verbatim account of the discussions that had taken place a few weeks earlier at a Warsaw Pact heads of government meeting, landed on the desks of British Prime Minister Edward Heath and of President Nixon, laying bare the Kremlin's cynical approach to detente. It gave account of how, at the Pact meeting, the East German leader warned his colleagues that, with all the dangerous talk of human rights and of detente, it was proving increasingly difficult for the East German leadership to keep the lid on their domestic cooking-pot and that unless the policy was abandoned, the whole situation could boil over and get out of hand.

The other Communist leaders voiced their agreement with the warnings of their East German colleague and called for an end to detente. Finally Mr Brezhnev himself weighed into the argument. After asserting his conviction that the Warsaw Pact would gain far more in a few months of detente than they had 'in a quarter of a century of "mailed-fist" confrontation with NATO', he bluntly declared:

> Trust us, Comrades, for by 1985, as a consequence of what we are now achieving with detente, we will have achieved most of our objectives in Western Europe. We will have consolidated our position. We will have improved our economy. And the shift in the correlation of forces will be such that, come 1985, we will be able to exert our will wherever we need to.

Neither the indisputable satellite evidence of a massive and accelerating Soviet military build-up, strategic as well as conventional – nor even the unique first-hand evidence showing up in stark and dramatic relief the contrast between what the Kremlin leaders say for public consumption in the West and what they say among themselves in private, including their brazen determination to use detente as a cloak to gain military supremacy over the West – in any way cooled the ardour of Western leaders, on either side of the Atlantic, to pursue the path of detente and bring about the unilateral weakening of NATO's capabilities. As if to make this clear, the United States and the Soviet Union signed in the following year a protocol to the 1972 ABM treaty, limiting ABM systems to a single site of 100 ABMs in each country and, in November, agreement was reached in Vladivostok limiting strategic offensive missiles on each side to 2,400 of which 1,320 might be MIRVed (i.e. have multiple independently targetable re-entry vehicles). This in turn was followed by the signing at Helsinki in August 1975 of the Declaration on Security and Cooperation in Europe.

Viewed from the Kremlin, detente, far from being a process for relaxing tension in the world, was nothing more than a skilfully, albeit thinly, disguised offensive of Soviet diplomacy, designed to persuade the West to lower its guard, reduce its armaments and accept that the Kremlin's intentions were peaceful and benign while, in reality, they were engaged in the biggest military build-up the world had ever seen. That they were so successful in getting away with their trickery was due in large measure to the lamentable weakness of Western leaders at this time and to their tacit connivance with the Soviets by their failure to tell their own peoples the truth and gravity of the situation for fear it might prove electorally unpopular.

Dr Kissinger was to comment that 'the ultimate test [of SALT] would be restrained international behaviour' (*The White House Years*, p.1253). It was precisely on this point that I pressed Soviet Foreign Minister Andrei Gromyko at a meeting I had with him, together with a small group of parliamentary colleagues, at the Soviet Embassy in London in 1975. The Foreign Minister, in response to a question about Soviet support for terrorism in Africa, had expounded with vehemence on the Soviet Union's determination actively to support 'Wars of Liberation' in Africa and elsewhere. When I asked him how such action could be consistent with the Soviet Union's commitment to the spirit of detente, he explained that the Soviet Union had not only a right, but a duty, to give full support to liberation movements. I thereupon ventured to enquire how it was that the Soviet Union presumed the right to interfere in the internal affairs of Third World countries yet took the strongest exception to even the raising of questions of human rights in relation to the countries of Eastern Europe. The last drop of blood drained from the Foreign Minister's heavily creased and already grey face. Shaking with anger and with eyes of penetrating coldness fixed on me he remonstrated: '*That* is an inadmissible question!' After a silence during which he sought to regain his composure he added: 'The two situations are entirely different. In the case of the countries of Eastern Europe, they are independent sovereign states!' The Foreign Minister did not vouchsafe what status the Kremlin accords the countries of Africa and Asia.

The impact of the Soviet Union's detente offensive on the balance of world power has been dramatic. In the space of a decade the West has moved from a position of strength to one of weakness. The United States, so long supreme in military nuclear power, has been decisively overtaken by the Soviet Union. Even in conventional strength the United States, so recently the equal of the Soviet Union in armed manpower, now has a strength less than half that of the Soviet Union and the once all-powerful US Navy had, by 1980, less than half the ships it had at the time of the Vietnam war.

The seventies – the 'Decade of Detente' – proved in reality to be the 'Decade of Appeasement'. These have been the years that the locusts have eaten, years in which the tide has been running strong and without respite against the interests of the West. Those who from the vantage point of high office among the nations of the West thought they were steering the fortunes of the democracies towards the safe havens of peace and reconciliation have, instead, brought them perilously close to the quicksands of danger and the rocks of catastrophe. By 1980 the world had become a far more dangerous place than a decade before, relations between the two superpowers far less cordial, the threat to the nations of the Third World infinitely greater and the prospects for world peace in the years ahead grimmer than at any point since the Second World War. Such have been the bitter fruits of 'Detente'.

Chapter Four

THE SOVIET WAR MACHINE

If the consequence of the Cuban missile crisis was to encourage America to turn her back on the cold war and to pursue the path of detente – a process encouraged and accelerated by her Vietnam involvement – in the case of the Soviet Union the reaction was exactly the opposite. However much the Soviet leaders may have invoked the language of detente to the world, and castigated as 'cold war warriors' and 'war-mongers' those who in the West presumed to warn of the existence of a 'Soviet threat', the brutal truth is that throughout this period no hint or even murmur of the word 'detente' was ever communicated to the Red Army, which was growing relentlessly and rapidly both in size and capability, let alone to Soviet armaments factories, which were churning out increasingly sophisticated weapons at a rate that can only be described as preparatory to war. The facts admit of no other interpretation than that ever since the mid-sixties the Soviet Union has been engaged in a giant one-sided arms race – for there was none other in the race – with the aim of creating the world's greatest war machine with which the Kremlin intends to threaten and, ultimately, dominate the rest of the world.

As we have seen, the turning point in Soviet policy may be traced to the fall from office of Nikita Khrushchev towards the end of 1964. Khrushchev was to die in disgrace in 1972 and was not even accorded a state funeral. Today, the chances are that a visitor to the Soviet Union, who happens to walk through the cemetery of Moscow's Novodevichye churchyard, will not even be informed by his Intourist guide that in an unkempt corner lies the grave of a man who for no less than eleven years, following the death of Stalin in 1953, had ruled the Soviet Union and who occupied a major role on the world stage. In Orwellian jargon he became an 'un-person', the fate of Soviet leaders fallen from grace since the days of Beria, the ruthless head of the NKVD, the forerunner of today's KGB.

Khrushchev was succeeded by a clique of very different men – dour, grey and unsmiling. His post as First Secretary and Chairman of the Council of Ministers was taken by Alexei Kosygin, and the more powerful office of General Secretary of the Communist Party of the Soviet Union was filled by Leonid Brezhnev. Smarting from the humiliation to which Khrushchev's headstrong blundering had led them, they determined to ensure that should comparable circumstances arise in the future, it would not be the Soviet Union that would be forced to withdraw under the gaze of a bemused world. While at home they sought to depersonalise the Soviet leadership and make it more collective, in the field of defence they concluded, rightly, that it was the combination of their weakness in strategic nuclear power and their inability to deploy their superior conventional power on a global scale that had enabled Kennedy to call their bluff in 1962. They determined to remedy these inadequacies. In retrospect this may now be seen as the moment when the Soviet Union's present military build-up began in earnest and the leaders in the Kremlin resolved to gain military superiority over the United States. In the course of the next fifteen years the Soviet Union, under the cloak of detente, was to create by far the greatest war machine the world had ever seen, displacing the United States from her much vaunted position as the world's No. 1 military power, not only in conventional capability but, more disturbingly, as a nuclear power as well.

Because of the obstinate refusal of Western leaders on both sides of the Atlantic to risk rocking the detente boat by telling their own peoples the truth for fear of courting political unpopularity for themselves and their parties, it has become very difficult indeed for the layman to grasp the true magnitude and gravity of the Soviet threat as it confronts the West today.

Generations brought up since the Second World War, who have learned of that conflict either from their parents who lived or fought through it or, at least from history books, war films or television, might be forgiven for imagining that Hitler had a lot of tanks, submarines and aircraft for, it is incontrovertible, that he was responsible for the deaths of more than forty million human beings (R.E. and T.E. Dupuy, *The Encylopaedia of Military History*, Macdonald, London 1977) and inflicting untold human misery.

Even leaving aside its vast and ever-growing nuclear arsenal, the Soviet Union has created a war machine that makes the efforts of Hitler's Nazis appear puny in the extreme. In May 1940, long after the occupation of Austria and Czechoslovakia, after the invasion of Poland and even as the Low Countries and France were collapsing under the weight of Hitler's Blitzkrieg, the total armoured strength available to Nazi Germany for its westward thrust amounted to no more than 2,574 tanks (British Army Historical Branch). Mr Brezhnev in 1980 had no fewer than 50,000 tanks at his command – 30,000 of them facing Western Europe – and each of far greater power and capability than their forerunners of four decades before. Future generations may find it difficult to understand how perfectly sane men, many of them holding the highest offices of state in their own land, could describe as detente a situation in which the foundations of democracy were threatened by a power – proclaiming as its goal the domination of the entire world if need be by force – which had built up an inventory of tanks *twenty times the number* (and each of them many times the power) of Hitler's Germany.

It took Hitler six years of single-minded rearmament to amass his 2,574 tanks. Yet today, that figure represents less than nine months' current production for the Soviet Union's three tank factories which have been building tanks at a rate of between 3,000 and 4,000 per year for more than a decade. Nor can the United States be cited as an excuse for the Soviet tank

build-up. With no more than 3,000 US tanks in
Europe – including its strategic stockpile of tanks for divisions
that would be flown to Europe in a crisis (*Military Balance 1980/
81*, IISS) – the stark reality is that the United States' entire
tank contribution to NATO is being outproduced by the Soviet
Union in a single year. In fact at one point in the late seventies
tank production in the United States had dropped to less than
300 per year – one-tenth of the Soviet rate. The numbers of
Soviet tanks are such that advancing in column, at 100-foot
intervals, they would stretch in one unbroken armoured traffic
jam more than 1,000 miles long from the Soviet border to the
English Channel. To back this incredible array of armour the
Russians are currently producing 500 122mm heavy artillery
pieces and an equal number of 152mm self-propelled guns a
year. Nor is it on land alone that evidence is to be found of the
scale of the Soviet build-up.

In 1942, at the height of the Battle of the Atlantic, Britain was
brought close to surrender through starvation by a force of
fewer than 50 Nazi U-boats operating in the North Atlantic.
The Soviet navy of today – leaving aside its huge fleet of
strategic ballistic-missile submarines – has no fewer than 189
attack-submarines, together with a further 68 equipped for
launching cruise missiles with nuclear warheads and could
concentrate twice as many submarines in the North Atlantic as
Hitler, each of them infinitely more potent. The current Soviet
Alpha-class submarine, for example, with a submerged speed
of 42 knots, is nearly five times as fast as the German U-boats,
can remain submerged and unreplenished one hundred times
as long and has a diving depth of over 3,000 feet – six times the
depth of Germany's wartime Type VIIB and substantially
deeper than any of NATO's present generation of submarine
(*Jane's Fighting Ships 1980*, Macdonald, London 1979).
Furthermore the new generation of Soviet attack-submarine is
armed with nuclear-tipped torpedoes. In 1942, even with a
ratio in the Allies' favour of four escort vessels for each Nazi U-
boat, the toll of Allied shipping was terrible. In June that year
no fewer than 170 Allied and Neutral merchant ships totalling
823,656 gross tons were sunk (Winston S. Churchill, *The Second
World War*). With a far less favourable ratio today, the NATO

allies, in spite of great advances in anti-submarine warfare (ASW), must expect far more grievous losses in the event of any future conflict. Over the fifteen years to 1980, the Soviets launched an attack-submarine at the rate of one every five weeks and a ballistic-missile or cruise-missile submarine every ten weeks.

While in numbers of major surface ships the United States had by 1980 dropped to less than 40 per cent of her 1965 strength from 493 to 191 (see Table 2, United States/Soviet naval balance, 1965-80, page 134), the Soviet Union had marginally increased its strength from 272 to 289 vessels over the same period. An example of the scale of current Soviet surface ship construction may be gained from the fact that it is building one KARA-class anti-submarine warfare cruiser every fourteen months, and the KARAs are only one of eight classes of major surface warships being built at the present time.

The Soviet build-up on land and sea has been more than matched by its efforts in the air. Ever since the mid-seventies Soviet aircraft factories, in addition to their production of interceptor aircraft and long-range bombers, have been building at a rate of 1,200 a year supersonic swing-wing aircraft, of which the Royal Air Force, in common with most NATO air forces, will have no equivalent until the Tornado GR-1 enters squadron service in late 1981. This is roughly twice the number of fast jets being produced in all the NATO countries put together, including the United States (Hansard, *Parliamentary Reply*, 22 April 1980).

In the strategic nuclear field – embracing all weapons with inter-continental range – the United States has not, since 1967, added so much as a single missile to its inventory of 1,710 missiles, which has been static at 1,054 ICBMs and 656 SLBMs. The Soviets, far from matching this restraint, over the same period *have added* 1,749 missiles to their arsenal, which has increased from 677 in 1967 to 2,426 in 1980 (*Military Balance 1980/81*, IISS). This represents a rate of production, over and above whatever is required for the replacement of older missiles, of no less than *three new strategic missiles per week*. In addition they are currently adding SS-20 mobile IRBMs, of which the West has no equivalent, at the rate of one every five days.

Put another way, the Soviet Union is outbuilding Britain's entire inventory of tanks, supersonic aircraft and nuclear missiles approximately *every twelve weeks*. However it is not merely the brute numbers of heavy weapons in the Soviet inventory that provide cause for alarm but, above all, the momentum and volume of production, which means the Soviet equipment is far more modern than that available to the NATO allies. Traditionally NATO, though heavily outnumbered in manpower and conventional military hardware, could count on the fact that it was superior in the calibre of its forces and equipment, which in every category was technologically more advanced. Today, in an increasing number of fields, this has ceased to be true. The T-72 tank, for instance, which has new armour and a new gun, is operational in large numbers with Soviet divisions in East Germany, where more than 7,000 Soviet tanks are deployed; it is more modern and more powerful than the American M-48 and M-60 currently in service with US forces in Germany. Yet, already another generation of Soviet tank, the T-80, is at the testing stage. In the judgment of Marshal of the Royal Air Force Sir Neil Cameron, until recently Britain's Chief of Defence Staff, Soviet tanks are now superior in quality to NATO's.

For its part, the Soviet Union maintains armed forces vastly larger than those of the United States and currently has under arms no fewer than 4·2 million men (if para-military forces such as the KGB border guards and MVD security troops are included) compared with the United States' 2 million, a figure that includes 150,000 women. But it is above all on mobilisation that the disparity between the two superpowers becomes most glaring. The mobilised strength of America's armed forces, including ready reserves (806,300) and those with any residual reserve obligation (1,616,800), stands at 4,473,100. The Soviet Union, which retains a two- to three-year military service, can mobilise no fewer than 25 million reserves, bringing her armed forces to nearly 30 million – more than six times those of the United States. In addition the Soviets claim the active membership of DOSAAF, a part-time training organisation, to be a staggering

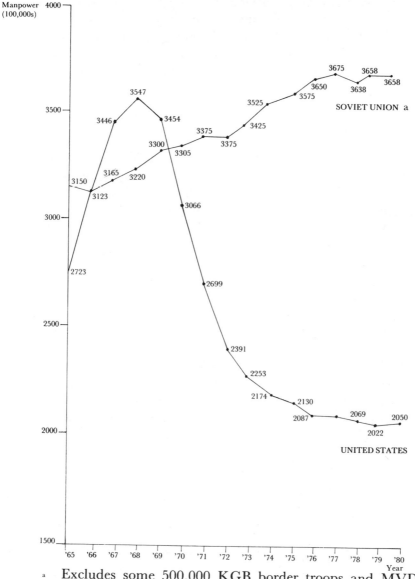

Fig 4   *United States and Soviet armed forces manpower*
1965–80

Manpower (100,000s)

SOVIET UNION a

UNITED STATES

Year

a   Excludes some 500,000 KGB border troops and MVD sercurity troops.

Source: *The Military Balance,* International Institute for Strategic Studies, London.

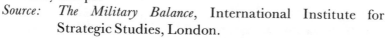

80 million.

The Soviet army is made up of 174 divisions, including 8 airborne divisions, supported by a force of 4,000 attack and transport helicopters. Of this total, no fewer than 1 million men in 116 divisions backed by some 30,000 tanks are deployed west of the Ural Mountains, facing Western Europe (*Military Balance 1980/81*, IISS). These figures do not include the forces of any of the Soviets' Warsaw Pact allies. Two features characterise Soviet forces facing NATO. The first is that, unlike NATO forces, they are deployed not for defence but for attack. The second is their colossal fire-power. Each front-line mechanised infantry division, consisting of three motor-rifle regiments and one tank regiment, which previously had six 122mm towed artillery pieces, is now equipped with eighteen 152mm self-propelled guns. This represents a trebling of artillery fire-power between 1976 and 1980. In addition the Russians have recently introduced a sixteen-tube multiple-rocket launcher, of which the West has no equivalent, firing rockets each with a warhead containing one-third of a ton of TNT. A single salvo from one battery of these monster weapons can dump a massive 72 tons of high explosive on a target within seconds.

Western military planners frequently make the assumption that any future war, if there is to be one, will inevitably be short. Precisely the same thinking pervaded the military mind prior to the outbreak of the First World War which was to last six years and involve no fewer than 65 million men (R.E. and T.E. Dupuy, *Encyclopaedia of Military History*, Macdonald, London 1970). However, given the pitifully small reserves available to NATO and the extreme inadequacy of many categories of war-reserve stocks, which in some cases would be exhausted in well under *one week* at the sort of wastage-rates seen in the 1973 Middle East war, it could be that, thanks to their own grossly inadequate dispositions, today's planners would prove themselves right in consequence of NATO's sheer inability to sustain a conventional war for more than a few days.

When, in the early sixties, President Kennedy set in train the abandonment of the 'trip-wire' strategy, based on the premise that even a conventional attack against Western Europe would invite an all-out nuclear response, in favour of the doctrine of 'flexible response', which provided for a conventional phase of several days without any automatic escalation to the use of nuclear weapons, the new doctrine was welcomed throughout the world as a step back from the brink of the precipice. Although NATO, as it enters the eighties, remains nominally committed to the 'flexible response' doctrine, this has become nothing but a hollow sham to which all pay lip service but few give credence. In consequence of the decisive shift against NATO in manpower and conventional military strength in Europe – the same shift that has caused NATO to reduce its estimate of the warning-time it could expect in the event of a surprise Soviet attack from thirty days to a bare forty-eight hours – the reality is that, with the forces NATO currently has in Central Europe, it would have no choice but to escalate within forty-eight or, at the outside, seventy-two hours to the use of tactical nuclear weapons (battlefield weapons with a destructive power measured in thousands of tons of TNT equivalent, rather than millions of tons as in the case of most strategic nuclear weapons). The dangers that such a decision would hold are imponderable and the possibility of a rapid escalation to all-out strategic nuclear war cannot be excluded. Though the politicians on both sides of the Atlantic, who have been responsible for allowing this grave erosion of Western conventional strength relative to the Warsaw Pact, may seek strenuously to deny it, the truth must be faced: NATO is back to the 'trip-wire'.

Beyond the sheer weight of numbers of the Soviet armed forces, a factor that causes NATO strategists extreme concern is the massive potential of Soviet forces for chemical warfare. Following the use of mustard gas, chlorine, phosgene and other agents by the Germans in the First World War and retaliation in kind by the British and French, the effects of chemical weapons and nerve gases were held to be so horrific that they provoked a widespread feeling that they should be banned as weapons of war, and indeed an international convention was signed in Geneva in 1925 outlawing them. Although Mussolini used gas against the Ethiopians when he invaded that country in 1936, as did the Japanese when they occupied Manchuria the same year, chemical weapons were never used in the Second

World War, above all because each side knew the other possessed them.

Today the Soviet Union is the only country with a major stock of offensive chemical agents, although the United States retains a limited and outdated stock of bombs and shells which have not even been test-fired since 1978. Other members of NATO possess only a defensive capability in the form of special suits with carbon linings and respirators to protect their pilots, ground crew, soldiers and sailors – though not their civilian populations – from chemical attack. In this field Britain is by far the most advanced of all the allies having developed excellent lightweight disposable Nuclear-Biological-Chemical (NBC) suits for her forces, including doctors and nurses in field hospitals and supply troops in rear areas, while key ground installations have filtered air to enable them to remain fully operational in a post-attack environment.

Bacteriological warfare, including the development and stockpiling of such weapons, has been outlawed under a convention signed in London, Washington and Moscow on 10 April 1972. However, notwithstanding that the Soviet Union is a signatory of the convention, there have in recent years been firm reports of at least one major incident in which substantial numbers of Soviet citizens living close to research establishments – of which the Soviet authorities resolutely refuse to allow any international inspection – died of mysterious diseases caused, almost certainly, by the escape of a biological warfare agent. The disaster occurred in June 1979 at a bacteriological weapons factory in the Siberian city of Novosibirsk, 2,000 miles east of Moscow. Hundreds of people are reported to have died and thousands to have suffered serious injury as a result of an accident at a factory.

Reports from the area told of thousands of people living near the factory coming down with a mysterious disease and many being killed. The authorities were swift to take action, ordering that streets and buildings throughout the neighbourhood be sprayed with disinfectant and forbidding the relations of the victims to see the bodies which were returned to them in sealed coffins. A cloak of secrecy descended and a ban on travel to the area was imposed in an attempt to cover up the accident.

Speculation has been rife among Western scientists and bacteriologists and was in no way allayed when, some months after the incident, the Soviet Government sought to sweep it under the carpet by informing Western governments (who insisted on an explanation of the facts) that the deaths had been caused by an outbreak of anthrax. Although it is well known that the Russians have been experimenting for some time with tropical viruses such as Marburg disease, Ebola disease and Lassa fever – and the discoloration of areas of the victims' bodies would be consistent with any of these – it is unlikely that an inadvertent release of such viruses into the atmosphere would have had such a devastating effect on the local population. A more plausible explanation may be that the Russian bacteriologists were experimenting with new strains of airborne virus akin to the bubonic plague or Black Death that killed 75 million people in Europe and Asia between 1347 and 1351.

If indeed the Soviet Union, in contravention of its international obligations, is going ahead with the research and stockpiling of biological weapons, this can only call in to question all agreements reached with the Soviets other than those that are strictly verifiable by independent means.

Surveying the incredible scale of the Soviet military build-up, it is difficult to avoid the conclusion that the Soviet Union is a nation which, in defiance of the wishes of its own peoples, is actively preparing for war. Among the most sinister and disturbing of its preparations is in the field of civil defence. The very suggestion that civil defence by any nation should be categorised as 'sinister' may puzzle the reader and requires explanation. There are many countries, especially neutral countries such as Sweden and Switzerland, that have also gone to great lengths to protect their civilian populations from the possibility of nuclear attack and there is no suggestion that *their* action is anything but prudent and laudable. The difference in the case of the Soviet Union rests in the fact that it is the only country in the world that, according to its own military doctrine, revealed in specialist military journals, believes it is possible to fight *and win* a nuclear war. It is at the bedrock of

Western political and military thinking that no nation can hope to win a nuclear war – that all mankind would be the loser. When every nuclear nation, other than Russia, holds such weapons for the sole purpose of *deterring* and *preventing* nuclear war it is inevitably disquieting in the extreme that one country should have plans for surviving and winning such a war.

There has been in recent years a division within the Western intelligence communities as to how serious Soviet civil defence preparations in fact are. On the one hand there is no doubt that the average Soviet citizen is unwilling to take civil defence exercises at all seriously and ignores the air-raid sirens when they sound. According to Vladimir Bukovsky, the leader of the human rights movement within the Soviet Union until, after ten years in assorted Soviet prisons, labour camps and psychiatric asylums, he was exchanged for the Chilean Communist leader Luis Corvalan on 18 December 1976: 'We all regarded the sirens as a huge joke and nobody would put on his gas-mask.'

At an official level, however, all the evidence points to the fact that civil defence is taken altogether more seriously. Some idea of the size of the Soviet civil defence organisation may be gained from the fact that at the summit of its organisational pyramid it is commanded by no less than fifty officers of the rank of general. The priorities in terms of protection are the Communist Party (CPSU) and military chains of command, armaments factory workers and essential services. In addition elaborate measures have been taken to protect the civilian population by the construction of specially hardened shelters in the basements of all apartment blocks and public buildings built in recent years. In many cases factories have nuclear-proof underground shelters sufficient to accommodate their entire workforce. Furthermore detailed plans have been laid for the evacuation of the civilian populations from all principal cities.

In consequence of these preparations – and the total lack of anything comparable in the United States – recent studies undertaken in the United States, where shelters identical to those used in the Soviet Union have been duplicated for test purposes, indicate that in the event of an all-out nuclear exchange between the two superpowers, the United States might expect to lose 140 million out of its 220 million population while Soviet losses might be no more than 40 million out of a population of 265 million, a figure that might be reduced to as low as 25 million in the event that the Soviets have time to implement their elaborate plans for city evacuation.

There can be no doubt that the non-existence or, at least, extreme inadequacy of civil defence measures in the NATO countries has the effect of reducing the credibility of NATO's own deterrent. Nevertheless, bearing in mind the extreme pressure on resources available for defence throughout the West, it is undoubtedly right that the nuclear nations of the West – the United States, Britain and France – should continue to concentrate their efforts above all on *preventing* a nuclear war, rather than seeking to survive it once it has happened. Certainly it is difficult to avoid the conclusion that, should it ever come to an all-out nuclear war, the survivors will envy the dead.

The size and dynamics of the Soviet war machine – the vast production of armaments far exceeding the combined output of the Western allies, the huge reserves of trained military manpower that dwarf the combined military strength of the NATO alliance, the emphasis on chemical warfare, continued experimentation in the field of biological warfare, its evident determination to overtake the United States in every field of nuclear power coupled with its proclaimed doctrine that it can survive and win a nuclear war – inevitably prompt the question in the Western mind: 'Why? What can it all be for?' Whatever its purpose, of one thing we may be certain: it is not for our benefit.

There are only two answers that provide any plausible explanation of the indisputable evidence of Western satellite photography and intelligence. The first may be called the Chinese or Keegan view. Both the leaders of the Chinese People's Republic and Lieutenant-General George J. Keegan, until recently Chief of US Air Force Intelligence, believe that the Soviet leadership has already taken the decision to attack and that the only question is: 'When?' Unpalatable and unpopular though such a view may be, there can be no doubt that it is one of the explanations that fits the evidence.

If I do not myself share this view it is certainly not because I doubt the facts, merely that, on the basis of a subjective judgment, I believe that the principal aim of the Kremlin – as it was of Adolf Hitler – is to win their objectives without a war. I find the most plausible explanation of the Soviet military build-up in the words of President Brezhnev already referred to in Chapter 3, which make clear that it is the aim of the Soviet Union to build up its military power to such an extent on the one hand, while on the other disarming the West, both morally and militarily, through the 'detente offensive', that to use Mr Brezhnev's words the 'decisive shift in the correlation of forces will be such that, by 1985 we will be able to exert our will wherever we need to'. What the Soviet leader evidently had in mind was that, by that date, the Western allies will have become so weak relative to the USSR, and divisions among the European members of NATO and the United States will have advanced so far, leading to a weakening of the United States' commitment to the defence of Western Europe, that a sudden Soviet move would present the NATO allies with two unacceptable alternatives: surrender or suicide.

PART III

THE WEST
VULNERABLE

Chapter Five

AMERICA THREATENED

As recently as the nuclear alert at the time of the Middle East war of October 1973, the United States still retained an overwhelming preponderance over the Soviet Union in strategic nuclear power. President Richard Nixon, reacting to evidence that the Soviet Union had emplaned 50,000 paratroops, a total of seven airborne divisions, at airbases in Eastern Europe and was preparing to intervene in the conflict, took the decision in the early hours of 25 October to place US forces world-wide – including nuclear forces – on alert to dissuade the Kremlin from any precipitate action. Even though the Soviet Union had by then gained a lead over the United States in numbers of silo and submarine-launched missiles (2,203 as against the United States' 1,710), none of the Soviet missiles was equipped with multiple warheads and, compared to the Americans', had a very poor level of accuracy. The United Staes with her superior technology had already converted many of her missiles to carry multiple independently targetable re-entry vehicles (MIRVs), enabling warheads from a single missile to strike with precision several different targets hundreds of miles apart. In consequence of this the United States, in spite of an inferiority of nearly 500 launchers, retained an advantage of nearly 4:1 over the Soviet Union in warheads, with a total inventory approaching 8,000.

Faced with this unambiguous demonstration of US resolve by Nixon, the Kremlin backed down as they had when similarly confronted by Kennedy a decade before. Fortunately for the Kremlin they were on this occasion able to avoid the humiliation of a public withdrawal, for their forces had not yet been committed overseas and the world – most notably the peoples of the Soviet Union themselves – remained largely ignorant of the circumstances that had prompted the US alert, unjustifiably attributed by the foolish or malicious to a plot by Nixon and his advisers to divert attention from the unfolding Watergate scandal.

However, by this time, the United States had already reached a plateau of strategic nuclear strength with the entry into service of the Minuteman III land-based ICBM with its three MIRVed warheads (0·17mt each) and the Poseidon C3 SLBM with ten MIRVed warheads (0·05 mt each). The Soviet strategic effort, on the other hand, was only just building up momentum. It was not until 1975 that a whole new family of Soviet land-based ballistic missiles, the SS-16, SS-17, SS-18 and SS-19 – significantly all ordered into development *after* the signing of the SALT I agreement of May 1972 – completed their test programme and were ready to enter service. Each of these new missiles carried multiple warheads with a demonstrated accuracy of some 400 yards over a range of up to 7,000 miles. The SS-18 with a throw-weight or payload of no less than 9 tons – ten times that of the US Minuteman and nearly three times that of America's heaviest missile, the twenty-year-old Titan II – can carry either a single 25 mt warhead or ten of 2 mt. Compared to America's latest Minuteman III, the SS-18 carries three times as many warheads, each with a destructive capability a dozen times greater.

Unlike the rest of the new generation of Soviet land-based missiles, all of which are protected in fixed underground silos, the SS-16 is a mobile missile designed to be transported and fired from a vehicle known as a transporter-erector-launcher. With this development the Soviet Union has achieved a major technological breakthrough, putting it potentially ten years ahead of the United States in this field. Its significance is twofold. First, while it is possible to pinpoint and therefore strike at an enemy's fixed silo-based missiles, it is infinitely more difficult in the case of mobile missiles, which can either keep on the move or remain effectively concealed. Thus a mobile missile is many times less vulnerable than a fixed one. (The same of course applies to the submarine-launched missile, of which the Soviet Union has an advantage of 56 per cent in numbers over the United States.) Secondly, the mobile land-based missile-launcher – and in this respect it holds an important advantage over the submarine – is capable of immediately reloading and firing again. Not only does this mean that a nation deploying mobile launchers could have many times more missiles than its launcher total would imply but it renders almost impossible the problem of verification, which alone can give confidence to arms-control agreements.

The mobile inter-continental-range SS-16, though it has completed its development and flight-test programme had, up to early 1981, not yet been deployed. This restraint evidently arose from a desire to avoid alarming or provoking the United States unduly while the SALT II negotiations were under way and was formalised under the terms of the SALT II protocol, due to expire at the end of 1981, whereby both sides undertook not to deploy or test mobile ICBMs such as the SS-16 or the United States' proposed new strategic missile the MX, a land-based ICBM designed by its mobility to resolve the problem of the new vulnerability of the Minuteman which, in the late eighties, it is due to start replacing.

While at the time of writing the American missile is still several years away from completing its development – 1986 has been set as the earliest in-service date for the first of the 200 MX missiles – the Soviet missile, minus its booster-stage, has already entered service with the Soviet Strategic Rocket Forces in the form of the SS-20 mobile intermediate-range ballistic missile (IRBM) of which by early 1981 more than 200 with a range of up to 4,000 miles had been deployed against Western Europe and China. The transporter-erector-launcher of the SS-20 is the same as for the SS-16, and all that is required to transform the SS-20 into the inter-continental-range SS-16 is the addition of a single booster-stage. If, following the US Senate's failure to ratify the SALT II treaty in the wake of the Soviet invasion of Afghanistan and in reaction to President Reagan's determination to renegotiate some of the terms of the treaty, there were to be a failure to secure agreement between the two superpowers, the Soviet Union is in a far stronger position than the United States, in the short term, to embark upon a new strategic arms race. In such an event one of the Soviet Government's very first steps is likely to be the operational deployment of the SS-16, which could come into service many years before America's MX.

However, there is yet another field in which the Soviet Union has stolen a march over the United States. Not only does the United States at the present time lack a mobile land-based missile, but her 1,054 land-based Titan and Minuteman silos, unlike those of the Soviets, have been designed to launch only a single missile each, for their construction is such that the blast of the rocket and the temperature of the exhaust gases cause severe damage to the silo-lining and wiring. Soviet technologists on the other hand, working to the instructions of political masters anxious to have more than one shot per silo, have pioneered and perfected a 'cold-launch' technique by which the missile is expelled from the silo by compressed gas before the rocket motors ignite, thereby enabling the silo to be reloaded one or more times. The capability of the Soviet Union to reload its mobile and land-based silo launchers presents the United States and the NATO allies with a major problem, making verification – in the absence of Soviet cooperation – an impossible task and threatening to lead to further instability and uncertainty in an already critically dangerous situation.

Satellite photography, in its present state of development, makes it possible for each side to know with precision both the number of missile silos, and, because they are observed being built, the number of submarine missiles tubes possessed by the other. However, if one side is capable of reloading its land-based silos and mobile launchers, while the other is not, there will inevitably exist the danger that it may be tempted to build and secretly store one or more reload missiles for each silo or launcher. Thus a whole new field of uncertainty has been

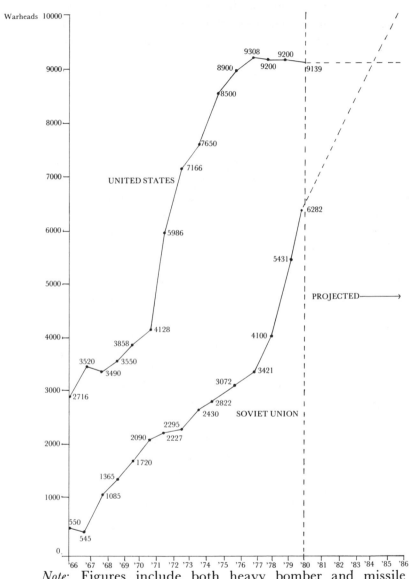

Fig 5   *United States and Soviet strategic warheads 1966–86*

Note: Figures include both heavy bomber and missile warheads and, beyond 1980, represent straight-line projections based on current trends.

Source: *The Military Balance*, International Institute for Strategic Studies, London.

opened up in which it is possible for a superpower that holds the aim of achieving strategic military supremacy over the other to build a strategic force several times its perceived strength. The adamant refusal of the Soviet Union to agree to any form of mutual on-site inspection – frequently proposed by Western governments over the years – adds to the dangers of duplicity in this field.

In consequence of these developments the Soviet Union had by 1980 achieved, not merely parity with the United States, but her displacement as the world's greatest military power. By that date the Soviet Union had secured a decisive advantage over the United States at every level of nuclear power including numbers, throw-weight and destructive potential of missiles deployed and it is clear that the surge and momentum of the Soviet strategic arms programme will see the United States eclipsed by the mid-eighties even in the numbers of warheads, her last remaining field of advantage. How remote from present-day reality now appears the confidence of Dr Henry Kissinger when, on 3 December 1974 he predicted: 'In the 1980s the greater flexibility of our force, and the greater vulnerability of their force is very likely to bring about a situation in which the threat to their forces is likely to be much greater than the threat to our total force – regardless of what the weight of the individual warhead is.' The truth is precisely the converse: it is the United States that is on the point of becoming vulnerable.

The most urgent crisis confronting the new US administration is the fact that, by 1983, the Soviet Union will have achieved a first-strike capability against the United States. It is estimated that by that date, warheads with a new generation of guidance systems – already flight-tested to an accuracy of less than 1,000 feet – will be fully operational with Soviet Strategic Rocket Forces. Indeed the most devastating indictment of President Carter's own administration is contained in US Secretary of Defense Harold Brown's *Annual Report to Congress (Fiscal Year 1981)* – the last of the Carter presidency – which declares:

The most immediate source of future instability is the

growing Soviet threat to our fixed, hard ICBM's. Although the Soviets have only just begun to deploy a version of the SS-18 ICBM with 10 MIRV's, within a year or two we can expect them to obtain the necessary combination of ICBM numbers, reliability, accuracy and warhead yield to put most of our Minuteman and Titan silos at risk (90%) from an attack with a relatively small proportion of their ICBM force. For planning purposes, therefore, *we must assume that the ICBM leg of our triad could be destroyed within a very short time as a result of a Soviet surprise attack* [author's emphasis].

It is difficult to conceive that President Carter would have scrapped production plans for the supersonic B-1 bomber and would have failed to press ahead at maximum speed with the MX mobile missile system had he been aware that by the early eighties the largest and most potent element of the United States' triad of strategic forces was to be rendered obsolete almost overnight. It is frequently alleged – usually by the enemies of democracy – that the Pentagon is guilty of regularly overstating Soviet strengths and capabilities so as to secure from Congress larger allocations for the US defence budget. The record does not substantiate the allegation. If guilty they be, it has more often been of *under*estimating the Soviet potential and, most critically, their ability to catch up in a short space of time with Western technology. There is no doubt that the speed with which the Soviets have been able to MIRV their missiles and dramatically increase the accuracy of their warheads took the Carter administration completely by surprise and represented a major failure, if not of intelligence, at least to act on intelligence, in a field where there is little room for error. In retrospect, the cancellation of the B-1 can only be seen as a major error of judgment. Both in the interest of the safety of the United States and the stability of the East-West balance, the development and deployment of America's MX missile cannot come soon enough.

The validity of the United States' thinking in basing its strategic defence on not one, but a triad of systems – land- and submarine-based missiles and long-range bombers – thereby guarding against any one becoming obsolete as the result of a Soviet technological breakthrough has been amply proved by events, in the light of America's stark realisation that 90 per cent of her 1,054 Titan and Minuteman land-based missiles could be taken out by a pre-emptive strike using only some 10 per cent of the Soviet missile force.

Nor is it only the land-based missiles that have become vulnerable. An important, though ageing, element of America's triad of strategic forces is her fleet of 348 B-52 bombers of Strategic Air Command. Even with their sophisticated array of electronic counter-measures (ECM) and their stand-off short-range attack missiles (SRAM) the chances of these twenty-year-old subsonic bombers getting through to their targets, in the face of the Soviet Union's vast in-depth air-defence array of more than 12,000 surface-to-air-missile (SAM) systems and radar-controlled guns, have been diminishing in recent years. It is for this reason that many of the B-52s are to be equipped from 1983 with twenty air-launched cruise missiles (ALCM) each, so as to enable them to strike their targets without having to penetrate Soviet air defences. However, the cruise missiles in their turn are also potentially vulnerable to the Soviets' new SA-10 surface-to-air missile which is believed to have an anti-missile capability and to interceptor-aircraft equipped with sophisticated 'Look-down/Shoot-down' radars and missiles, though the cruise missile's small radar cross-section (claimed to be no larger than that of a seagull) and the potentially large numbers in which it will be deployed, thanks to its comparatively low cost ($1 million a missile) will render the problems of countermeasures formidable indeed.

With technology advancing at an ever-accelerating pace new areas of breakthrough and, therefore potentially, of instability will continue to appear. One such threat to the stability of the strategic balance between East and West comes from recent developments in the field of high-energy lasers and charged particle-beam technology. In spite of warnings over many years by Major General George Keegan and a small team of specialists in US Air Force Intelligence that the Soviet Union had under way a major programme in this field, the Pentagon, the CIA and the Carter administration refused to take these reports seriously, relegating the possibility of such weapons to the realms of science fiction. As early as 1975 General Keegan disclosed to the then CIA director, William Colby, his findings on Soviet development of beam-technology weapons aimed at neutralising the United States' entire ballistic missile force. Colby formally convened the CIA's Nuclear Intelligence Panel to consider the evidence and, subsequently, prepare a report. According to the authoritative US magazine *Aviation Week and Space Technology*:

> The report said that there were no technological errors in the USAF's analytical work. It was agreed by the board that there is a massive effort in the USSR involving hundreds of laboratories and thousands of top scientists to develop the technology necessary for production of a beam or other energy weapon for use against US ICBMs and SLBMs. The report also said the board was unable to accept USAF's detailed conclusions regarding the experimental site at Semipalatinsk. *It reasoned that since none of the key sub-technologies involved had been perfected in the US it was implausible that the Soviets could be so far ahead* [author's emphasis]. In any event the US scientific advisers to the CIA were unwilling to concede that the Soviets could harness such advanced technology into a working weapon. . . .

When, in the late seventies, it was learnt that the Soviet Union had already stolen a march over the United States with the development of a 'killer-satellite', capable of destroying US satellites in orbit by effecting a rendezvous with them in space and triggering an explosive device once alongside, the administration was forced to take a closer look at this and other areas of Soviet effort in the field of advanced military technology. The value to an aggressor of being able to blind an adversary by the destruction of his 'Spy-in-the-Sky' satellites would be incalculable, though at the same time it would represent the most direct warning possible to a potential victim to bring his own forces to the highest levels of alert. In this field, as in the field of lasers and beam-technology, the United States is now engaged in a major effort to make up lost ground.

The significance of lasers and beam-weapons rests in their potential to concentrate a pencil-beam of energy to great distances through the atmosphere or in space, burning up anything in its path. In the event that such a beam could be directed with precision against an attacking missile or warhead it is theoretically possible that a brief burst of energy, probably from a nuclear source, could destroy the triggering mechanism and turn the missile into a useless lump of molten metal. In October 1980 the US Department of Defense made public a film of an experiment conducted by the United States earlier in the year in which a pilotless aircraft was shot out of the sky in flames by a laser weapon. Suggestions that the timing of this disclosure had any, even remote, connection with the approaching US election day might justifiably have been attributed to the mischief-making of irresponsible journalists or the opportunism of political opponents of the Carter administration, were it not for the fact that it came hard on the heels of the government-authorised disclosure of yet another supposedly top-secret US defence programme (codenamed 'Stealth') which, by new design techniques and energy-absorbing coating materials, is intended to render American bombers of the future and new cruise missiles virtually invisible to an enemy's radar. It is difficult to imagine that such disclosures, which came close to prompting resignations among senior air force officers, would have been made in anything other than an election year and is evidence of a cynical subordination of national security to the exigencies of domestic party politics, giving the Russians, at least in the case of the 'Stealth' programme, plenty of time to develop countermeasures.

Destroying a nuclear warhead travelling at several thousand miles per hour outside the earth's atmosphere – and being sure of being able to do so whatever the atmospheric conditions on earth – presents problems far removed from incinerating an aircraft at short range on a clear day. But the principle is the same. Clearly even the Soviet Union has some way to go before it can deploy a laser-beam system that could provide an effective defence against an all-out missile attack thereby rendering the United States' and Britain's entire ballistic-missile force obsolete, but that it will before long be achieved there can be little doubt. The most promising platform for such a weapon would be an orbiting satellite, or space station, given its far greater horizon of view of any enemy attack and the fact that there would be virtually no degradation of the weapon's effectiveness, even at great range, due to the absence of cloud cover, storms and the usual interference of the earth's atmosphere. The problems involved in placing a sufficiently powerful energy source and beam-direction equipment in orbit are substantial but it could well be that the great effort invested by the Soviets in recent years in developing and testing heavy orbiting space stations are channelled in this direction. Belatedly, the United States is taking the threat of a Soviet breakthrough in this field far more seriously and the US effort in directed-energy weapons technology has now been brought together under the Defense Advanced Research Projects Agency (DARPA). The United States' space shuttle Columbia, with its ability to lift large payloads into earth orbit and subsequently recover them, will make an important contribution to the US research programme in this field, which is one the Reagan administration is likely to treat far more seriously than did its predecessor.

As weapons become more sophisticated the importance of technology over brute force becomes more evident. A breakthrough in this field could be worth dozens of tank divisions or hundreds of missiles in deciding the outcome of any future conflict. The fact that the Soviet Union has been turning out five times as many high-quality engineering graduates in recent years and is currently spending more than twice as much on research and development – 25 per cent as against the 11 per cent of Britain and the United States – from a defence budget that is half again as large as that of the United States (DOD, *Annual Report to Congress (Fiscal Year 1981)*) is a matter that should not be overlooked. Though there are vast gaps in Soviet technology, especially in the civil field which trails years behind the West, it cannot be doubted that Soviet investment in advanced military technology of human and economic resources on so vast a scale will, inevitably, lead to technological advances and breakthroughs that could leave the West in a dangerously exposed situation.

The election of President Reagan in November 1980 with a landslide majority may be expected to have a profound effect upon American – and no doubt upon Soviet – policies in the strategic arms field. However, this is a sphere that is not susceptible to quick change. Therefore, no matter how far-reaching the decisions taken by President Reagan and his advisers may be, it is impossible for such decisions to bear fruit, in terms of military hardware, before the mid-to-late eighties. Given the momentum of the Soviet military build-up, under way already for some fifteen years, the balance of power will inevitably continue to shift in favour of the Soviet Union throughout the early eighties and – however frustrating it may be for Americans who expect results, if not yesterday, at least today – there is little that the United States will be able to do about it. President Reagan will find himself the prisoner of the misjudgments and weaknesses of his predecessors who, by their lack of foresight, by their worldly innocence and by their utter failure to see through the Russian game, have put America at risk.

There is an obvious danger that the new administration of President Reagan, spurred on by anxiety at the potential threat to the US land-based missile force, might over-react and assume that this represents, if not the sole, at least the principal threat to peace at the present time. Such a judgment could lead to an excessive concentration on remedying the deficiencies in American strategic systems at the expense of addressing even more pressing dangers. For the foreseeable future (at least until the Soviets are able to deploy an effective beam-technology anti-missile defence) the United States will retain sufficient strategic capability in her formidable force of Poseidon and Trident ballistic-missile submarines, backed by the B-52s with their ALCMs, to deter any Soviet attack against the continental United States. As Churchill rightly observed during the wartime years: 'There's no point in making the rubble bounce!' The United States will continue to possess, as will the Soviet

Union, the capability of making the rubble bounce many times over in the other's backyard.

Short of a catastrophic accident, arising from a major failure of one of the superpowers' command and control systems, or the implausible scenario of supreme authority in either the Kremlin or the White House being gained by a group of madmen or fanatics, it is difficult to conceive circumstances in which one side might decide to launch an all-out attack on the other, except as a consequence of the escalation of a conflict arising out of instability *elsewhere on the globe*. For this reason, if for none other, the people and government of the United States have no choice but to be directly involved in developments beyond the confines of their own continent, however remote or insignificant they might appear to be. The lessons of the past – learnt at such cost already twice this century – should not be forgotten. The way in which the action of a single revolutionary Gavrilo Princip, hurling a bomb at Archduke Francis Ferdinand of Austria-Hungary in the remote Balkan village of Sarajevo on 28 June 1914, triggered a world war in which more than 20 millions were to die is an object-lesson of how easily a situation can escalate out of control and is one that should not be lost on those who have the awesome responsibility of guiding the destiny of the world in the nuclear age.

The Second World War only reinforced the truth learnt in the First World War, that however much the English-speaking democracies (Britain, the United States, Canada, Australia and New Zealand) might wish to remain aloof from Europe and the conflicts of others, as throughout the twenties and thirties they struggled desperately to do, they utterly failed. Indeed it was the very isolationism of all these nations, but most especially of the United States, that, by giving Hitler free rein in Europe, led so directly to yet another world war, the one thing they had sought to avoid. How much less in today's world can it be imagined there is any hiding place where a nation may cut itself off from the dangers that beset the world, by seeking to cocoon itself from reality with a policy of isolation? Europe can no more pretend that it is not involved in the Middle East on which it is dependent for more than two-thirds of its oil supplies – the very life blood of its industry and defence potential – than the United States separated by barely thirty minutes' flying time from the Soviet Union's land- and submarine-based inter-continental ballistic missiles, can afford not to recognise that all its hopes for the peace, prosperity and continued freedom of its own people are inextricably bound up with the fate of the peoples of Europe.

Far graver than any possibility of a Soviet pre-emptive nuclear strike against the United States is the danger that, in a crisis involving an East–West clash over oil or mineral resources elsewhere in the world, the Kremlin might feel tempted to exploit the critical and growing imbalance of power that exists today in Central Europe. If at any time the Soviet leadership were to conclude that the invasion and subjugation of Western Europe could be accomplished without invoking the strategic deterrent of the United States – and, with it, unacceptable damage to Mother Russia – the stage could be set for the Third World War.

Chapter Six

CRISIS IN EUROPE

The NATO allies have long been reconciled to the fact that in conventional military power they are severely outnumbered in Europe by the Soviet Union and its Warsaw Pact allies. Indeed ever since the end of the Second World War, the Soviet Union has maintained far larger forces in Europe, outnumbering NATO in troops, tanks and combat aircraft by a factor of approximately 2:1. More recently, the disparity has increased to nearer 3:1. Although menacing, this was a situation that NATO could live with, with equanimity if not enthusiasm, so long as the West retained an overwhelming preponderance of nuclear power at inter-continental, Euro-strategic and battlefield level. But in the space of a single decade – the disastrous decade of detente – every one of these offsetting advantages has been lost. These developments hold grave implications for the stability of Europe and threaten to undermine the credibility and the strategy of the NATO alliance.

Following the rapid demobilisation of British and American forces at the end of the Second World War, which left both short of ground troops (an action in no way matched by the Soviet Union), and in the wake of the United States' newly acquired supremacy in nuclear weapons, the original NATO strategy that grew up under the presidencies of Truman and Eisenhower was based on massive nuclear retaliation by the United States in the event that the Soviet Union should ever seek to take advantage of its superior conventional strength to launch an attack on Western Europe. The plan provided for first use by NATO of nuclear weapons, irrespective of whether or not the Soviets used such weapons themselves, and came to be known as the 'trip-wire' strategy.

In the early sixties, as the Soviet Union grew in strength as a military nuclear power, the dangers inherent in such all-out retaliation increasingly came to be recognised and there was an urge to pull back from the nuclear brink. This led to the evolution under President Kennedy of the doctrine of 'flexible response', formally adopted by NATO in 1969, and which, to this day, remains the official strategy of NATO. The new strategic doctrine, instead of being premised on the immediate use of nuclear weapons, required NATO to maintain in Central Europe conventional forces sufficient in strength and readiness to be able to withstand and hold, for several days at least, an all-out conventional attack from the East. Only in the event that NATO forces proved unable to hold their ground with conventional weapons, or, that nuclear weapons were used against them, would NATO escalate to the use of tactical nuclear weapons, colloquially known as 'battlefield nukes'. Should even these weapons prove inadequate to stop the massed armoured advance of Soviet and allied forces across West Germany towards the Low Countries and France, then and only then would resort be had to strategic nuclear weapons aimed at the Soviet heartland.

Military doctrines such as these may be excellent in theory, but would they work in practice? Regrettably the answer to that cannot be known, except when it is already too late. Robert McNamara, US Secretary of Defense under Kennedy and later under Johnson, was foremost in acknowledging the dangers and inadequacies of such doctrines. In one of several meetings I had with him in the mid-sixties in his vast Pentagon office, into which one would be ushered at the split second of the appointed hour, McNamara gave me his views on the dangers involved in the first use of tactical nuclear weapons:

The problem is that the bomb does not drop out of the sky wrapped up with a label saying: 'I'm only a tactical nuke – please retaliate only in kind.' There is a real danger that the battlefield commander would radio back to the Soviet High Command: 'We are under nuclear attack' – period. There would be no guarantee whatever that the Soviet Union would confine its retaliation to military targets alone or to the use of only tactical warheads.

Be that as it may, the basic strategy of NATO over the first thirty years of its existence, whether based on the 'trip-wire' or 'flexible response' doctrines, has been to rely in the last resort on its overwhelming superiority in the nuclear field to make up for its many inadequacies at the conventional level. Throughout this period it was confidently assumed that the Soviet Union would never dare embark on any major adventure against Western Europe so long as it meant risking catastrophic devastation of the Soviet Motherland, for the cost to Russia would far outweigh any possible advantage that could be hoped for by the occupation of part or all of a devastated Western Europe. Thirty years or more of peace are eloquent testimony to the validity of the strategy. However, by the beginning of the eighties the situation in Europe had changed drastically to the point where the entire credibility of NATO's defence posture was in question.

Not only, as has been mentioned in a previous chapter, has the West – which inevitably and overwhelmingly means the United States – lost the strategic nuclear advantage that had been hers for more than thirty years but, even lower down the scale of nuclear might, the Soviet Union has succeeded in establishing a decisive preponderance. Just as the restraint demonstrated by the United States in not adding a single missile since 1967 to its strategic inventory conspicuously failed to persuade the Soviet Union to limit its own strategic build-up, so at the level of Euro-strategic weapons (nuclear missiles with strategic warheads but without inter-continental range and

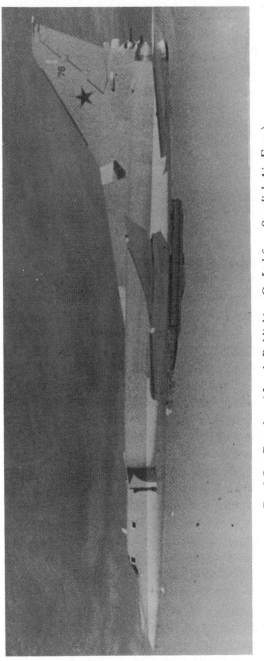

Backfire Bomber (*Jane's Publishing Co Ltd from Swedish Air Force*)

therefore not covered by the SALT negotiations) the fact that the NATO allies have actually reduced their strength in this field has utterly failed to prompt any reciprocal gesture by the Soviet Union.

Between the mid-sixties, when the United States withdrew its medium-range Thor and Jupiter missiles together with its force of B-47 bombers from Europe, and the mid-seventies there was a rough balance in land-based theatre-nuclear systems between NATO and the Soviet Union (which, significantly, does not entrust nuclear weapons to its own Warsaw Pact allies). The Soviet Union's 600 medium-range SS-4 and SS-5 missiles, two-thirds of them targeted against Western Europe, were offset by Britain's 56 RAF Vulcan bombers and a force of some 170 F-111 fighter bombers of the United States Air Force stationed in Britain. Apart from a gradual increase in the modest French capability, which is not even committed to NATO, the Western allies have not added in any way to their Euro-strategic capability for well over a decade, having previously significantly reduced it. Thus the massive Soviet build-up in this field since the mid-seventies has been entirely unprovoked and may be seen as further evidence, if any were needed, of the Soviet Union's determination to achieve not merely parity with the West, but to gain supremacy.

The development and deployment since the mid-seventies of two deadly new weapons systems, the Backfire supersonic nuclear strike-bomber and the SS-20 intermediate-range ballistic missile (IRBM), have drastically increased the Soviet threat against America's European allies. By early 1981 180 Backfires and more than 200 SS-20s were already in service with Soviet forces, two-thirds of them facing Western Europe, one-third against China and Japan. So far as NATO is concerned, the deployment to date of Backfires and SS-20s represents an increase in the destructive potential targeted against the cities and the civilian population of Western Europe equal to more than *10,000 Hiroshima bombs*, even allowing for the destruction of approximately 200 of the older SS-4s and SS-5s and the fact that half the Backfires facing Europe are in an anti-shipping rather than a nuclear-strike role. President Brezhnev was technically correct when, towards the end of 1979, he claimed that he had added not a single missile to those arrayed against Western Europe. However the fact is that NATO has no land-based missile in Europe capable of reaching the Soviet Union, while the Soviets' one-for-one replacement of the older generation of missiles represents a trebling of warheads targeted against Western Europe. In addition the Backfire is a completely new system, in effect also a missile system given that it can launch its nuclear weapons up to 400 miles from its target. In consequence of this development the Soviet Union had by 1980 established an advantage in Euro-strategic weapons of no less than 3·5:1. Evidently even this margin does not satisfy the men in the Kremlin for construction rates are currently running at one Backfire every twelve days and one SS-20 every five, and the balance of advantage in this field will continue to shift heavily in favour of the Soviet Union for the foreseeable future. Such has been President Brezhnev's peculiar contribution to the process of detente in Europe.

The Backfire bomber, which is a military development of the Soviet Union's TU-144 supersonic transport, nicknamed 'Concordski' by the British for its close resemblance to the Anglo-French Concorde, is capable of flying at 1,750 m.p.h., or two and a half times the speed of sound, and has a radius of action of 2,000 miles, nearly double the USAF's F-111 (*Military Balance 1980/81*, IISS). By making use of its in-flight refuelling capability Backfire can be given inter-continental range, although *the Russians promised Mr Carter they will not do this* and, evidently, he took their word for it. It is equipped to carry four AS-4 Kitchen air-launched cruise missiles, subsonic jet-propelled guided missiles with a range of 375 nautical miles, each armed with a nuclear warhead. By early 1981 some 180 of these bombers were operational, equally divided between the Soviet Long-Range and Naval Air Forces. Though some are deployed against the Chinese border, the great majority face the NATO allies in Western Europe. The naval Backfires from their bases on the Baltic and Black seas can dominate the sea-lanes of the Mediterranean, and present a new and deadly threat to the NATO navies and to all merchant shipping bound for Europe. Meanwhile the Backfires of the Long-Range Air

Legend:
- The Iron Curtain
- Soviet satellite states established by the Red Army after 1945 and subsequently incorporated into the Warsaw Pact
- NATO member countries
- Neutral countries

FINLAND

Vyborg

Leningrad

Revalo

SWEDEN

ESTONIA

LATVIA

DENMARK

LITHUANIA

U.S.S.R.

Vilna○

○Minsk

HOLLAND

EAST
Berlin○

POLAND

Warsaw○

BELGIUM

FEDERAL

GERMANY

○Bonn

Prague○

○Lvov

LUXEM
BOURG

REPUBLIC

CZECHOSLOVAKIA

of GERMANY
Munich ○

FRANCE

SWITZ
ERLAND

AUSTRIA

HUNGARY

○Budapest

ROMANIA

ITALY

Belgrade
○

Bucharest

Black Sea

YUGOSLAVIA

BULGARIA

○Sofia

CORSICA

Rome

ALBANIA

○
Tirana

SARDINIA

GREECE

TURKEY

Mediterranean

100,000
Native   Men~includes full-time members
100,000   of armies and paramilitaries;
Foreign   reserves are not included

1,000
Native   Tanks
1,000
Foreign

The Balance of Conventional Forces in Central Europe 1980

Force, which have the capability of striking any target in Western Europe and even of attacking Britain via the 'back door' from the west, could wreak devastation on Western Europe's ports, airfields and centres of civilian population.

In the case of the SS-20 the Soviet Union has achieved an important breakthrough in ballistic-missile technology for, unique of all the land-based systems deployed by either side at the present time, it is mobile. Moving on its transporter-erector-launcher, it can be concealed under camouflage in forests or in buildings. Its ability to move makes it difficult to find and almost impossible to destroy. With a range of 2,700 nautical miles it is comparable to Britain's Polaris missiles but its three MIRVed warheads of 0·5 mt (*pace* the IISS) are more powerful than Polaris' three 0·2 mt multiple-re-entry vehicle (MRV) warheads which, unlike the fully MIRVed SS-20, cannot be independently targeted. An especially threatening attribute of the SS-20 is its ability to reload and launch additional missiles, on the existence of which it is difficult to establish precise information. This uncertainty in itself lends a dangerously unstabilising effect to the situation. In the event that the present rate of SS-20 deployment is maintained the Soviets could have 500 of these missiles in service by 1985, including over 300 with some 1,000 nuclear warheads targeted on Western Europe. However, if each launcher were to be equipped with just two reloads the number of warheads would be increased to no less than 3,000.

It is the scale and strength of the Soviet build-up, combined with the decaying capability of Britain's twenty-year-old V-bombers which are scheduled for retirement by 1983 to be followed not long after by the US F-111s, that prompts NATO's current theatre nuclear forces (TNF) modernisation programme, which is long overdue and urgently needed to restore even a severe imbalance of power. However, the United States has no medium- or intermediate-range ballistic missile in its inventory, or even on the drawing board, equivalent to the Soviets' SS-20. The 108 Pershing II short-range ballistic missiles (SRBM), due to become operational in Western Europe from 1983 onwards, will have only a fraction of the SS-20s' 2,700-nautical-mile range. Similarly, the 464 Tomahawk ground-launched cruise missiles (GLCM) that will come into service with US forces in Europe at the same time are scheduled to have only tactical, not strategic, warheads and a range that would cover only Eastern Europe and the very western extremities of the Soviet Union. Thus, while the Soviet Backfires and SS-20s can already strike all the capitals of Europe from their home bases in the Soviet Union, the American Tomahawks and Pershings, even when they come into service, will not have the range to strike the Soviet heartland.

One of the more disquieting elements of the SALT II agreement, as presented to the US Senate by President Carter in late 1979, rested in the fact that while no restriction whatever was placed on Soviet medium-range systems such as Backfire and SS-20, the treaty imposed severe restrictions on the only medium-range system readily available to NATO to counter them, namely the US cruise missile. The treaty effectively ignores a whole range of Soviet strategic systems of which the US has no equivalent. Furthermore it took no account of the realities of the geography of Europe and the substantially lesser range of US theatre-nuclear systems compared to those of the Soviets. In addition the protocol to SALT II restricts the deployment of ground- and submarine-launched missiles (GLCM/SLCM) to a maximum range of no more than 375 miles. The Carter administration argued that this restriction was unimportant because the protocol was due to expire at the end of 1981 which anyway was well ahead of the earliest possible date the United States could bring the missiles into service and that this part of the protocol was therefore meaningless. If, indeed, it was meaningless, it is difficult to know why such a clause was included in the first place, unless it was the intention of the Carter administration, subsequently, to extend it into the future.

However, the most severe restraints on Western medium-range systems come not from the temporary protocol but from the treaty itself, which automatically classifies any aircraft carrying a cruise missile with a range of more than 375 miles as an inter-continental strategic launch-vehicle – a figure no doubt chosen to suit the convenience of the Soviet Union whose

Backfires would otherwise have been designated inter-continental given the 375 mile range of their AS-4 cruise missiles. Thus, if to counter the growing Soviet strategic build-up against Western Europe, the United States wished to arm some of its F-111 fighter-bombers, or other aircraft based in Britain, with cruise missiles, this could only be done at the expense of standing down B-52 bombers in the United States, for America legally to remain within the SALT II ceiling of 1,320 MIRVed missiles and heavy bombers equipped for cruise missiles. Article II of the treaty specifically includes among the definitions of 'heavy bombers' under paragraph 3(c): 'Types of bombers equipped for cruise missiles capable of a range in excess of 600 km', that is to say 375 miles.

In every field the Soviet nuclear build-up against Europe has been unrestrained. In addition to the 350 Badger and Blinder bombers, now supplemented by some 90 Backfires, deployed against land-based targets in Western Europe, the numbers of Soviet nuclear-capable tactical aircraft facing the NATO countries have trebled in a decade, rising from under 1,000 in 1970 to close on 3,000 by 1980. Even at battlefield level, yet another area of traditional Western superiority, the Soviet Union with its vast array of 1,300 Frog, Scud and Scaleboard short-range missiles deployed in Central Europe dwarfs NATO's 270 Pershing I and Lance tactical missiles by a factor of 5:1 (*Military Balance 1980/81*, IISS). Not content with this, the Russians are currently replacing these with a whole new generation of tactical weapons known to NATO as the SS-21, SS-22 and SS-23, respectively. Even until quite recently the growing Soviet advantage at battlefield level had been more than offset by NATO's clear superiority in nuclear-capable artillery. Only recently has NATO become aware that the Soviet Union which, together with its allies, outnumbers NATO by a factor of no less than 5·5:1 in artillery (*Hansard*, Parliamentary Reply, 23 April 1980) has also developed a capability of firing nuclear projectiles from many of its heavy guns and howitzers. Altogether the Warsaw Pact's conventional artillery facing Western Europe totals 14,800 guns compared to NATO's mere 2,700 artillery pieces (*ibid*).

The importance and value of NATO is amply proved by the

fact that to date it has been instrumental in maintaining the peace of the world at the highest level for more than thirty years – an era of tranquility unprecedented in this century that has enabled the peoples of the Western democracies to enjoy both freedom and a growing prosperity. Unquestionably the most decisive factor in realising this achievement has been the fact that, throughout this period, the NATO allies were at all times able to count on US nuclear superiority to offset NATO's weaknesses in conventional power. The dawn of the eighties ushered in an era in which every single one of NATO's offsetting advantages in the field of nuclear weapons – at strategic, Euro-strategic and at battlefield level – has been lost. The inherent stability that previously existed in the balance of world power, most especially at its fulcrum in Central Europe where 1,590,000 Warsaw Pact soldiers with 32,700 tanks confront 780,000 NATO forces with only 6,600 tanks across the Iron Curtain border (*Hansard*, Parliamentary Reply, 23 April 1980) has now ceased to exist.

The fact that the Soviet Union, while lulling the West with sweet words of detente, has been exerting itself to the limit of its technological, industrial and economic capabilities to establish a clear lead over the United States in the field of military nuclear power has not in any way led to a slackening of effort in terms of conventional power.

Heedless of the fact that since 1962, US land, sea and air forces in Europe have been reduced from 434,000 to barely 300,000 and, in defiant violation of the spirit of the MBFR (Mutual Balanced Force Reduction) talks which had as their specific aim the reduction in the concentration of conventional military strength in Europe, the Soviet Union has throughout this period been building up its armed manpower as well as its tank and artillery strength in the forward areas. The very purpose of the MBFR talks was to achieve a reduction of tension, by making a surprise attack by massive concentrations of armour and manpower less likely, if not impossible. But by 1980 it had become abundantly clear, to all that had eyes to see, that the Soviet Union, far from cooperating in this exercise had from the very start been working to subvert it. Soviet strength in Eastern Europe increased from twenty-six divisions in 1967 to

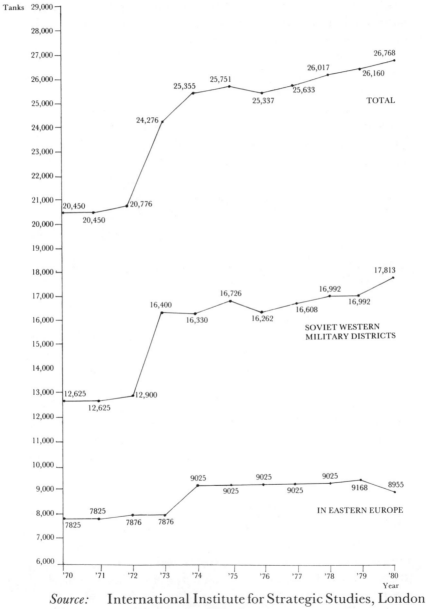

Fig 6   *Soviet tanks in Eastern Europe and Western Military*
Districts of the Soviet Union
1970–80

Source: International Institute for Strategic Studies, London
(previously unpublished).

thirty-one by 1979; later the same year one of these divisions was withdrawn from East Germany by the Soviets with a fanfare of television publicity as a 'gesture towards peace'. It seems likely – though the naive Western apologists for the Soviet Union who hailed the Soviet action could scarcely have foreseen it – that the true reason it was withdrawn was to form one of the six Soviet divisions that took part in the invasion and subsequently the occupation of Afghanistan. At the same time the strength of Soviet forces in the Western Military Districts of the USSR, adjacent to Eastern Europe, was increased from sixty-four to sixty-seven divisions in twelve months. More significantly, Soviet divisions in Eastern Europe are not only more numerous but each is substantially stronger in manpower, tanks and artillery than a decade ago. Indeed even if an entire Soviet tank army, consisting of three armoured divisions, were to be withdrawn from the Group of Soviet Forces in (East) Germany (GSFG), there would still be several hundred more Soviet tanks in Central Europe than a decade before as the MBFR talks were first being mooted. The remarkable fact is that all this has come about during a period when the Soviet Union was adding no less than twenty-five divisions to its forces along the Chinese border.

A measure of the gravity of the Soviet conventional build-up and, by the same token, of the utter failure of the MBFR dialogue, is the fact that, whereas at the start of the Vienna talks NATO felt it could count upon no less than thirty days' warning of any impending Soviet attack against Western Europe, the warning-time has today been reduced to *no more than seventy-two hours*. The assumption of a thirty-day 'warning-period' had been made on the basis that, previously, Soviet and Warsaw Pact forces facing NATO on the Central Front were judged to be inadequate, of themselves, to launch an attack without first being strengthened by the mobilisation of reserves. It was NATO's conviction that such mobilisation, which it was estimated would take not less than thirty days, could not go unnoticed in the West and would give NATO precious time in which to mobilise as well. Thirty days also happened to be the timescale required before the very first seaborne reinforcements might be expected to arrive from the United States. Today however, NATO strategists believe that in consequence of the remorseless Soviet build-up of recent years, Soviet and Warsaw Pact forces in East Germany, Czechoslovakia and Poland are now so strong that they have achieved what is known as a 'standing-start' capability or, in other words, the ability to launch an attack without prior mobilisation or reinforcement. It has been this disturbing development that has forced NATO to the conclusion that it can now rely on no more than seventy-two hours warning-time which, allowing optimistically only twenty-four hours for the political leaders of the NATO countries to take decisive action and give the order for mobilisation without delay, would provide no more than forty-eight hours 'military warning-time' for the troops to mobilise, outload their war-stores and move up to their battle-stations (in many cases, far removed from their peacetime billets). Indeed, in recent years several major units of Britain's 55,000 strong Rhine Army have for long periods been out of West Germany altogether on detached duty in Northern Ireland.

In this scenario Soviet forces would mobilise 'on the roll' once an attack was under way. The thirty Soviet divisions in Central Europe, maintained all the time at full strength, would be reinforced by a further sixty-seven Soviet divisions in the adjacent Western Military Districts of the Soviet Union as they mobilise. The problems of reinforcement are infinitely greater for NATO than for the Warsaw Pact as the United States has to transport her forces across the Atlantic, mostly from the Southern or Western states, a distance of some 5,000 miles or more while the Russians have barely 500 miles to cover from their western border to West Germany, and only 300 in the case of Austria, whose neutrality would almost certainly be violated in the event of a Soviet attack. Some idea may be gained of the Soviets' massive and rapid reinforcement capability from the fact that they maintain in the Western USSR sufficient tank transporters to move forward simultaneously no less than four tank armies amounting to twelve armoured divisions with some 4,000 tanks – one-third more in fact than the United States' entire tank strength in Europe.

The consequence of this swift and grave development has been to cause all the NATO allies to look once again at the state of readiness of their forces and the speed with which reinforcements can be called up and deployed. Foremost in this exercise has been the United States, which plans, by an increase in the number of its divisional stockpiles in Europe, together with a major overhaul of its air transport resources, to step up its current capability of moving a single division and forty squadrons of tactical aircraft to Europe within ten days, to a total of no less than five divisions with sixty tactical air squadrons in the same timescale. This will represent an impressive improvement in capability. Nervertheless the reality has to be faced that the doctrine of 'flexible response' could be sustained only so long as the NATO allies maintained sufficiently strong conventional forces relative to those deployed against them, furnished them with equipment that was technologically superior and, in the last resort, retained superiority in battlefield, theatre and strategic nuclear weapons. Those days have gone. 'Flexible response' is a dead duck, not because the concept is outdated, nor even because the allies have consciously wished to abandon it, but from weakness and, above all, from the fact that NATO's politicians have not willed the means to make it a reality. For better or for worse – and who can doubt but that it is the latter – NATO is back to the 'trip-wire'.

Chapter Seven

BRITAIN: THE UNSINKABLE CARRIER?

'Although the British military situation is hopeless, they do not show the least sign of giving in.' With these words Hitler in July 1940 launched preparations for Operation 'Sea Lion' – the invasion of Britain. Orders were given for the assembly in German, Belgian and French ports of more than 4,000 transports, barges, trawlers and assorted vessels that would convey the 260,000-strong invasion force across the narrow waters of the English Channel to Britain. At the same time the German Luftwaffe launched its air offensive aiming to shatter the Royal Air Force and gain superiority over the skies of Britain which, as Hitler recognised in his very first directive on 'Sea Lion', was the key to the invasion plans.

The courage and skill of the immortal 'Few' who, in the summer of 1940, saved Britain from invasion is legend, and every schoolboy has heard of how, in those brilliant summer months now known as the Battle of Britain, the pilots of RAF Fighter Command, many fresh out of school and with a brief training, managed, by a hair's breadth, to turn the tide against the Luftwaffe's superior strength and change the course of history. However, by comparison with the scandalously run-down state of Britain's air defences in the eighties, the 'Few' constituted a veritable armada of air power.

Throughout the battle that raged over the skies of southern England and the Channel coast during the months of July, August and September 1940, the RAF's front-line operational strength, including aircraft available at four days' readiness, averaged 1,000 fighter aircraft, dropping at its lowest point to 875 in the third week of September, at the climax of the battle (Winston S. Churchill, *The Second World War*, vol. II). Were there to be any future 'Battle of Britain', the fighter-pilots of the Royal Air Force would have to face an even more deadly enemy against far more adverse odds.

In consequence of the adamant refusal of successive British governments to provide sufficient resources to meet the requirements of an adequate air-defence, there had been an utter failure to anticipate the consequences for Britain of the introduction into the Soviet Air Force of an entire new generation of aircraft since the mid-seventies. Up till then, the only aircraft with sufficient range to strike Britain's shores from the Soviet Union were the long-range Bear and Bison bombers and the medium-range Badgers and Blinders of the Long-Range Air Force. Because of their limited numbers and, except in the case of the Blinder, their subsonic speed, it had long been presumed by RAF planning staff that this force was insufficient to present any serious conventional air threat to the United Kingdom. It was therefore concluded, no doubt rightly, that were they to be used, it would be to carry only nuclear weapons, the counter to which was not to be found in a fighter defence but in the retaliatory capabilities of the RAF's V-bomber force and the Royal Navy's Polaris submarines.

At that time none of the Soviet Union's tactical air force, or Frontal Aviation as it is known, had the capability of reaching Britain's shores; indeed, as its name implies, its role was to provide air support for the Red Army on and immediately behind the front line. However, the replacement of the older short-range fighter bombers by a new generation of supersonic swing-wing aircraft – Fencers, Fitters and Floggers – each with treble the range and double the payload of the aircraft they were replacing, has meant that in the space of five years the tonnage of bombs that could be dropped on Britain had increased *tenfold* and that, for the first time, the Soviet Union had acquired the capability of launching a conventional air attack against Britain. By 1980 85 per cent of Soviet Frontal Aviation fighter bombers had been replaced by new-generation equipment of which the Royal Air Force had at the time no equivalent in operational service. Given the fact that Soviet aircraft factories have for some three years been building these aircraft at the rate of more than a thousand a year – a staggering twenty per week – it would clearly be possible for the Soviet High Command, in the event of any future conflict, to task against Britain up to a thousand of these aircraft or approximately one-third of the number currently facing Western Europe. Under such circumstances the pilots of the Royal Air Force could find themselves outnumbered *over the skies of Britain* by a factor not of 2 or 3:1 as in the Battle of Britain but by more than 10:1.

Today, the Channel remains as formidable a tank-ditch as ever, but only to a nation that retains naval superiority round its shores and supremacy in its skies. There was a time, as recently as the 1950s and 1960s, when United Kingdom air space was referred to glibly by certain military strategists as the 'UK sanctuary', so minimal was thought to be the Soviet capability of launching a conventional air attack against Britain. In accordance with this thinking, coupled with the premature belief that missiles had rendered manned aircraft largely obsolete, the Royal Auxillary Air Force was abolished in 1957 and a decade later RAF Fighter Command was merged with Bomber Command to form Strike Command. Meanwhile the resources available for the air defence of the United Kingdom were allowed to fall from 52 squadrons with more than 900 aircraft in 1955, to a mere 7 squadrons with not even one-tenth as many aircraft in 1980. By the late seventies Britain had no more than 70 front-line aircraft – Phantoms and Lightnings, built with the technology of the fifties – for the air defence of the entire United Kingdom and coastal waters. Indeed the situation had become so critical that a single RAF station (RAF Wattisham in East Anglia) with a squadron of ten Phantoms, of which only seven could be guaranteed operational at any one time, had responsibility for defending all of London, the entire southern half of England, the southern part of the North Sea, the English Channel and the western approaches towards the Atlantic.

It is not mere bravado but a statement of fact to say that Britain's armed forces in calibre of manpower are second to none in the world. Much of their equipment, too, especially the Army's new Challenger tank, Blowpipe and Rapier surface-to-air missiles, and the Royal Navy's Sea Dart and Sea Wolf anti-air and anti-missile missiles, are among the finest in the world. Indeed Sea Wolf is so precise as a point-defence system for surface vessels that it can even knock out of the air a 4·5-inch shell inbound to a vessel at several times the speed of sound. The principal weakness of Britain's armed forces rests, rather, in their very small numbers and the inadequate volume of modern equipment with which they are armed.

Although the Royal Air Force is shortly to receive into squadron service the supersonic, swing-wing Tornado GR-1 interdictor/strike aircraft of which 220 have been ordered, it will not be until the mid-eighties that the air-defence variant, the Tornado F-2, is due to enter service. Equipped with the British medium-range air-to-air Skyflash missile and the latest look-down/shoot-down radar, the air-defence Tornado is more of a bomber-destroyer than a dog-fighting interceptor, and will radically improve the RAF's capability of fighting against heavily adverse odds. However, unless for some unforeseen reason the Soviet Union ceases building up its Frontal Aviation forces, the RAF's total buy of 165 air-defence Tornados – *equivalent to eight weeks' Soviet production at its current rate* – appears to be woefully inadequate to meet the danger of the hour.

The attraction of Britain as a prime target both for the Soviet High Command in the event of war and to the KGB even in peacetime is not far to seek. Nor does it rest solely in the fact, as activists of the Campaign for Nuclear Disarmament assert, that Britain is herself a military nuclear power and that she provides base facilities in Scotland's Holy Loch for US nuclear submarines and, shortly, for 160 ground-launched cruise missiles in Berkshire and Cambridgeshire, as she has over many years for an equal number of F-111 fighter-bombers at Lakenheath and Upper Heyford.

Britain's importance in the struggle that is already joined for the future of Western Europe extends far beyond the provision of base facilities for US forces in Europe. To many she is seen as a symbol of freedom and a bastion of democracy. Alone of the nations of Europe she refused to submit to the Nazi tyranny. And alone, except for her loyal Empire spread around the globe – Canada, Australia, New Zealand, India, South Africa and Rhodesia, together with forces from East and West Africa – she fought on for three long years until the United States joined in the fray. Then, from being the citadel that had stood firm against the Nazi fire that had engulfed all of Europe, Britain was transformed into a vast armed camp and became the springboard from which the assault for the liberation of occupied Europe was ultimately launched.

To this day Britain remains in the eyes of NATO the unsinkable aircraft-carrier that, in the event of any future crisis in Europe, would play the key role in the US reinforcement of Europe which rests at the heart of the defensive strategy of NATO. Not only does Britain contribute important land and air forces to the front line in Central Europe, but the Royal Navy provides the lion's share of NATO's 'Ready Forces' in the Eastern Atlantic and would have a vital part to play, together with the RAF's Nimrod anti-submarine aircraft, in any conflict in ensuring that the vast convoys of troops, hardware and supplies complete their journeys to British and other West European ports in safety, in the teeth of the Soviet submarine and bomber threat.

Under the NATO plan, several thousand aircraft would stage through British bases and British air space on their way from the United States to Europe. The prize to the Kremlin of knocking out Britain in the earliest days of a conflict, or, better still, of securing her defection from the NATO alliance in advance by subversion, would be very great indeed. At a stroke the very foundation of NATO's defensive plan would have been undermined and Europe's defence potential shattered.

Given the importance of Britain as a target and the desperate weakness of her air defences, the fact that the Soviet Union maintains no fewer than eight divisions of airborne forces, consisting of some 56,000 paratroops – equivalent to the entire peacetime strength of Britain's Rhine Army – should not pass unnoticed. By comparison, the United States maintains no more than a single airborne division of 16,000 men. The Soviet Union's massive airlift capability provides her with the means of deploying large numbers of troops complete with artillery, armoured fighting vehicles and light tanks to any point on the globe, as has been demonstrated in recent years in Angola, Ethiopia, Vietnam and, most recently, Afghanistan. There can be little doubt that an airborne attack launched against Britain at the outset of a conflict would almost certainly meet with failure. However NATO's belt of Hawk anti-air missile defences in Central Europe has little depth (unlike its Soviet counterpart with more than 12,000 defensive missiles and radar-controlled guns) and it is unlikely to prove effective in preventing the breakthrough of a sustained Soviet air attack, coupled with strikes by SS-20 missiles armed with tactical nuclear warheads against British air bases and port installations; the clear possibility exists that the RAF might lose air supremacy over the skies of Britain and the way would be open for a Soviet airborne invasion backed from the sea by elements of the Soviets' 70,000-strong naval infantry with their formidable array of assault ships.

Present plans call for the British Army on the Rhine, on mobilisation, to be more than trebled in strength to over 180,000 men. Thus some 70 per cent of the readily available forces of the British Army would be in Europe together with more than three-quarters of Britain's 900 Chieftain tanks. The British Isles would be virtually denuded of troops. Barely 100,000 men, plus 50,000 reservists not yet assigned a war-role, would be left to guard the home base. This may have been a quite justifiable policy in the days when the United Kingdom could still be regarded as a 'sanctuary' but, given the attraction to the Kremlin of attempting to deliver a knockout blow to Britain and the temptation to do so offered by the run-down state of Britain's air defences, it would be foolish in the extreme to rule out the possibility of an attempted invasion of Britain in the event of hostilities.

In these wholly new circumstances there is an urgent need for Britain to re-examine the security of her home base. There is no sense in Britain deploying large ground and air forces in Germany and basing her plans on assigning no less than 70 per cent of her regular army and readily available reserves to Central Europe, if Britain herself is to be left wide open to attack and invasion. The threat to Britain in the 1980s in consequence of the Soviet Union's dramatic enhancement of its tactical air power in the late seventies is an entirely new situation. Britain has become intensely vulnerable. Her military installations, ports, cities and, above all, her civilian population are open to aerial bombardment – even with *conventional bombs* alone – on a scale far beyond anything experienced in the Blitz.

It was in recognition of this new situation that on coming to office in May 1979 the Conservative Government under the leadership of Margaret Thatcher and her Secretary of State for Defence, Francis Pym, took the stop-gap decision of ordering that a squadron of Lightning interceptors be taken out of the crates in which they had been mothballed for a decade or more and returned to operational service to supplement the RAF's threadbare front-line strength of seventy aircraft – the total available for UK air defence. However even this step was countermanded before it could be implemented with the announcement in January 1981 of £200m ($450m) worth of defence cuts, following Pym's replacement as Secretary of State for Defence by John Nott, previously Minister for Trade. One importance decision not rescinded was the commitment to provide a second line of defence, with the arming of ninety Hawk trainer aircraft with the AIM9-L Sidewinder air-to-air missiles for base defence. The addition of these aircraft represents a desperately needed strengthening of the RAF's capability; however it is no more than the beginning of a major undertaking if Britain's home base is to be made secure.

The problems involved in strengthening Britain's home defences to the point where a potential attacker would be forced to conclude that the cost would be very high indeed and probably not worth risking are by no means insuperable. Furthermore it could be achieved without undue cost and without succumbing to the temptation of weakening Britain's contribution to NATO on the Central Front in Europe, which, at the time of writing, is an option that is being given serious consideration. Admittedly Britain's commitment under the terms of the Brussels Treaty to contribute 55,000 troops to NATO's forward defence on the Central Front was made under different circumstances from those of today, but for Britain to reduce her contribution to Europe at a time when the Soviet Union and their Warsaw Pact allies have vastly increased their capability against Western Europe would have the effect of lowering still further the nuclear threshold of Europe. It would set a very bad example indeed to other members of the alliance at a time when there is a need for the maximum steadiness on parade.

It is urgent that the highest priority be given to a major strengthening of Britain's air defence and this will require both an acceleration and an expansion of the RAF's order for 165 Tornado F-2 air-defence aircraft, which are at present not scheduled to enter squadron service until 1985 and beyond. Together with this there must be an expanded pilot-training programme and an increased provision for airfield hardening, with the construction of aircraft shelters, which would largely be funded by NATO. In addition it would seem only prudent that the United States be invited to play a part in the defence of Britain's air space which, in wartime, would be every bit as much an American concern as a British one, especially as there would be many times more American aircraft at UK air bases than British.

It is a common misconception among many in Britain that the United States Air Force already has a planned and trained role in the air defence of the United Kingdom. This is not so. The seven squadrons of USAF F-111 fighter-bomber based at Upper Heyford and Lakenheath are all nuclear-capable strike-aircraft whose targets would be airfields, railheads and munition stores in Eastern Europe and the western extremities of the Soviet Union, while the six squadrons of 108 A-10 Thunderbolt II aircraft are earmarked for a tank-busting role in Central Europe. Only the so-called 'Aggressor Squadron', with its small complement of F-5s at RAF Alconbury, painted to look like Soviet MiGs and used for the tactical training of US and NATO fighter-squadrons in Europe, would even have the capability of engaging an enemy aircraft. In a crisis a vast array of USAF and Air National Guard squadrons would be flown across the Atlantic and stationed in Britain at bases already identified and provided for. Given the very limited manned bomber threat to the continental United States, the USAF would undoubtedly have substantial air-defence resources available that could be put to good use in Britain but, unless their use is planned and regularly exercised in advance, their contribution to UK air defence would be limited and, meanwhile, the several hundred US aircraft at British bases would be intensely vulnerable.

Allied to air defence, priority must be given to the provision of missile defences against air attack. Apart from a few squadrons of ageing Bloodhound surface-to-air missiles, providing limited coverage over air bases in East Anglia and Lincolnshire and a handful of Rapier squadrons deployed to guard key airfields against low-level attack, the United Kingdom is at present devoid of missile defences. In addition to the many air bases, command and communication centres that are uncovered, there is no protection whatever afforded to Britain's vital ports, let alone her cities with their vast civilian populations. Not only is a more extensive deployment of Rapier required, there is an urgent need for the British Government to give the go-ahead for the deployment of British Aerospace's Land Dart, an area air defence missile providing a wide radius of coverage, already well proved in its naval version known as Sea Dart.

An evident requirement is for the creation of a large pool of trained reserve manpower, separate from Britain's existing reserve forces and Territorial Army, most of which are earmarked for service in Germany and therefore have to be trained and equipped to Rhine Army standards. This would involve the establishment of an entirely new category of reservist, combining the roles of the wartime Home Guard and Civil Defence of the Second World War. Given the present level of threat, it is a dangerous absurdity that, under present plans, any future crisis would find barely one per cent of the British people trained and equipped to fight, while 55 million would be condemned to watch on television. The problems and costs involved in recruiting, training and arming such a force of volunteers – desirably at least a million strong – would not be great since they would require no more than light infantry weapons including man-portable anti-tank and anti-air missiles, which could in peacetime be held at local police stations under lock and key. In wartime they would have the effect of turning the whole British Isles into a most formidable armed camp and would ensure a traditionally warm welcome for any so bold as to invade her shores. And in the event that Britain did ultimately succumb, it would provide a formidable basis on which to launch a campaign of guerrilla warfare against any occupying forces – the only hope of securing the country's ultimate liberation.

The lack of a substantial pool of trained reserve manpower to meet any future unforeseen crisis represents a major weakness in Britain's defences though it is the armed forces themselves that are the most strongly opposed to any suggestion of conscription or to the creation of a new category of reservist, for they are convinced that, whatever politicians may say, it will have to be funded out of existing resources at the expense of some other programme. Regrettably successive governments have convinced them that they are right, therefore almost every idea for innovation is resisted. But no matter how excellent Britain's armed forces may be, the harsh reality has to be faced that their mobilised strength, including all reserves, is less than 600,000 men and women, one-third of what it was in 1960 (*Hansard*, Parliamentary Reply, 28 January 1980) and fewer than that of Switzerland, Sweden or even tiny Finland with one-twelfth of Britain's 56 million population. It is of course only right to point out that Britain's armed forces are full-time professional volunteers, more experienced and more highly trained than the part-time 'citizen armies' maintained most notably by the neutral countries of Europe, who rely on conscription and on a continuing reserve liability to the age of fifty to maintain their greater strength in numbers.

Finally attention needs to be given to the strengthening of Britain's naval forces, for although the Royal Navy remains the third largest in the world, after the Soviet Union and the United States, and currently contributes no less than 90 per cent of the ships to NATO's 'on call' forces in the Eastern Atlantic, the truth is that it is but a shadow of its former strength. There is an incontestable requirement for Britain to maintain a strong naval building programme if she is to maintain her seaward defences while at the same time strengthening her capability to assist the United States in patrolling the vital oil routes that carry Europe and America's life-blood from Arabia and the Persian Gulf across the Indian Ocean, round the Cape of Good Hope and through the waters of the South and North Atlantic. In the event of a Soviet attack against NATO, the United States would require all the assistance Britain could give her in keeping open the sea-lanes and above all the vital reinforcement link across the North Atlantic, which, had it been severed in the last war, would have brought Britain to surrender through starvation. Britain's shipyards, suffering severely from a world-wide collapse of civil orders, have caused the British Government some embarrassment by, unprecedentally, completing vessels for the Royal Navy one or even two years ahead of their expected delivery date which, contractually, have to be paid for, causing Britain's Ministry of Defence to cut back sharply in other fields. One of the principal casualties has been the Navy's future shipbuilding programme, which has, effectively, been brought to a standstill, with little prospect of even a single order being placed for a major ship until 1982.

With idle shipyards and steelworks operating far below capacity at a time of rapidly increasing external danger, logic requires that the Government, far from cutting back on its orders, should initiate a major shipbuilding programme. There are few who would question the need for Britain, whose national debt doubled in the five years before the Conservative Government took office in 1979, to live more nearly within her means, but with well over £3,000 million ($7,000 million) a year of taxpayers' money being given in subsidies and grants to Britain's ailing nationalised industries as well as £8,500m ($18,000m) being paid out to the unemployed, a strong case can be made for the Government switching some of these resources to the placing of actual orders for ships. This would provide work for the shipyards, orders for Britain's recession-hit engineering and electronics industries, take up slack in the steel industry, reduce both the extent and the cost of unemployment *and build a navy*.

The British Government's attitude to defence, at the present time, can only be described as one of acute schizophrenia. The Cabinet appears to be well aware of the threat confronting the NATO allies today; indeed none has been more outspoken than the Prime Minister herself who, delivering the Winston Churchill Memorial Lecture in Luxembourg on 18 October 1979 declared: 'The Soviet armies in Europe are organised and trained for attack. Their military strength is growing. The Russians do not publish their intentions. So we must judge them by their military capabilities.' But, although the threat is recognised, little is being done about it. Rhetoric alone is not enough. Soon after the Conservative Government came to office in 1979 General Alexander Haig, Secretary of State in the Reagan administration, prior to his retirement as Supreme Allied Commander, Europe (SACEUR), called on Mrs Thatcher, her Defence Secretary Francis Pym and Foreign Secretary Lord Carrington at Downing Street. They outlined for him the British Government's thinking in the field of defence. Following the meeting General Haig was heard to make the shrewd comment: 'What they said was music to my ears – but will they find the dough?'

The budget constraints on defence expenditure are very great indeed in all the democracies, with almost irresistible pressures from electorates (on governments anxious to secure a further term of office) to devote any resources that may be available – and even resources that are not available but have to be borrowed – to provide a high and ever-rising standard of living and level of social benefits. A comparison of defence expenditure in the United States and Britain in recent years as against spending on social benefits tells its own story with the trend running strongly in favour of *social* security at the expense of *national* security. In the case of Britain, over the twenty-five-year period to 1980, defence has declined from 27·4 per cent of total government expenditure to a bare 11·6 per cent, while expenditure on social security has increased from 17·7 per cent to no less than 28 per cent of total expenditure. In the United States the trends have been the same. Since 1960, when the percentage of government (including both federal and state) expenditure on defence and social services stood at an equal level of 30 per cent, defence has slumped to a mere 19·8 per cent of total outlay, while expenditure on social services increased to 49·1 per cent in 1977, the most recent year for which figures involving state as well as federal expenditure are available.

Currently Britain is spending approximately 5 per cent of her gross domestic product on defence, a figure that in percentage terms is higher than in any other European member of NATO, and which even in real terms places her second only to West Germany. However, if we take into account the cost of service pensions, together with the provision of education, medical services and married quarters for forces' families overseas, the levying of rates (local taxes) and value added tax (sales tax), not to mention the absurdity of the Treasury being allowed to exact petroleum tax every time an RAF Phantom is refuelled for the air-defence of the United Kingdom – a total amounting to £1,500 million or 15 per cent of overall defence expenditure – the percentage that Britain devotes to actual defence would drop to about 4·3 per cent of GDP. More significantly, Britain's defence expenditure would need to rise by *no less than 50 per cent* from its present level if the Conservative Government of Mrs Thatcher were to devote as great a proportion of overall government expenditure to defence as the Labour Government of Harold Wilson was doing in the mid-sixties.

Until recent years Britain's armed forces could justifiably boast not only a higher calibre of manpower than any other in the alliance – a position they retain to this day – but also they were armed with equipment that was the equal of any of the allies and far superior to anything available to Soviet or Warsaw Pact forces. However, in recent years the forces' equipment programme has suffered severely to the point where, today, even the Soviet Union has overtaken Britain and indeed all the Western allies, not merely in numbers, in which it has long enjoyed an overwhelming advantage, but increasingly in calibre of equipment in many fields on land, sea and in the air. Although the British Government remains committed to a 3 per cent increase in defence expenditure in real terms in the years

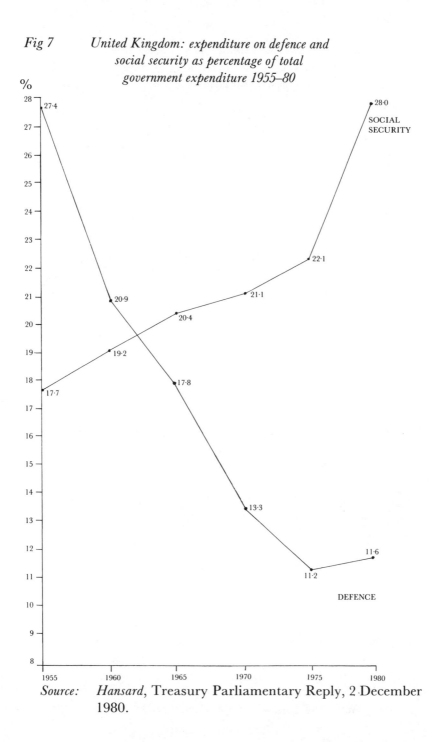

Fig 7   *United Kingdom: expenditure on defence and*
             social security as percentage of total
             government expenditure 1955–80

%

28 ·0

SOCIAL
SECURITY

27·4

22·1

21·1

20·9

20·4

19·2

17·8

17·7

13·3

11·6

11·2

DEFENCE

1955   1960   1965   1970   1975   1980

Source: *Hansard*, Treasury Parliamentary Reply, 2 December
             1980.

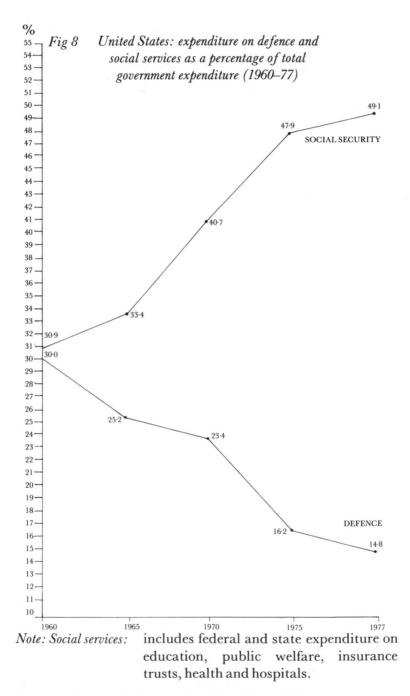

%

Fig 8   United States: expenditure on defence and
social services as a percentage of total
government expenditure (1960–77)

49·1

47·9   SOCIAL SECURITY

40·7

33·4

30·9
30·0

25·2

23·4

DEFENCE
16·2

14·8

1960   1965   1970   1975   1977

Note: Social services: includes federal and state expenditure on
education, public welfare, insurance
trusts, health and hospitals.

Source: Statistical Abstract of the United States 1979.

ahead, with 'technological' inflation – for instance the cost of replacing aircraft of 1950s technology with that of the 1980s – running well over 3 per cent a year ahead of 'consumer' inflation rates, Britain's planned expenditure is not even enough to enable her armed forces to hold their ground, let alone to improve their capability in the face of a sharply mounting threat. The point is well made in Britain's Defence *White Paper* for 1981 which shows that the cost of replacing an existing Leander class frigate with a modern Type 22 frigate is three times as much in real terms; in the case of a modern jet fighter the differential in price, again allowing for inflation, is fourfold.

'How much is required?' is a question often asked and one that is impossible to answer with precision. What is certain is that the sums required to ensure the maintenance of peace and freedom in the years ahead cannot be measured by two or three fine percentage points. Can anyone doubt that it is better to err on the side of safety than to gamble with catastrophe by risking falling narrowly short of the mark?

It is often argued that Britain's prewar Prime Minister Neville Chamberlain was right in his decision to postpone the day of reckoning with Hitler's Nazi Germany, thereby earning for Britain precious months, even years, in which to rearm and make good the neglect of previous years. However, although by the end of 1937 Britain was producing 118 airframes and 250 engines each month, Germany was outbuilding her by a factor of 4:1 with a construction rate of 500 airframes and 1,010 engines per month (Martin Gilbert, *Churchill*, Heinemann, London 1976, vol. 5). As each month passed, as today in the 1980s, the potential aggressor was increasing his lead while the democracies fell back in the race.

Nevertheless history has failed to give Chamberlain proper credit for the major rearmament programme he launched on becoming Prime Minister in May 1937. The reason lies no doubt in the fact that, extensive though Britain's rearmament was, it proved insufficient and, above all, too late to prevent the Second World War. It is nonetheless a fact that Chamberlain, who has gone down in the history books as the arch-appeaser, quadrupled Britain's defence expenditure in the space of just three years, increasing it from £172 million in 1936 to £743 million (at current prices) in 1939, putting up the proportion of Britain's gross domestic product spent on defence from 3·5 per cent to 12·5 per cent (Cmnd 6623, April 1945, C.H. Feinstein, *National Income Expenditure and Output of the United Kingdom 1855-1965*, Cambridge University Press, 1972).

Though Chamberlain's rearmament programme, coming late as it did, was not adequate to deter Hitler from launching what Churchill was to term the 'Unnecessary War', there is no doubt that his foresight saved Britain, if only by a hair's breadth, from losing it. As the wave upon wave of Luftwaffe attacks reached their crescendo on 15 September 1940, with flashing lights on the wallpanel of the underground bunker of No 11 Fighter Group at Uxbridge signalling raids by German bombers and fighters of '40 plus', '60 plus' and '80 plus', Churchill, Prime Minister since only four months before, noticed that all twenty-five of the Group's squadrons were airborne, either engaging the enemy or returning to base to refuel and rearm. He turned to Air Vice Marshal Park, the Group Commander, to enquire how many squadrons remained in reserve. Park replied simply: 'There are none'. Churchill in his war memoirs comments, 'What losses should we not suffer if our refuelling planes were caught on the ground by further raids of "40 plus" or "50 plus"! The odds were great, our margins small – the stakes infinite.'

Chamberlain's successors would do well to ponder what might have been the outcome had Britain, in those hours that decided the fate of the world, had fifty Hurricanes or Spitfires fewer, had the development of a fledgling radar system not been pioneered or had the elaborate underground command and control system linking Fighter Command's stations not been prepared. Britain owes Chamberlain an unacknowledged debt of gratitude. The 300 per cent increase in defence expenditure for which he was responsible in that crucial three-year period leading up to the outbreak of the Second World War stands in stark contrast to the efforts of his successors forty years on who, together with their NATO allies – under conditions of peril every bit as great – are struggling to achieve even the modest NATO goal of an annual increase of 3 per cent in real terms.

Because the rate of technological inflation in military replacement costs is running so far ahead of the ordinary rate of inflation, even a 3 per cent annual increase on Britain's current budget of £12.27 billion ($27 billion) is so seriously short of what is required to maintain even the present strength and capability of Britain's armed forces that major cuts are inevitable unless the pledge given by the Conservative Party before the May 1979 election to make a major transfer of resources from other fields to defence is honoured. The present gravity of the international situation is such that it is urgent that Britain should today give to defense at least as great a degree of priority as did the Socialist Government of Harold Wilson which in the mid-sixties – at a time when the perceived level of threat was far lower than it is acknowledged to be today – was devoting 17·8 per cent of public expenditure to defence compared to the mere 11·5 per cent under Margaret Thatcher in 1980/81. Anything less would risk falling seriously below the level of events.

Such an increase would represent no more than half the British Government's estimated annual receipts from North Sea oil and gas in the five years to 1985 and could easily be found from within the overall total of Britain's current public expenditure programme by reducing other Goverment expenditure by five per cent and specifically by transferring, to defence, resources presently earmarked for subsidies to the nationalised industries, and government make-work or 'Job Creation' schemes, as well as from savings on unemployment and social security benefits in respect of large numbers of men and their families who would cease to be a burden on the taxpayer.

The spin-off of a major rearmament programme would be to provide a defence-led way out of the slump that is today crippling British industry. Through defence orders, resources would be pumped into private industry, especially in the engineering and electronic industries, boosting Britain's high technology enterprises which, otherwise, risk losing their foremost research teams to California or Texas. Nationalised industries such as shipbuilding, aerospace and steel would all benefit and Britain's defence industry manufacturers would be enabled to capture valuable export orders which, all too often, fail to materialise when the home government shows no apparent interest in placing orders for their equipment. Above all, it would provide a way out of the recession, based on an expansion of the free enterprise sector and of Britain's high-technology industries.

Britain has the opportunity, indeed the duty, to give a lead in Europe. It would be nothing less than a tragedy if, after all Mrs Thatcher's brave words on defence and the excellent start she made in boosting forces' pay by 54 per cent within twelve months of coming to office and courageously deciding to buy Trident and accept cruise missiles on British soil, she were now to falter, when so many hopes in Britain and abroad are pinned on her resolve. What shall it profit a nation if it shall conquer inflation, yet lose peace and freedom?

Part IV

THE GLOBAL THREAT

Chapter Eight

ADMIRAL GORSHKOV'S NAVY

'For the Soviet Union, the main goal of whose policy is the building of communism . . . , sea power emerges as one of the important factors . . . .' (Admiral Sergei Gorshkov, *The Sea Power of the State*, Pergamon Press, 1979).

January 1981 marked the twenty-fifth anniversary of Admiral of the Fleet Sergei Gregorovich Gorshkov's taking up command of the Soviet Navy. Under the guidance of this officer, who had a distinguished career in what the Russians refer to as the Great Patriotic War of 1941–5, when he was especially involved in amphibious operations in the Black Sea and the recapture of Novorossisk, the Soviet Navy has been transformed from an ageing and ramshackle fleet, having little capability beyond the coastal confines of Soviet home waters, into the most modern and most powerful navy in the world, deploying Soviet power to every corner of the globe. Justly he is regarded as the architect and father of Russia's new ocean-going navy.

It was only after the Second World War that the United States' Navy took over from the Royal Navy, which for three centuries had ruled the waves supreme, the mantle of the world's greatest naval power. This was the consequence both of the terrible losses suffered by the Royal Navy in the six long years of war, especially in the Battle of the Atlantic and the Arctic convoys to Russia, and the colossal level to which United States naval construction was increased when she joined in the war, following the Japanese attack on Pearl Harbour on 7 December 1941. Regrettably, the unchallenged supremacy that the United States' Navy enjoyed in the postwar years in the Mediterranean as well as the Atlantic and Pacific oceans was to prove shortlived.

It was the vision of Admiral Gorshkov to build a navy that would rival that of the United States and indeed, ultimately, surpass it as an instrument of global power. Drawing on his experience of the Second World War he early concluded: 'The main, most universal and effective kinds of forces of the Fleet have become submarines and aircraft.' It is evident that this has been his guiding principle in the shaping of the Soviet Navy of today. Although he has at his command a large and very modern fleet of surface ships totalling 289 – compared to the United States' 191 – like the iceberg, the most formidable strength of the Soviet Navy is to be found beneath the waters. In terms of underwater strategic power, the Soviet Union today deploys no less than 87 ballistic-missile submarines (SSBNs) with 1,003 missiles (SLBMs) – 48 in excess of the limit allowed under the terms of the SALT agreement – while the United States has only 41 comparable submarines with 656 missiles (*Military Balance 1980/81*, IISS).

Already by mid-1980 10 ballistic-missile submarines of the Delta III class, each armed with 16 S-N-18 missiles, were in service with the Soviet Navy, yet the in-service date of the first of the United States' comparable vessels, the Ohio class with 24 Trident C4 missiles, had been delayed until at least mid-1981. The Trident missiles have a lesser range than their Soviet counterparts, 4,000 nautical miles as against 4,500, and 8 warheads of 0·1 mt each compared to the Delta's 3 warheads each of 1·2 mt. Although only 11 submarines of the Ohio class are currently planned for the US Navy, the Russians are continuing to build Delta IIIs and have recently launched the first of the new Typhoon class which, like Trident, has 24 missiles. Apart from a formidable force of 189 hunter-killer or attack-submarines, designed to destroy surface shipping or

Soviet Delta Class III Submarine (*Jane's Publishing Co Ltd from US Navy*)

other submarines, a category in which the United States has only 81, the Soviet Union deploys no fewer than 68 cruise-missile submarines, of which there is no equivalent among Western navies. The latest Soviet cruise-missile submarines, the Echo II class, each have 8 SS-N-12 missiles with a range of 2,000 nautical miles armed with nuclear warheads, and pose a formidable threat to the NATO allies' air and missile bases both in Europe and the United States with their ability to make low-level attacks underneath the ballistic-missile radar warning screens. The problems involved in targeting the SS-N-12, which were first deployed in 1979 and of which 48 were operational by July 1980, are substantial, especially in view of the missile's range which is greater than that of the planned US Tomahawk SLCM with a range of 1,500 nautical miles. At present long-range aircraft such as Russia's Bears and Bisons, and possibly the supersonic Backfire, are used to provide mid-course guidance to the missiles in flight, although the Russians are believed to be working on a system of directing their cruise missiles by space satellite.

In accordance with Gorshkov's strategic concept, the air power of the Soviet Navy has been increasing dramatically, especially with the deployment since the mid-seventies of the supersonic Backfire nuclear strike-bomber, which has been delivered in equal numbers to the Soviet Naval Air Force and to the Long-Range Air Force and is currently being produced at a rate of thirty per year – a limit set by President Brezhnev in a written undertaking given to President Carter at their meeting in Vienna in the period 14–18 June 1979. Second only to the attack- and cruise-missile submarines, this growing force of Backfires, of which there are already more than eighty in the Soviet Naval Force, armed as they are with 400-nautical-mile range AS-4 Kitchen cruise missiles with nuclear warheads, presents the greatest threat to NATO's surface fleets and shipping.

In addition to land-based naval air power, the Soviet Union is now building up a seaborne capability. Already two 43,000-ton carriers of the Kiev class are at sea, each equipped with fourteen Yak-36 Forger vertical take-off aircraft, an inferior version of Britain's Harrier jump-jet, and a further two vessels are under construction. However there is already evidence that the Soviets intend to enter the field which has for so long been the preserve of Western navies with the construction of an attack-carrier. By the spring of 1980 the keel of a nuclear-powered flat-top aircraft-carrier, with a probable displacement of 75,000 tons, was reported to be in place at the Nikolayev yard in the Ukraine.

The Russians have evidently recognised the formidable ability of the United States' attack-carriers to deploy power on a global scale without reliance on land bases – a factor of some consequence bearing in mind the Russians' abrupt ejection from naval and air bases in Egypt and Somalia in recent years. In peacetime, for flag-waving purposes, and in the case of limited war, the attack-carrier remains without question the most potent vessel on the high seas today and the determination of the United States' Navy to maintain a force of fifteen such vessels will be welcomed by the allies and friends of the United States world-wide. But in conditions of all-out war, their importance must be assumed to be substantially less, given their great vulnerability to attack by submarines equipped with nuclear-tipped torpedoes or by Backfire bombers attacking in regimental strength (the Soviet counterpart of NATO's squadrons) of twelve aircraft or more. Already almost half a US carrier's combat aircraft have to be devoted to the defence of the carrier itself, reducing the vessel's offensive capability.

Admiral Gorshkov has no doubts about the role of a navy in peacetime, declaring:

> Remaining a very effective and an essential means of armed struggle, they [navies] are constantly used as an instrument of the policy of states in peacetime. The sea is no-man's-land and, therefore, the fleets do not encounter in their activity the many limitations which stand in the way of the use for political purposes of other branches of the armed forces in peacetime.
>
> The fleets in this regard have assumed special importance in modern conditions in connection with the growth of their strike power. The mobility of the fleet and its flexibility where limited military conflicts come to a

head enable it to exert an influence on coastal countries, employ and extend a military threat at any level starting from a show of military force and ending with the mounting of landings (S.G. Gorshkov *The Sea Power of the State*).

This new Soviet capability was recognised in the US Department of Defense *Annual Report to Congress (Fiscal Year 1981)* which declared:

> The Kiev-class carriers, with their vertical takeoff and landing Forger aircraft, Hormone helicopters, long-range anti-ship missiles, and ASW weapons, could engage in limited power projection missions. They have the capability to provide escort for Soviet sealift operations and a measure of air support for amphibious assaults. *Perhaps more important, they can make the risk of outside interference with these activities look high* [author's emphasis].

The balance of sea power in the world cannot be looked at solely in terms of the capabilities of the two superpowers, for while the Soviets' Warsaw Pact allies make a substantial contribution in terms of ground forces and air power, they lend little weight at sea. When, however, the contribution of the United States' allies is taken into account, the overall balance swings back in NATO's favour, though it is an advantage that is remorselessly being eroded by the Soviet Union's very high rate of construction on the one hand and, on the other, the unwillingness of Western governments to find the resources required to maintain NATO's naval capability, let alone strengthen it.

Britain's Royal Navy remains the third largest in the world and, although today concentrated in the north-eastern Atlantic, continues to patrol world-wide with regular deployments to the Mediterranean, Indian Ocean and Pacific. In addition to seventy major surface combat vessels, among the best-equipped in the world, the Royal Navy has twenty-seven attack-submarines, twelve of them nuclear, as well as four

Polaris ballistic-missile submarines, scheduled to be replaced by the mid-nineties with a new generation of submarine equipped with the longer-range Trident missile from the United States. HMS *Invincible*, the first of a new generation of smaller aircraft-carriers, equipped with Sea Harrier vertical take-off aircraft, has recently entered service and is to be followed by HMS *Illustrious* and HMS *Ark Royal*.

Although no longer formally a member of the military organisation of NATO, France too maintains important naval forces consisting of forty-eight major surface ships, including two medium attack-carriers of the Clemenceau class, each with forty aircraft, as well as twenty-one diesel attack-submarines and six ballistic-missile submarines equipped with ninety-six French-built M-20 missiles with a range of 1,600 nautical miles. It is to France's credit that thanks to General de Gaulle's determination she has, without outside help or access to US technology, developed and deployed her own triad of nuclear forces made up, in addition to her ballistic-missile submarines, of eighteen intermediate-range ballistic missiles (IRBMs) buried in the rock of the Plateau d'Albion in southern France and thirty-three Mirage IVA bombers. However, although France's conventional naval forces regularly take part in NATO exercises, they make no contribution to NATO's 'on-call' peacetime patrols. In addition to Britain and France, Italy, West Germany and the Netherlands all make important naval contributions to the alliance. Nor can the growing naval strength of Japan be ignored in the equation with its forty-eight destroyers and frigates and fourteen submarines, though it is high time she were brought into closer relationship with the NATO alliance and encouraged to make a greater contribution to Western defence.

Apologists for the Soviet Union are to be found in every country and the argument is often advanced that it is only right that the Soviet Union should have a navy the size of the United States or indeed, as it now happens, double the size. However, it is not sufficient to judge only the number and quality of the vessels deployed by each side; consideration must also be given as to their purpose. The United States and Western Europe depend entirely on the high seas for access to their sources of energy and raw materials in the Third World. Without safe and uninterrupted passage for these vital cargoes across the sealanes of the world, the industrial economies of North America, Europe and Japan would collapse and, with them, their defence capability. It is to protect these lines of communications that Britain for four centuries, and more recently the United States for four decades, has felt the need to maintain major naval forces across the ocean trade routes. Many have been the nations that have benefited from the presence of the White Ensign and the 'Old Glory' on the oceans of the world.

The Soviet Union on the other hand, self-sufficient for energy and most raw materials, and enjoying overland communications with all her major allies, has no similarly obvious need for a blue-water navy. Of course an important element of that navy is undoubtedly earmarked to counter the United States' force of forty-one ballistic-missile submarines. However, given that the Soviets themselves have more than twice as many of that category of submarines, it is difficult to conclude other than that the massive number of 257 Soviet attack- and cruise-missile submarines has as its prime objective the interdiction, in the event of war, of passage on the high seas to merchant shipping, and especially supertankers, bound for Western countries.

That Soviet policy on the high seas has been one of 'denial' to the West in the event of war, has been indisputably reinforced by the relentless efforts made in recent years by the Soviet Union to establish not merely base facilities but to achieve actual political and military control of countries at strategic points on the trade routes of the West. One need look no further than the writings of Admiral Gorshkov for confirmation of this strategy: 'Together with one of the most important and all-embracing tasks of the fleet – destruction of the enemy's ships – a qualitatively new task has appeared: the curbing of the enemy's military-economic potential by directly acting on his vitally important centres from the sea' (S.G. Gorshkov, *The Sea Power of the State*).

However, in the light of Russia's relentless naval build-up and the substantial presence her fleets now maintain in the Mediterranean as well as the Atlantic, Indian and Pacific oceans, it is clear that the Soviet Union's ambitions have progressed from a strategy of mere 'sea-denial' to one of 'sea-control'. It has undoubtedly drawn great encouragement from the massive run-down in recent years of the United States Navy which by 1980 had less than half the strength of major vessels it had at the time of the Vietnam War. This sharply adverse trend calls into question the entire reinforcement strategy of NATO. These plans require the transportation from the United States to Europe, in a period of tension or in the event of attack, of no fewer than 1 million men, 10 million tons of equipment and 100 million tons of stores. This volume is so great that even if all civil air transports were co-opted, no more than 5 per cent of the requirement could be airlifted. For the 95 per cent to arrive safely by sea depends on the ability of NATO (principally the United States and Britain) to retain control of the North Atlantic. The extent to which this could be achieved in face of the ability of the Soviets to deploy no fewer than eighty attack- and cruise-missile submarines in the Atlantic, Barents and Norwegian seas, backed by supersonic Backfire aircraft which can, even without air-to-air refuelling for which they are equipped, range far out over the Atlantic, must be a matter for surmise.

It is the fervent hope of NATO commanders that it would prove possible to complete the bulk of this reinforcement during a period of tension, before the outbreak of hostilities – the Russians, and their own politicians, permitting. However, now that NATO can count on no more than seventy-two hours' warning-time of an impending Soviet attack against Western Europe (compared to a minimum of thirty days previously anticipated) such a scenario appears increasingly unrealistic. Even the most optimistic NATO naval authorities concede that if such a volume of equipment and stores had to be transported across the Atlantic in conditions of all-out war – not to mention the likelihood of ports and airfields in Britain and continental Europe being under air bombardment and missile attack – losses of naval and merchant vessels as well as of equipment and men would be devastating. The combination of the drastic reduction in expected warning-time and the significantly higher level of Soviet threat to surface vessels in the North Atlantic has forced the NATO allies, especially the United States, to look again at the problems of reinforcement, and decisions have already been taken to increase the size of US tank holdings and pre-positioned stocks in Europe as well as the speed and scale of airborne reinforcements from the United States.

In one field the West for the time being continues to retain an important advantage over the Soviets at sea and this is in underwater detection technology. Because of the physical properties of water, despite efforts to use magnetic anomaly detection devices to pick up a submarine's mass under-water or infra-red equipment to sense the waste heat from a nuclear submarine's cooling pumps, sound waves remain to date the only practical way of detecting and locating submarines under the sea. This can be done by surface ships with sonars or by aircraft and helicopters dropping sono-buoys. These operate either in a 'passive' mode, in which they listen out in silence for the sound of a submarine, or, alternatively, in an 'active' mode when they emit a signal and wait for the echo to bounce back from a submarine, any return being registered on the ship's or aircraft's sonar display. However, because seawater forms itself into different layers of uneven temperature and salinity, surface sonars frequently are able to look down to only a limited depth before the horizontal saline layers act as mirrors that reflect the sonar wave, concealing anything at a greater depth. To see deeper a variable-depth sonar towed behind and below a surface ship is required or, more effectively, another submarine, able to look upwards from below. In this respect the latest Soviet Alpha-class attack-submarine, which with a speed of 42 knots is both faster and able to dive deeper than any of NATO's, has a distinct advantage. But in spite of this recent Soviet advance, thanks to their superior propulsion technology, British and American submarines remain substantially more silent than their Soviet counterparts – a vital factor in the battle for advantage under water that continues uninterrupted even in peacetime.

Underwater detection techniques by sonar have advanced to the point where a US or Royal Navy submarine on patrol, coming across another submarine, or for that matter a surface

Table 1   *United States and Soviet major surface ships and submarines (active) 1965–80*

United States	1965	1980
Aircraft-carriers – attack and support	27	14 (3n)
Aircraft-carrier - assault and transport	30	
Battleships/command ships	6	–
Cruisers	40	25 (17gm 8n)
Frigates	30	72 (8gm)
Destroyers	360	80 (37gm)
Submarines – ballistic missile	31n	41n
– cruise missile	–	–
– attack	169 (29n)	81 (75n)
– Total:	693	313

Soviet Union	1965	1980
Aircraft-carriers – attack and support	–	2
Aircraft-carriers – assault and transport	–	2
Battleships/command ships	–	1
Cruisers	22	36 (8gm)
Frigates	100	173 (63gm)
Destroyers	150	75 (39gm)
Submarines – ballistic missile	40 (15n)	87 (71n)
–cruise missile	40 (12n)	68 (45n)
–attack	345	189 (46n)
–Total:	697	633

n   nuclear-powered
gm   guided missile
Source: Jane's Fighting Ships, 1965–66, 1980–81,
   Macdonald, London.

Table 2   *United States/Soviet naval balance*
1965–80

	United States	Soviet Union
1965		
Major surface ships	493	272
Submarines – ballistic/ cruise missile	31n	80 (27n)
Submarines – attack	169 (29n)	345
Total:	693	697
1980		
Major surface ships	191 (11n)	289 (1n)
Submarines – ballistic/ cruise missile	41n	155 (116n)
Submarines – attack	81 (74n)	189 (46n)
Total:	313	633

n   Nuclear -powered

Source: *Jane's Fighting Ships, 1965–66, 1980–81,*
        Macdonald, London.

vessel, is able, by feeding into their ship's computer the 'noise print' given out by the engines and propellers of the other vessel, to establish not only whether it is friend or foe, but the class and, very often, the name of the vessel. Like a human finger-print or voice-print, no two underwater 'signatures' of a vessel are *precisely* identical. In recent years the United States has secured a decisive lead over the Soviets in this battle of wits being played out in the cold dark waters of the deep with an invention called Sosus, which involves littering the seabed with millions of miles of spaghetti-like cable and enables the United States to keep close track of Soviet submarines and, especially, of their ballistic-missile submarines or 'Boomers', as they are more colloquially known to the US Navy.

If the West still retains a key advantage in this vital field today, the ability of the Soviet Union to catch up with Western technology in a short space of time by devoting its far greater resources to military research – curently twice the proportion spent by the United States from a budget 50 per cent greater – and its vast output of science and engineering graduates, should not be underestimated. CIA and Pentagon forecasts have, invariably, underestimated the speed with which the Soviets can make up lost ground.

By contrast with the clear political resolve of the Kremlin to build the most powerful navy in the world, the great momentum of their naval armaments programme and the sure guidance of a single man over quarter of a century to shape it, Western efforts have suffered from an inconstancy of political direction, an absence of drive and a total lack of continuity, the result of the etiquette of military bureaucracy that requires a change of military leadership every two or three years so as to provide 'jobs for the boys'.

For the West, the maintenance of the freedom of shipping on the high seas is, simply put, a matter of life or death, yet the NATO allies have looked on with complacency as the Soviet Union in the space of fifteen years has transformed the balance of world power at sea. NATO's supremacy in the Atlantic and United States' dominance in the Pacific, unchallenged until the sixties, have both now disappeared, and even the Mediterranean, so long regarded as a Western pond by the

British and American navies, today regularly has more Soviet ships in its waters than those of the NATO allies. Nor has serious account been taken of the more than 400,000 sea mines the Soviet Union has built which can be laid by ships or aircraft (even in peacetime) and subsequently activated for war.

The sea-lanes on which the West depends are today at mortal risk. In conditions of war the NATO navies would be hard put even to hold their own, let alone provide protection for the vast tonnage of merchant shipping and vital oil supplies on the high seas at any moment. The trends at sea, as in other fields, remain unremittingly unfavourable to the West and it is a matter of urgency that Western political leaders take stock of the terrible transformation that has taken place on and beneath the oceans of the world.

Chapter Nine

THE SOVIET MASTER PLAN

The determination of the Kremlin to project Soviet power on a global scale has led them not only to construct the most modern and most powerful navy in the world, but also to acquire a formidable airlift capability. The scale of the Soviet Air Force's transport force, consisting of more than 1,000 long- and medium -range transport aircraft, enables it to deploy a force of 50,000 troops from the Soviet Union to, for instance, the Persian Gulf or Middle East within forty-eight hours. In a crisis, this force could be supplemented by some 1,450 Aeroflot civil transports. These recent developments have drastically changed the Soviet Union's relationship with the newly independent countries of the Third World, which it is now able to treat with brashness and forcefulness. In retrospect the Soviet invasions of Hungary in 1956 and of Czechoslovakia in 1968 may be seen as having been, at least from the Soviet viewpoint, 'defensive' actions in which the Soviet Union was doing no more than respond to a challenge to its hegemony over Eastern Europe. However, in the seventies, Soviet imperialism shifted gear and went unashamedly onto the offensive with the evident determination of imposing a new hegemony over the Third World nations of Africa, the Middle East, South-East Asia and Latin America.

Throughout the late fifties and sixties the Soviet Union relied on a thrusting arms-sales policy and on its support for terrorist organisations to strengthen its influence in the Third World. More recently it has come to use intervention forces, usually in the form of Cuban and Vietnamese surrogates, stiffened by Warsaw Pact and even by Soviet forces. As a consequence of this policy of aggressive expansionism, the seventies, far from being a decade of detente for the Third World, saw bloodshed and starvation increase sharply while some 100 million people in Laos, Cambodia, Vietnam, Angola, Mozambique, Ethiopia and Afghanistan fell under the rule of Marxist dictatorships allied to Moscow.

Ever since the Soviet Union first cast down its gauntlet to the West in the Middle East with the Soviet – Egyptian arms deal of 1955 – cleverly dressed up as a 'Czech' arms deal so as not to arouse Western suspicions – it has relentlessly sought not only to remove Western influence from the area but to replace it with its own in the economic, political and military spheres. It cannot be doubted that the choice of Egypt as the initial vehicle for Soviet penetration and expansionism in the Middle East was a shrewd one given the powerful influence exerted by Egypt throughout both the Arab world and the African continent as well as its strategic position standing astride the Suez Canal which not only links the Mediterranean and Indian Ocean but, at that time, constituted Western Europe's principal supply route of oil from Arabia and the Persian Gulf. However although Egypt might have been the Kremlin's initial target, the ultimate goal, even from the very outset, was to gain physical control of the West's vital energy sources in the oil-rich deserts of the Arabian peninsula and the Persian Gulf. If, early on, Soviet attentions appeared to be devoted above all to wooing the Arab countries on the Mediterranean shore, it was merely a recognition of the fact that Western influence – reinforced by a powerful British military presence in Aden and throughout the Persian Gulf – was so strong in the Gulf area that there was little prospect for advancing Soviet interests there for the foreseeable future.

Although Karl Marx was to be proved disastrously wrong in his prediction in the mid-nineteenth century that Britain, the world's first industrialised nation, would also be the first to go Communist, his spiritual heirs in the Kremlin were sounder in their judgment when they saw the potential for using Egypt, with by far the largest population of any Middle East country, for spreading a brush-fire proletarian revolution throughout the Arab world; the newly ensconced Egyptian dictator, Colonel Nasser proved only too eager to be the serviceable tool of the Soviet cause.

In July 1956 Nasser, encouraged by his growing military strength and by his new-found Soviet friends, seized the Suez Canal, which belonged to an Anglo–French consortium and declared it nationalised. This action prompted the disastrously conceived Anglo–French operation, ostensibly mounted to protect the Egyptians from Israeli forces advancing west across Sinai but, in truth, aimed (secretly in league with the Israelis) at toppling Nasser. Egyptian resistance was light and the Anglo–French forces were within hours of gaining all their objectives when, under intense international pressure, most especially from the United States, the politicians' nerve cracked and the order was given for the military operation to be halted in its tracks. The failure of the operation to achieve its intended objective and the subsequent humiliating withdrawal only served to inflame and fuel the latent fires of Arab nationalism from Morocco to the shores of the Persian Gulf and had the effect of raising Nasser to the status of near-deity in the eyes not merely of his own countrymen but of peoples throughout the Arab world.

The Russians, as Nasser's backers, gained much credit among nationalist elements throughout the Middle East and were able to bask in the Egyptian dictator's reflected glory as his influence and power spread far and wide. It seemed at times that Nasser's dream of creating a Pan-Arab movement, which would unite the Arab world under the leadership of Egypt and of Nasser himself, might become a reality. In ensuing years the Soviet Union poured vast quantities of tanks, fighter-aircraft and other war materials into countries throughout the Middle East. These arms deliveries had the desired effect of destabilising the entire area and led directly to the Middle East conflicts of 1967 and 1973, both triggered by aggressive military build-ups against Israel backed by a massive volume of Soviet military equipment. By 1980, in consequence of this Soviet policy, Syria had 2,920 tanks, Iraq 2,650 and even Libya, with a population of less than 3 million, had 2,400 – each two or three times as many as Britain's tank strength of 900 Chieftains and close to the level of the United States' total commitment to NATO of 3,000 tanks in Europe.

However Nasser's Pan-Arabist dreams came to an abrupt halt with his defeat at the hands of the Israelis who, in their brilliant Six Day War campaign of 1967, succeeded in destroying four Arab air forces and defeating three armies in inside a week.* Nasser's come-uppance was not viewed with universal regret throughout the Arab world, indeed in the Gulf States the rulers greeted it with unconcealed delight as they saw his power, which menaced their authority and their nations' independence, spectacularly broken.

The Soviet position in Egypt, surprisingly, given the fact that it was as a result of deliberate Soviet misinformation that Nasser made his fatal decision to move an army of 100,000 men with 1,000 tanks into the Sinai desert, did not immediately suffer. Indeed, in the wake of defeat, the Russians became even more essential to Nasser's domestic political survival and they used the opportunity of moving into Egypt no less than five fighter and bomber squadrons of the Soviet Air Force, an army of 15,000 military 'advisers' in addition to large numbers of civil technicians. Soviet tactics were taught in Egyptian military academies and the Russians established a missile defence screen along the entire length of the Suez Canal to protect the main base areas. Even after Nasser's death in September 1970 and the succession of Anwar Sadat as President, Soviet influence in Egypt continued to grow, reaching its zenith in May 1971 with the signing of a fifteen year 'Treaty of Friendship and Cooperation'.

Between the end of the Six Day War and the outbreak of the

---

*A fuller account may be found in the author's book *'The Six Day War'*, written in conjunction with his late father Randolph S. Churchill, published in the United Kingdom by Heinemann and in the United States by Houghton Mifflin.

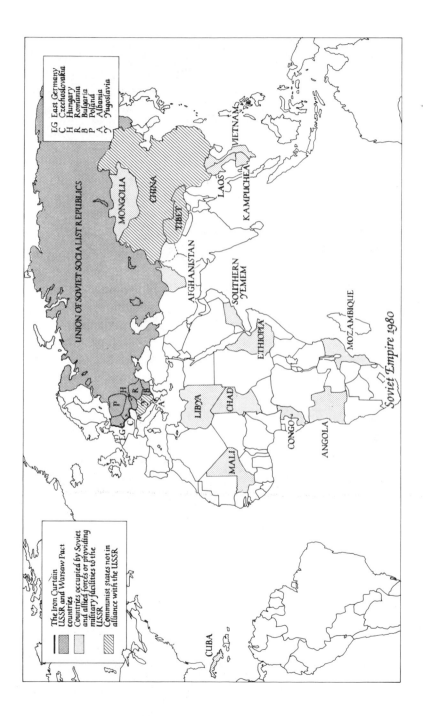

Soviet Empire 1980

The Iron Curtain
USSR and Warsaw Pact
countries
Countries occupied by Soviet
and allied forces or providing
military facilities to the
USSR
Communist states not in
alliance with the USSR

EG East Germany
C   Czechoslovakia
H   Hungary
R   Romania
B   Bulgaria
P   Poland
A   Albania
Y   Yugoslavia

UNION OF SOVIET SOCIALIST REPUBLICS

MONGOLIA

CHINA

TIBET

LAOS

VIETNAM

KAMPUCHEA

AFGHANISTAN

SOUTHERN
YEMEM

ETHIOPIA

MOZAMBIQUE

LIBYA

CHAD

CONGO

ANGOLA

MALI

CUBA

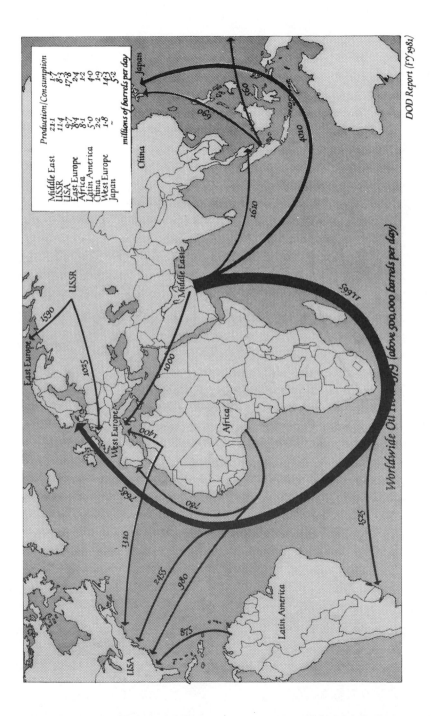

Middle East	Production/Consumption 21·1	1·7
USSR	11·4	8·3
USA	9·7	17·8
East Europe	8·4	2·4
Africa	8·1	1·2
Latin America	5·0	4·0
China	2·2	1·9
West Europe	1·8	14·3
Japan	–	5·2

millions of barrels per day

China

USSR

Middle East

East Europe

West Europe

Africa

Latin America

USA

Japan

1590

1025

560

680

4010

1610

1665

1310

245

980

1400

780

765

1685

875

525

1000

Worldwide Oil movement (above 500,000 barrels per day)

1973 conflict, the Soviet Union launched a massive new Middle East arms race, delivering 2,100 modern tanks to Egypt and 1,700 to Syria. This combined tank force represented more than four times Britain's total armoured strength, including the British Army of the Rhine. In air power Egypt received some 630 combat aircraft – principally MiG-21, MiG-17 and Sukhoi-7 fighter-bombers. A further 350 aircraft went to the Syrians. Russian supplies of new aircraft to Egypt and Syria alone totalled very nearly 1,000 – more than three times Britain's tactical combat aircraft strength. Meanwhile, Israel had obtained from Britain and the United States some 850 tanks, in addition to 100 captured Russian T-54/T-55s, 95 F-4 Phantoms and 160 subsonic A-4 Skyhawks. However United States deliveries of military hardware to Israel during this period amounted to one-quarter of what the Soviet Union was pumping into Egypt and Syria, let along Iraq and Algeria. By October 1973, the Egyptians and Syrians between them were able to field three times as many tanks and nearly twice as many aircraft as in 1967. The Russians, having set the stage, bear a heavy responsibility for the renewed outbreak of war. President Sadat, who masterminded the coordinated Egyptian and Syrian assault of 6 October 1973 which took Israel by surprise with an attack on two fronts, gained much credit in the Arab world for the way in which he placed the hitherto invincible Israelis on the defensive and pressed them very hard indeed until they had time to mobilise their reserve army fully. However by the end of the conflict the Israelis had so far turned the tables that their forces were within striking distance of the gates of Damascus and the city of Cairo. Indeed so critical had the situation become that the Russians threatened to intervene with airborne forces to save the Egyptians, triggering in turn a worldwide United States alert.

Even before this latest round in the Middle East conflict, the Soviet presence and behaviour had succeeded in arousing enormous local resentment and, within a year of coming to power, Sadat, who was determined to establish once again Egypt's national independence, gave the Russians their marching orders and expelled them with ignominy from a country they had sought to dominate with an ever-growing arrogance and an army larger than the British ever had at the height of their colonial power. It was a process not finally completed until March 1976 when he denounced the Soviet–Egyptian Treaty.

It would be a mistake to imagine that the Soviet Union is purely opportunist in its actions. While it is true that the Soviets are liable to lean heavily against any half-open door, they do so, not at random, but with a sense of purpose and by design. As one whose lot it has been to report events throughout the world – regrettably for the most part, wars – for almost two decades, I have been left with few illusions about the aims of Soviet policy. However, when I visitied the Somali Republic in the Horn of Africa in February 1978, I must confess to having my breath taken away by the directness and ruthlessness of what was described to me as the Soviet 'Master Plan' for Africa and the Middle East. It was laid bare for me by the Soviet Union's most recent ex-ally, President Siad Barre who, just three months before, had expelled the Russians and their 3,500 'military advisers', a presence that amounted to one Russian for every fifteen soldiers of the Somali army.

For many years Somalia had been the Soviet Union's principal ally in Africa. A Soviet–Somali Cooperation Agreement signed in 1961 had been followed by an Arms Agreement in 1963 and the arrival of Soviet 'military advisers' in 1967. In the wake of a formal Treaty of Friendship and Cooperation signed in July 1974 Somalia agreed to provide the Soviet navy with important base facilities including a floating dock towed all the way from Russia equipped to reload Soviet submarines in the Indian Ocean with nuclear missiles. But as President Barre explained to me the Soviet interest in Somalia by no means stopped there. The Soviet plan was to use Somalia as its principal base for engineering the subversion of all the independent governments of East Africa: northwards towards the Mediterranean, across the Red Sea to Arabia and the Persian Gulf, and southwards towards central and southern Africa. The reason that Somalia and, specifically, its President, had been made privy to the Soviet plan was that Somalia was billed to play the star role in the Soviet subversion of its neighbours. Thus in the course of numerous visits to Moscow, which frequently involved lengthy sessions in the Kremlin with Mr Brezhnev and other leading members of the Politburo, the Soviet leaders set out their grand design.

In outlining their 'Master Plan' to President Siad Barre of Somalia, the Kremlin leaders explained how one of the principal targets for Somalia-based subversion was to be President Nimeiry of Sudan, a friend and immediate neighbour of Sadat who shared the latter's strong distaste both for Communism and Soviet imperialism. In the case of the Sudan, where the Russians had already made two serious though unsuccessful attempts to overthrow Nimeiry, the Kremlin looked to what they claimed to be the 22,000 members of the Sudanese Communist Party and other disaffected elements to achieve success. Although the operation was to be mounted principally from Somalia, as in the two previous coups Libya was also to play a direct part in infiltrating men and arms into the country from Sudan's north-western border. Once the Government of Sudan had been overthrown the next step was to isolate Egypt and overthrow President Sadat. 'Who does Sadat represent anyway?' Brezhnev demanded scathingly of President Barre, adding rhetorically in reply to his own question: 'Only the *petit bourgeoisie* – he has no support among the masses.' The toppling of Sadat and the establishment of a Marxist government in Egypt is something that the Kremlin will wait its opportunity to achieve but is unlikely ever to abandon.

When, late one night, I had a three-hour meeting with President Barre in his heavily guarded military headquarters in Mogadishu he told me:

> There were to be two phases to the Soviet plan. First, to gain control of as much coast-line as possible with a view to securing naval and air bases from which the Soviet Union might dominate and, when it chose, interdict the flow of Western and neutral shipping upon the high seas, especially on the route through the Red Sea and the Suez Canal and, above all, the West's vital oil supply routes from the Persian Gulf round the Cape of Good Hope, the very lifeline of Western Europe and the United States.

The second phase of the Soviet plan looking to the longer term was, through a combination of subversion and outside intervention, to gain physical control of the great treasure-houses on which the prosperity of the Western economies is based, the energy treasure-house of Arabia and the Persian Gulf, and the mineral treasure-house of Central and Southern Africa.

The Somali President added, with an evident sense of retrospective distaste: 'We were to be but the stepping stone for their expansionist plans in Africa and the Middle East.'

It is evident that the strategists of the Kremlin have had a far shrewder appreciation of what constitutes the vital interests of the West than have their counterparts in the US State Department or the Chancelleries of Western Europe. Long ago the Russians recognised the almost total dependence on imported oil supplies of all the non-Communist industrialised nations, with the exception only of the United States which, like the Soviet Union itself, had traditionally been self-sufficient for oil. Further they foresaw that the rapidly growing prosperity of the entire Western world in the fifties and sixties, combined with its increasing scarcity of energy resources, would lead to this dependence on imported oil supplies becoming even more marked and afflicting even the United States, though they could scarcely have anticipated the speed and the scale of this latter development.

The postwar period was one that saw a massive switch from indigenous coal to imported oil as the principal fuel source of the industrialised nations. Whereas in 1950 Western Europe depended on oil for only 12 per cent of its energy needs, by 1980 this dependence had increased to no less than 80 per cent. Meanwhile three successive closures of the Suez Canal due to Middle East wars, together with the construction of supertankers which, already by the early 1960's, exceeded 100,000 tons and had a draught too great to pass through the Canal laden, led to the much longer route round South Africa's Cape of Good Hope becoming the principal supply line for the energy needs of Western Europe and, increasingly, of the

United States. By 1980 the Suez Canal was open once again, having been widened and deepened at the direction of President Sadat to accommodate fully laden tankers up to 150,000 tons deadweight, and, carrying some 20,000 vessels each year, though it seems unlikely it will ever succeed in attracting back more than a fraction of its former oil tanker traffic.

Overwhelmingly the greatest volume of trade on the high seas today in tonnage, value and strategic importance is in oil. South Africa's Cape of Good Hope is the route by which 70 per cent of Western Europe's oil and already more than 30 per cent of the United States' imports must travel from the Persian Gulf and Arabia. In 1979 no less than 622 million tonnes of oil travelled the Cape route – more than two-thirds of it destined for Western Europe. The dependence of the United States on imported oil, which reached 46 per cent in 1979 (Department of Defense, *Annual Report to Congress Fiscal Year 1981*), and hence, on the Cape route, is rapidly increasing.

It should not be forgotten how, in the Second World War, a handful of German naval vessels succeeded in sinking nearly 250 Allied vessels between Lourenço Marques – now Maputo – and Cape Town alone. Against this background the recent construction and deployment world-wide by the Soviets of a powerful surface fleet backed by a force of no fewer than 257 attack- and cruise-missile submarines (more than 90 of them nuclear powered) represents a grave threat to the free flow of commerce upon the high seas on which both the economies and military potential of the industrialised Western nations depend.

In the course of the seventies the strength of the Soviet Navy in the Indian Ocean increased substantially with standing deployments of Soviet naval forces far exceeding Western forces, at least until the Soviet invasion of Afghanistan and the seizure of the American Embassy hostages in Tehran prompted a major US and Western naval build-up.

Chapter Ten

THE ENERGY
TREASURE-HOUSE

In the wake of Britain's military withdrawal from the Gulf after 1968 it was foreseeable and inevitable that the centre of gravity of Soviet intrigue would shift to the Persian and Arabian Gulf which, from the very outset, had been the true goal of the Soviet 'Master Plan' in the Middle East. Across the waters from Somalia and the Horn of Africa, the Soviet Union by the early seventies had already gained control of South Yemen, formerly the British protectorate of Aden, and from there the Soviet plan called for a stepping up of terrorist activities by the Marxist Dhofar Volunteer Forces against the neighbouring oil-rich Sultanate of Oman as well as the reactivation of the civil war in North Yemen which shares a common border with Saudi Arabia. North Yemen in turn was to be used as a stepping-stone to overthrow the ruling royal family of Saudi Arabia on which the United States remains dependent for the lion's share of its Middle East oil supplies.

Another special target of Soviet intrigue was Iran where, following the departure of British forces from the area, the Shah had with the full approval and encouragement of the British and Americans taken on the role of protector of the entire Gulf region. Western governments, mostly notably Britain and the United States, sought to offset their huge trade deficits with

Iran by relentless efforts to force more and more arms on the Shah. The British succeeded in selling him no fewer than 875 Chieftain tanks – nearly 50 per cent more than the entire inventory of Britain's Rhine Army, on top of an equal number supplied by the United States. The United States' Navy, warned that approval for its own purchase of the supersonic F-14 Tomcat fighter-bomber designed for carrier operations was dependent upon securing at least one foreign order for the aircraft, went to extraordinary lengths to persuade the Shah to purchase four squadrons totalling eighty of these excellent but most expensive aircraft complete with their long-range Phoenix missiles, even though he had not a single aircraft-carrier from which to operate them. In addition, among a huge inventory of other military equipment, the Shah allowed himself to be persuaded of the need for no less than 800 military helicopters. In the latter period of the Carter administration, when the suggestion was made that the US Government was letting down in his hour of need an ally – to whom President Carter at a 1978 New Year's Eve banquet in Tehran had pledged his personal support – the myth was skilfully put about by the US media and emphasised time and again that the Shah was a tyrannical ruler who oppressed his people and shamefully squandered the vast wealth of his nation on armaments and useless militaristic baubles, instead of applying it to the benefit and advancement of his people. This unedifying chorus was joined even by certain people of distinction who just a few years earlier had been only too happy to accept the lavish hospitality proferred by the King of Kings. If the Shah placed too great an emphasis on military hardware, the governments of Britain, the United States and France bore with him a full share of responsibility. But in spite of this and the lavish personal style in which the Shah and his family lived, the fact is that by the closing years of the Shah's reign no more prosperous or industrially advanced society was to be found anywhere between Tel Aviv and Singapore.

At the time of my discussions with President Barre in February 1978 – a time when the Shah appeared to be as secure as ever on his throne – he told me of the Russian leaders' designs against the Shah. In the secrecy of the Kremlin the

Soviet leaders had, only a few months before, told him of their confidence that they could count upon the allegiance of a large number of pro-Soviet activists to overthrow the Iranian leadership, confiding, 'It is only a matter of time before the Shah meets the bullet that is destined for him, given the major elements of disaffected young people, many of them already active members of the Communist Tudeh Party, which will ultimately take over.'

Although the Russians were proved right in their forecast that the Shah's government could not survive his personal demise, they can scarcely have credited the possibility that it would come about so soon, let alone that the government of the United States – supposedly the Shah's principal ally – would be instrumental in his downfall. Yet by January 1979 the Shah, on the advice of the Carter administration, had gone into exile abroad, letting rip the full fury of the Iranian Revolution, in which the Tudeh Party, equipped with large numbers of Soviet-supplied weapons, played a key role, although content initially to accept an interregnum in which the Ayatollahs and the fanatics of Muslim fundamentalism would be allowed the semblance of authority.

With the coming to office of the Carter administration in January 1977 the United States developed an advanced state of schizophrenia in her relationship with the Shah who, a year before, had embarked on a policy of liberalisation and reform, releasing from jail certain opponents of his regime and allowing others to return from exile. While the new President personally appeared to support the Shah, important elements of his administration regularly made statements to the press expressing concern about the authoritarianism of the Iranian Government and deploring the strong-arm methods of SAVAK, the Iranian Secret Police. Indeed the Bureau of Human Rights, until eventually overruled by Brzezinski, was allowed to hold up for several months supplies of riot-gas destined for Iran. In the fateful months when the future of Iran as a key ally of the West was hanging in the balance, the open warfare raging in Washington between the State Department and the National Security Council through their respective heads, Cyrus Vance and Zbigniew Brzezinski, was to do untold damage to the Western cause in one of the most strategically vital areas of the globe. In the absence of any leadership from President Carter, the conflicting policies and personal rivalries involved in the power struggle within the administration conspired to deprive American policy of all coherence and resolve at a crucial time when only clarity of view and strength of purpose by her principal ally could save Iran from the twin perils of chaos or Communism.

In the face of growing disorder and rioting the Iranian government, on 7 September 1978, declared martial law and on the next day more than one hundred rioters were shot by troops when they ignored orders to disperse – a day that came to be know as 'Black Friday'.

The Shah was evidently shocked, even angered, at what had happened and for a critical time appeared to hesitate between the courses of repression and continued liberalisation. For a while, half-heartedly, he allowed the military to continue their efforts to restore order, but the rioting in the cities and the strikes by workers in the oilfields only became more widespread, especially when it became clear that the military had been ordered to be more circumspect in their handling of the rioters. The Shah's indecision was due not only to the fact that he was mortally ill with cancer, a factor not widely appreciated at the time, but above all to his unwillingness to sanction bloodshed in a bid to retain power. Indeed after he had gone into exile he declared: 'A Sovereign cannot save his throne by spilling the blood of his people.' Abruptly the Shah switched to a policy of conciliation, arresting those members of SAVAK believed to have been guilty of excesses, and making important concessions to the striking oil-workers. But by then it was too late.

On 5 November in the face of renewed and widespread student rioting led by activists of the Communist Tudeh Party, which culminated in the burning of the British Embassy in Tehran, the Shah agreed to the formation of a military government under General Reza Azhari in place of the civilian administration which had clearly lost control of the situation. A major factor behind the rioting in addition to the activities of the Tudeh Party was undoubtedly the inflammatory declarations by the Ayatollah Khomeini living in exile in France at Neauphle-le-Château. This septuagenarian mullah had long been an outspoken critic of the Shah's programme for the industrialisation and modernisation of Iran and was bitterly hostile to the Western influences which had led to the emancipation of women, the abandonment of the veil and a far less strict observance of the dictates of Koranic law. He saw in Western culture and morals the works of the Devil and harboured a deep and impassioned determination to lead Iran back to an eighth century Muslim state in all its rigour and fanaticism.

Far removed from the scene of action in Iran it might have been thought that the ageing Ayatollah was powerless to influence events, however that would be to misjudge the power of the Western news media and the willingness of certain elements of it, wittingly or unwittingly, to allow themselves at a critical juncture to become the vehicle for propaganda designed to achieve the overthrow of governments friendly to the West. Regrettably the Overseas Service of the Britsh Broadcasting Corporation can, almost invariably, be relied upon to be foremost among offenders. When in July 1975 I was reporting for the London *Daily Telegraph* the struggle that was raging in Portugal between the Communist Party and the forces of democracy, in the wake of the previous year's revolution, I had been struck by the vehemence with which the Socialist Party leader Dr Mario Soares, and other democratic party leaders with whom I had meetings, denounced what they described as the pernicious and extremely damaging daily news bulletins being broadcast from London, in which those presenting the programmes, by deliberately twisting stories through mistranslation or sometimes by a mere change in intonation of voice, were distorting the news and commentaries and introducing a pronounced pro-Communist bias.

A few days later, following an all-night sitting in the House of Commons, I had occasion to buttonhole the then Prime Minister, Harold Wilson, coming out of the chamber after a vote and, in a half-hour meeting with him in his room, I had the opportunity of conveying the anxiety expressed to me by his friend Dr Soares at the singularly unhelpful line being transmitted by the Portuguese service of the BBC. It is an oft-reiterated fiction that the Overseas Service of the BBC, although funded by the Foreign Office, is wholly independent and entirely beyond the control of government. Suffice it to say that within days two ultra-Left Portuguese employees of the BBC were suspended from duty and subsequently dismissed and the offending broadcasts ceased abruptly upon their departure.

There is little doubt that in similar circumstances of crisis some three years later, when the fate of another close ally of Britain hung in the balance, the BBC's Iranian Service did untold damage to the Western cause by providing the fanatically anti-Western Ayatollah Khomeini not merely with a platform but with a daily communications link with the Iranian mob. In many cases, but for the BBC, the Ayatollah's fire-brand speeches and calls for public demonstrations in defiance of the authorities would never have reached the ears of the student activists in Iran. The Overseas Service of the BBC has long been the repository of disaffected elements from different countries, anxious to use the resources of the British taxpayer and the transmitters of the BBC to politic against their own governments. No doubt reflecting the Foreign Office's own viewpoint, the censorship imposed on Soviet and East European dissidents broadcasting to the USSR and Eastern Europe during the period of supposed detente of the seventies was substantially greater than the control exercised over anti-Western dissidents broadcasting to countries which were the allies of the West.

As the rioting in Tehran got worse, so relations between the National Security Council and the State Department in Washington became exacerbated. The State Department favoured a return to civilian government and sought to urge this upon the Shah in a signal to Tehran. However, when Brzezinski saw the draft telegram, he superseded it with his own which affirmed that the United States would back the Shah 'to the hilt' in any action he might take to restore his authority. At one stage relations between the National Security Council and the State Department became so strained that Brzezinski took the unprecedented step of cutting off the State Department from all further consultation. The result was a flood of inspired leaks to the press attacking both the Shah and the policies of the National Security Council. Meanwhile Mr William Sullivan, US Ambassador in Tehran, proposed entering into negotiations with Ayatollah Khomeini, whose return to Iran was viewed with favour by many officials of the State Department. Indeed UN Ambassador Andrew Young so far exceeded himself as to describe the plotting prelate who was soon to have so much blood on his hands as a 'Saint'. Sullivan's suggestion was promptly vetoed by Brzezinski. However when the latter's Special Coordinating Committee, which included, among others, Secretary of State Cyrus Vance, Secretary of Defense Harold Brown and Stansfield Turner, Director of the Central Intelligence Agency, proposed that Energy Secretary James Schlesinger, also a member of the Committee, be sent to Iran to assure the Shah of the United States' fullest support, their proposal was in turn vetoed by President Carter, on the advice of the State Department. The name of General Robert Heuyser, a US General and NATO Deputy Supreme Allied Commander Europe, was substituted for that of Schlesinger and, far from being sent to assure the Shah of continued American support, he was, amazingly, charged with the task of persuading the Iranian military commmanders that, under no circumstances, following the departure of the Shah from Iran – a decision by then already taken in Washington – should they seek to take power and that, if they did so, they could expect only the strongest disapproval from the United States.

Unlike their Turkish counterparts who, in comparable circumstances of growing disorder a year later, were to take decisive action to keep Turkey in the Western camp, the Iranian generals and air force comanders, to their cost, did the bidding of the American President as conveyed to them by General Heuyser. Following the Shah's departure into exile on 16 January 1979, many of them pleaded with Heuyser not to allow the return to Iran of Ayatollah Khomeini who they warned would make the task of Dr Sharpoor Bakhtiar's civilian government impossible, but their pleas fell on deaf ears. Within weeks of the Ayatollah's return and the revolution that ensued, they were delivered to revolutionary justice and all but four tortured and put to death.

Right up to his departure into exile, the Shah placed total faith in the United States. With catastrophic consequences for himself and Iran, he placed himself and his country in the hands of the officials of the Carter administration. To the very end the Shah was convinced that the United States, at least out of self-interest, if not of friendship towards himself and Iran, had a determination to ensure that Iran remained firmly in the Western camp. He clung doggedly to the conviction that the Americans must have somewhere a plan of action for safeguarding Iran from chaos or Communist takeover, even if they had no role for him in that plan nor felt able to confide its details to him. He evidently failed to appreciate the abrupt change in US policy that followed in the wake of President Carter's election nor did he have any understanding of the extent to which America's Central Intelligence Agency – the West's first line of defence in peacetime – had been reduced to near impotence in the wake of Watergate, let alone the ins and outs of the power struggle in Washington between the hawks and doves of the Carter administration, in the absence of any firm guidance from the Oval office.

The departure of the Shah and his subsequent death in exile in Egypt in the sanctuary offered by President Sadat who, alone of all the presidents and prime ministers who had fawned on him at the height of his power, was to prove a constant and true friend in adversity, led directly to the loss of Iran to the West and its descent, through the orgy of blood-letting that followed Ayatollah Khomeini's accession to power, to the chaos of a primitive religious fanaticism, making it a ripe target for Soviet intrigue. It was not only the generals but countless thousands of patriotic Iranians who were murdered as the mob went on its wild rampage inspired by the hate-filled exhortations of the Ayatollah and his supporters. Others were executed following 'show trials' that bore no relation to justice.

Among the first victims of the chaos that ensued were to be the staff of the United States' Embassy, which was overrun and ransacked by a well-organised mob that included not only activists of Iran's Communist Tudeh Party but, significantly, members of the Palestine Liberation Organisation, the closest allies and willing surrogates of the Soviet Union in the Middle

East. The Embassy staff themselves were taken prisoner and in defiance of international law were to be held hostage for more that fourteen months – an act unparalleled in diplomatic relations in modern times, given the Iranian Government's overt complicity with the captors.

After many months of frustrating and abortive negotiation, direct and through intermediaries, the patience of the American Government and people ran out and an operation that had tentatively been set in hand within weeks of the hostages being taken was launched on 24 April 1980 with the aim of securing their rescue by military force. The venture was attended by ill-luck from the very start, when an unforecast dust storm caused mechanical failure that resulted in only five of the original eight Sea Stallion helicopters from the aircraft-carrier USS *Nimitz* arriving in servicable condition at Desert One, the rendezvous point in the Iranian desert. The plan had been drawn up on the basis of at least six serviceable helicopters being the minimum needed to assure the success of the rescue mission and, accordingly, the decision was taken by the Pentagon, with the concurrence of President Carter, to abort the mission. It was at this point that tragedy struck. As one of the helicopters lifted off in the darkness to allow another to be refuelled from one of the C-130 Hercules transports, its rotor blades sliced into the transport plane. Both aircraft burst into flames causing ammunition to explode and destroying two other helicopters. No less than eight members of the specially trained combat team lost their lives and the survivors clambered aboard the remaining three Hercules, leaving their dead comrades behind in the blazing wreckage that lit up the night sky for miles around.

As in the case of the Franco–British fiasco at Suez, so too in the case of the abortive US rescue mission, responsibility for failure rests heavily on the political leadership. Undoubtedly the operation was attended by more than its share of ill-fortune but the excuse that the mission had to be aborted due to the lack of sufficient serviceable military hardware is difficult to accept, especially when made by the United States of all countries. It is impossible to avoid the conclusion that the direction of the operation at the highest political level was lacking in the calculated ruthlessness and single-minded determination (exhibited so dramatically by the Israelis in the Entebbe raid of 3 July 1976) which alone might have achieved success in circumstances even more hazardous than those confronting the Israeli rescue attempt. If the attitude of the President's close advisers is any guide, the mission was born less from a resolve or any sense of conviction that it could indeed succeed than from frustration among those in the White House, plagued by the daily enquiries of newshawks and the increasingly outspoken demands by the hostages' families and political opponents that action be taken, so that at least they would be able to claim: 'Goddamit, we tried!'

Not long afterwards, in September of the same year, the situation in the Persian Gulf took a further downward spiral towards disintegration and chaos with the invasion of Iran by neighbouring Iraq whose President Sadam Hussein sought to seize back by force control of the Shatt-al-Arab waterway, which had previously been ceded to the Shah in return for the latter's agreement to cease supporting Iraq's Kurdish rebels. Though the Iraqi attack took the disorganised Iranian army by surprise and, initially, Iraq made rapid gains, it was not long before Iranian resistance stiffened and the Iraqi advance ran out of steam. However, on 30 September there was an intriguing report, which did not receive much notice at the time, of an attack by two 'Iranian' Phantom jets on an Iraqi nuclear facility being built with French assistance not far from Baghdad. It is in fact more probable that the two Phantoms, which inflicted considerable damage on the plant, were not Iranian at all but Israeli, seizing upon the general chaos of the conflict to strike at what the Israeli Government sees as a potentially mortal threat to the people of Israel.

For some time now a time-bomb has been ticking away in the Middle East, a bomb that hold momentous, potentially catastrophic, implications for the future peace of the area as well as for the interests of the West. The French Government has taken upon itself, with a recklessness not shared by any other nuclear power, including the Soviet Union or the People's Republic of China, responsibility for giving Iraq a nuclear bomb. Though there has been much talk in recent years of the so-called 'Gaddafi bomb' which Libya is helping to finance Pakistan to build, Iraq is undoubtedly the most advanced Arab country in terms of nuclear development. Iraqi scientists have gained a growing expertise in this field ever since the supply to Iraq by the Soviet Union in 1968 of a research centre and a Soviet-built IRT-2000 reactor. However, the Soviet Union has always been scrupulous in taking firm steps to ensure that what they supplied to Iraq could be used solely for peaceful purposes.

France in its lust for oil appears to have thrown to the wind all constraints of morality, good sense, or even self-interest. It is no secret that the French for some time now have been assisting the Iraqis in the provision of a far more advanced nuclear research centre and two reactors appropriately codenamed Osiris after an Egyptian god who was always represented as a dead king and traditionally regarded as the Ruler of the Dead. In view of the bad relations existing between Iraq and the Egypt of President Sadat, especially since the latter's assent to the Camp David agreements and his momentous pilgrimage to Jerusalem and Israeli soil, the Iraqis have changed the name of their reactors to Osiraq. To the Israelis, who harbour bitter feelings against the man who as Prime Minister of France from 1974 to 1976 initiated the project, it is better know as 'Oh! Chirac!'

The Iraqis have been less brazen about their intentions than Libya, whose President Gaddafi declared in 1974: 'Some years ago we could hardly procure a fighter-squadron. Tomorrow we will be able to buy an atomic bomb with all its parts. The nuclear monopoly is about to be broken.' However, there can be no doubt that, given Iraq's lack of industrial base and its consequently limited requirements for electrial power, their intention has been, and remains, to acquire nuclear weapons. Under such circumstances it defies all understanding that France should have agreed – in its pursuit of oil and arms deals – to supply Iraq with a nuclear reactor that uses as its fuel highly enriched weapons-grade uranium.

When, in 1978, President Carter made a strong protest to President Giscard d'Estaing of France in respect of this project, and in particular at the nature of the fuel to be used, the French agreed to 'caramelize' the fuel, a process that involves treating it in such a way as to render it suitable only for peaceful, not weapons, application. However, President Carter was scarcely in a strong position, himself, to criticise the French since it had been an American Government that had enabled India, through the provision of reactors that also made use of highly enriched uranium, to become a member of the nuclear 'club' with the explosion of a plutonium device in May 1974. But following insistence by President Saddam Hussein that Iraq was interested only in weapons-grade fuel and that arms contracts with France valued at more than £1,300 million ($3 billion) would be cancelled, the government of France went ahead with the supply of weapons-grade material.

To suggest that the Israelis are deeply anxious about the project would be an understatement. The fact that in 1979 a top-security plant at Toulouse in France was broken into and two reactor cores intended for Iraq were subsequently found to have been damaged beyond repair came as no surprise to those who know the gravity with which Israel views the matter. Israel's intelligence service, the Mossad, was almost certainly responsible for this sabotage though, intriguingly, there is reason to suspect that the Israeli agents enjoyed the active assistance of elements of the French security service, although it is impossible to say whether they were acting in defiance of their own Government or, with true Gallic Machiavellianism, on its instructions.

In spite of this sabotage, which set back the Osiraq programme at least six months and the subsequent assassination in his room at the Meridian Hotel, close to the Arc de Triomphe in Paris in May 1980, of Yahia el Meshad, the Egyptian nuclear physicist in charge of the Iraqi nuclear programme, the new research centre was already well advanced when the two Phantom jets made their attack under cover of the Iran–Iraq war. An amazing aspect of the Franco–Iraqi contract is that under its terms France has delivered to Iraq no less that 72 kg (158 lb) of weapons-grade uranium, amounting to three years' advance supply. Such a quantity of fissionable material also happens to be enough to make three nuclear bombs.

The importance of the Iraqi contract to France is

undoubtedly great for, under its terms, France has been
assured of a least one third – 30 million tonnes in 1980 – of its
oil supplies to be paid for by sales of French arms, which since
1975 have secured more than a 50 per cent share of the Iraqi
market displacing the Soviet Union which, until then, had held
a virtual monopoly. There remains the possibility that the
interruption of oil supplies from Iraq, in consequence of Iraqi
aggression against Iran, will cause the French Government to
reflect upon the wisdom if not the morality of its action, though
under President Giscard d'Estaing this appears unlikely.

What is certain is that the Israelis cannot and will not allow a
situation to come about in which Iraq – which continues to be
in a state of self-proclaimed belligerence with Israel – has a
nuclear weapon standing in one corner of a hangar with a
Soviet-supplied Tupolev TU-22 Blinder nuclear strike-bomber
in the other. In a country as small and so obviously vulnerable
as Israel, with its entire population concentrated into a coastal
strip, in places no more than nine miles wide, the devastation
that could be wreaked by even a single nuclear weapon does not
bear contemplation. The world may be assured that, for
whatever varied reasons they may have emigrated from Europe
and from Soviet Russia to the Middle East, the survivors of the
Holocaust and the children of the victims of Auschwitz, Belsen
and Babi Yar did not come so as to fall victim to any modern-
day megalomaniac who might seek to fulfil Hitler's avowed
intent of exterminating the Jewish race.

In addition to a military capability that, in conventional
terms, far exceeds what is normally associated with a nation
with a population of three million, including more than three
times as many tanks and air-defence aircraft as Britain, Israel,
though careful never to admit the fact let alone boast of it,
undoubtedly has had nuclear weapons of its own for many
years. Those who know Israel and the Israeli people are well
aware that there are no lengths to which its leaders will not go in
order to ensure the security and protection of their civilian
population, and that they would not hesitate to authorise
whatever action may be necessary to this end. Once again the
Middle East, and the stability on which the interests of the
West are so heavily dependent, appears to be heading

remorselessly towards a crisis of major proportion.

The rivalry of the industrialised nations for Middle Eact oil in the latter part of the twentieth century makes the 'Scramble for Africa' of the colonial powers of Europe in the nineteenth century appear like a picnic. The determination of the Soviet Union to gain control of the sources of the West's oil supplies through vast arms deliveries, subversion and overt intervention has disastrously destabilised the whole area, spreading wars and triggering a near 2000 per cent increase in oil prices in the space of a decade – the direct cause of an economic slump unprecedented since the thirties. The tensions to which these policies give rise will ensure that the Middle East continues to be a cockpit of intrigue and conflict and that it remains the most obvious potential cause of a world war between the superpowers. This already dangerous situation is now to be aggravated by the French Government's unbridled lust for the Black Gold of the desert.

Chapter Eleven

AFGHANISTAN AND AFTER

Over Christmas 1979 Soviet forces invaded Afghanistan in strength seizing control of the capital, Kabul. They claimed they came at the request of Afghanistan's President Hafitsullah Amin who had been repeatedly described by Radio Moscow as 'a great friend of the Soviet Union'. Two days later, on 27 December, the Soviet Ambassador in Kabul, Fikryat Tabeyev, and the Soviet Minister of Transport, Mikolai Talytsin, called on President Amin at his office. They told the President that with fighting still going on in the city centre his life was in jeopardy from hostile insurgents and rebels and suggested that, for safety, he should move to the Darulaman summer palace, located on the outskirts of Kabul not far from the Soviet embassy where the Red Army would 'protect' him. That same evening at 7 p.m. a Soviet military unit arrived at the Darulaman palace to take up their protection duties. Just four hours later Radio Kabul announced that Hafitsullah Amin had been executed and that Babrak Karmal was the new President of Afghanistan. The former President was suddenly now described as the 'bloody hangman of the people' and the 'wild slaughterer and unworthy spy of the American CIA'. In his first press conference, Babrak Karmal was full of praise and gratitude for those who had secured him such swift promotion, declaring: 'It is as clear as the sunlight that the Soviet Union is the most honest friend of all suffering peoples, including the Moslems of Afghanistan' (Hans Graf Huyn, *We all are Afghanistan*, Institute of American Relations, Washington DC 1980).

Up to 1978 Afghanistan had maintained an independent and, for the most part, neutral stance, though it had long had close relations with its large and powerful neighbour on its northern borders, the Soviet Union. In April of that year Moscow had engineered a coup in which President Sadar Mohammed Daoud, who had dared to seek to ban the Afghan Communist Party which enjoyed the closest links with Moscow, had been assassinated and a pro-Moscow puppet regime installed. Mohammed Taraki, Communist Party Chairman, had been proclaimed President. However, not long afterwards, Taraki himself was murdered and his place taken by Hafitsullah Amin, also an accomplice of the Kremlin, though they were to murder him in turn.

From the moment of the April 1978 coup Western influence in Afghanistan declined sharply and the Soviet Union became pre-eminent, though the internal situation remained unstable with widespread fighting among tribal factions opposed to Afghanistan's new rulers. It was this continuing unrest that led to the Kremlin's decision of December 1979 to occupy the country and assert its authority. A factor triggering the invasion was no doubt the seizure by Muslim rebels two months before of the Salang Pass and tunnel, the only major overland route leading from the Soviet Union to Afghanistan. The Salang tunnel is one of the most remarkable, yet virtually unknown, feats of modern civil engineering. More than 11,000 feet up in the Hindu Kush mountain range, whose peaks tower to more than 20,000 feet, Soviet engineers in the late sixties completed a 2 mile-long tunnel with massive steel doors at either end some 100 miles north of Kabul. The tunnel and road linked the Afghan capital with the Soviet Union by a direct overland route. (On those rare occasions when the Soviet Union deigns to give Third World countries civil, rather than the more usual military aid, experience suggests that such countries need to be even more circumspect than when accepting military aid, for there is almost invariably some sinister reason for it.) Another part of the Soviet Union's far-sighted civil aid to Afghanistan involved the construction of a major airfield at Bagram, 30 miles outside the capital. Both these projects were evidently conceived by Kremlin strategists with only one aim in mind: the eventual occupation of the country by Soviet forces.

On 8 December the United States' reconnaissance satellites showed major and unusual troop concentrations close to the Soviet border with Afghanistan and it was reported that a Soviet combat battalion had landed at Bagram airport outside Kabul. Their mission, as soon became clear, was to attack from the rear the Afghan rebel forces holding the Salang tunnel thereby opening the way for the intended Soviet invasion. This objective was achieved by 15 December and the invasion was able to go ahead as planned, over Christmas when it was evidently thought (rightly as it turned out) that the NATO allies might be least able to make any coherent and coordinated response to the Soviet action.

By mid-January 1980 the Soviet invasion force had built up to an estimated 80,000, made up of five motor-rifle or mechanised divisions as well as one airborne division. Later in the year as the Soviet troops met a strong and stiffening resistance from the fierce Afghan tribesmen, Soviet forces, including support troops, increased to close on 100,000.

The reaction in the West to the Soviet invasion was one of profound shock. President Carter described that action as the most serious threat to world peace since the Second World War and went on to make the frightening admission that he had learnt more about the Soviet Union in the past week than ever before in his lifetime. Although Mrs Thatcher joined the American President in making a forceful denunciation of the Russians, the reaction in certain other European countries was noticeably more muted. West Germany's former Chancellor, Willy Brandt, declared the world still suffers from too little and not from too much detente and went on to suggest that NATO must share part of the blame for the Soviet invasion by the fact that the West had not pressed ahead far enough in disarmament talks with the Russians!

However even the British and American governments, in spite of their outspoken verbal condemnation, were decidedly restrained when it came to proposing the possible application of sanctions against the aggressor. Not prepared to go so far as to withdraw their ambassadors from Moscow nor even to seek to impose any form of general economic or trade sanctions against the Soviet Union, the two governments decided to make the centrepiece of their protest an appeal to their athletes not to participate in the Olympic Games due to take place in Moscow that summer. This noticeably low-key Western response to Soviet aggression, backed up, in the case of the United States, by a temporary grain embargo and a proposal that other Western nations should agree not to assist the Soviet Union in circumventing that embargo or enter into new commercial contracts with the Russians, was the sum total of the punishment exacted on the Soviet Union by the West. But when even these limited proposals were put to the other NATO allies, it proved impossible to obtain any forthright or united stand by the alliance as a whole. At the end of the day only twenty-nine nations, including the United States, Canada, West Germany, Japan, China, Kenya, Israel, Thailand, Argentina, Uruguay, Paraguay, Hong Kong, and most of the Muslim states including Turkey, Saudi Arabia and Pakistan were prepared to go so far as formally to boycott the Olympics, another thirty-five failed to attend, while eighty-five national committees took part. In spite of repeated requests to British athletes not to participate, the British Government recognised it had no power to prevent its athletes participating and that therefore it could do no more than issue exhortations, though in the case of the British Olympic Committee these fell on deaf ears. Nonetheless many individual atheletes with a greater sense of national honour, together with some of the intended team participants, notably the fencing, yachting and equestrian teams, chose not to take part and to support the boycott.

Meanwhile the European Economic Community agreed not to increase it sales of food and, specifially, grain to the Soviet Union so as not to compensate the Russians for the grain they were unable to obtain from the United States under the terms of the embargo. But it is clear that absolutely nothing can persuade the EEC to abandon its determination to pursue its absurd policies of selling beef and butter to the Soviet Government, through a middle-man who is a French Communist millionaire, at one-quarter the price it is available to consumers within the Common Market countries, the difference being made up to the farmers by massive subsidies financed by the European taxpayer – a trade in which the Soviet Government makes a profit estimated at 200 per cent or more on the re-sale of these commodities to the Soviet consumer, the difference in part financing the Soviet Union's expenditure on armaments. Thanks to the Common Market the Soviet leaders no longer have to make the choice between guns or butter; the feckless Europeans, to finance the over-production of their farmers, virtually give the Russians the butter, the sale of which is used to purchase guns!

The feeble and farcical nature of the Western response to naked Soviet aggression, far from being seen in the Kremlin as a positive deterrent to future acts of aggression must have appeared instead more as an open invitation to repeat the action elsewhere, as occasion should serve, sure, as they no doubt suppose, in the knowledge that the democracies are too weak, divided and self-seeking to formulate a serious or coherent protest that would be damaging to the interests of the Soviet Union. The reason for the failure of the Western allies to rise to the level of events is not far to seek. Unlike the Warsaw Pact in which a single country dictates its party line and enforces its rule upon its involuntary allies, the NATO alliance is a voluntary grouping of fifteen independent nations with a disparate, and frequently conflicting, outlook upon the world. Indeed NATO reflects the weaknesses and strengths of the democratic system on which the constitutions of all its member states are founded. As Churchill once observed: democracy is the worst form of government – except for all the others. There can be no doubt that democracy is at an extreme disadvantage, especially in peacetime, in dealing with the wiles of a totalitarian dictatorship. However in a crisis and, as has already been proved decisively twice this century, in wartime, nothing is more formidable than the determination and anger of a free people in defence of their homes, their liberty and their loved ones. But the converse is also true, namely that there are few institutions more short-sighted or improvident for safeguarding them in peacetime. If it is difficult for a single democracy to pursue a steady and sensible course, confronted by external threats, blandishments, flattery and cajoleries from abroad, while plagued with economic crises and party political strife as successive election contests come round at home, how much less is it realistic to expect all members of a fifteen-nation alliance such as NATO or a ten-nation partnership, as the EEC has now become with the accession of Greece in 1981, to share a common view, let alone to adopt a positive course of action, except in the most dire of emergencies.

The Western allies with their pusillanimous response to deliberate, overt and large-scale Soviet aggression have been put to shame by the courage and resolve of the fierce, proud tribesmen of Afghanistan. Untrained, largely undisciplined and with no clear focus of national unity round which they are able to rally and unite, they have held their ground against a superpower equipped with the most technologically advanced weapons of modern warfare. Virtually bare-handed, armed for the most part with nothing more than some 100,000 antiquated breech-loading Lee Enfield rifles of the Second World War and a handful of bazookas of Korean War vintage, they have confonted Soviet forces equipped with the whole panoply of modern warfare including T-72 tanks, Hind helicopter-gunships, MiG jet fighters and Tupolev bombers. The patriotic forces, mistakenly and all too frequently described by the Western media as 'rebels', and above all the civilian population of the mountain villages where resistance is strongest, have suffered terrible casualties at the hands of the invaders, but many Russians have also been killed. Some idea of the treatment to which the civilian population is being subjected, with close on 100,000 Soviet troops actively involved in the fighting, may be gleaned from the reported actions of Soviet forces at a time when there were no more that a few hundred Soviet 'military advisers' in Afghanistan. *The Washington Post* reported on 7 February 1980 what it termed the 'Kerala Massacre', describing how in the town of Kerala in eastern Afghanistan on 20 April 1979 about twenty Soviet advisers supervised Afghan troops in the killing of an estimated one thousand or more unarmed people suspected of supporting the anti-government Moslem resistance. After being forced to line up in crouching positions they were shot from behind by machine gun and the bodies bulldozed. The order to shoot was given by a Pushtu speaking Russian soldier.

It is plain that such systematic and cold blooded slaughter was part of official Soviet policy to strike fear into the hearts of the Afghan population and to quell resistance at any cost, although this was quickly denied by the Soviet authorities who branded the news accounts 'monstrous misinformation' but refused to allow impartial observers to go to the scene.

Since the Kerala Massacre Soviet forces have increased a hundred-fold in numbers and Soviet bombing and strafing attacks on the civilian population in many of the mountain areas defying Russian rule have been frequent. For the most part the Russians have established themselves in heavily defended base areas, such as the strategic air base of Bagram outside Kabul, and in fortresses in the capital and other provincial towns from which they venture out only with the protection of either tanks, jet-fighters or bombers and armoured helicopter-gunships from which they are able to inflict heavy casualties on the Afghan tribesmen and civilian population, but in which they are themselves virtually impervious to attack, as a result of the shameful failure of the West to supply the Afghan resistance fighters with modern anti-air and anti-tank weapons. Thus the contest is a wholly unequal one. It is rare indeed that a chance machine-gun round succeeds in bringing down one of the Hind helicopter-gunships by penetrating a fuel tank or damaging some vital linkage on the aircraft's control system or engine; and, only occasionally, have the resistance fighters succeeded in destroying a Russian tank – usually by blowing off one of its tracks with a bazooka and then setting the tank on fire with petrol. For the most part, given the inadequacy of their equipment, Afghanistan's patriotic forces have had no choice but to concentrate their efforts on ambushing the 'soft' vehicles of the Russian supply columns which now dare to move only in heavily armoured convoys.

But in spite of all the Russians' military resources, there is little evidence at the present time to suggest that the invaders are making headway in their efforts to subdue the tribespeople of this wild and magnificent land. The resistance fighters continue to control the overwhelming majority of the country and the Russians have few friends. In mid-1980 the Russians, sure in the knowledge that neither the America of Mr Carter, nor the timid nations of Western Europe, would dare equip the resistance fighters with sophisticated and effective weapons of war, were shocked at the sudden loss in the space of a few weeks of several tanks and helicopters to missile attack. They were even more shocked when they discovered that the missiles were Russian, evidently passed on to the patriotic forces by elements of the Afghan army which the Russians had mistakenly supposed to be loyal to their puppet President, Babrak Karmal. An immediate purge of Afghan units was ordered and they were forthwith stripped of all guided weapons and sophisticated equipment. But, in the case of certain units, this was not accomplished without a fierce fight in which the Russians turned their massive fire-power including tanks, artillery, multiple-rocket launchers and unchallenged air power against their supposed 'allies'.

Many have been the apologists in the West who have sought to make excuses for the Sovet aggression. It has been variously suggested that the Russians felt threatened by developments in Afghanistan with which they share a common border, but this is implausible in light of the fact that, for several years, Afghanistan has had a Marxist government and that under President Carter, America's CIA had become such a shadow of its former self as to rule out any danger that it might stir up trouble for the Russians in one of its neighbour states. More far fetched yet was the alternative suggestion that the Russians invaded Afghanistan because they were frightened of the development of Muslim fundamentalism among the Soviet Union's own very large Muslim community, which amounts to a total of some 47 million out of an overall population 263 million and whose birthrate is soaring while that of the Russians proper is falling. If indeed the Russians do hold such fears, it is difficult to understand the logic that impels the

Kremlin to incorporate within the Soviet empire an even greater number of potentially dissident Muslims while, at the same time, uniting the Islamic world against them in hostility.

The explanation of the Soviet action is almost certainly more straightforward. The Kremlin ordered the invasion of Afghanistan as a deliberate act of policy, forming part of its grand design to encircle, subvert and, eventually, to dominate the key areas of Arabia and the Persian Gult, so vital to the West. It is certain that the Soviets did not invade Afghanistan for anything they might hope to find in that poor and, for the most part, desolate land which, so far as is known, has few resources beyond natural gas which, even before the Soviet invasion, was pumped by pipeline to the south-eastern regions of the Soviet Union. Since the Soviet occupation the pipeline has been sabotaged on at least three occasions by the Afghan resistance forces, principal among whom are the more than 100,000 tribesmen of the National Islamic Front of Afghanistan (NIFA) under the military command of Hassan Gailani, who reports that the Soviet soldiers are for the most part very young (seventeen or eighteen-year-old conscripts) and that their morale is so low that they are not above selling their weapons.

It is a common, yet mistaken, assertion in the West, especially among Americans drawing upon their own country's experience, that Afghanistan will be Russia's 'Vietnam'. It could indeed be made so, but only if the West is willing to give its fullest moral and material backing to the Afghan resistance, which it has conspicuously failed to do thus far.

Those in the West who believe that the Russians must now recognise that they have made a costly mistake evidently fail to appreciate that their action in Afghanistan is tying down no more than one-twentieth of the Soviet army – for which it is providing invaluable active-service training – and that, meanwhile, the Kremlin is forging ahead towards its strategic objectives. Following the Soviet takeover of Afghanistan, Russian forces are at the Khyber Pass on the Pakistani border and no more than 300 miles now separate them from India. Playing on India's antagonism for Pakistan and fear of China, and throwing in for good measure the unspoken threat that, unless the Indian Government is compliant with Soviet wishes, the latter is in a powerful position to stir up massive unrest in India with its 670 million population and its intractable problems of extreme poverty and hunger, the Soviet Union has concluded a £700 million ($1.6 billion) arms deal with the Indian Prime Minister Mrs Indira Ghandi, reportedly at heavily discounted prices.

Pakistan, the only remaining Western ally in the area with armed forces of any size, which already has to face two-thirds of the vastly larger Indian army stationed along its southern borders, now finds itself with the Russians for neighbours to the north-west, while a growing volume of Soviet military hardware flows into India. The Pakistani Government of President Zia has made clear that they would welcome Western military aid and that they are eager to cooperate in any Western plan for the coordinated defence of South-West Asia. However, even after the Soviet invasion of Afghanistan the Carter administration displayed a marked reluctance to give full support to its would-be ally. President Zia was offered a mere £80 million ($200 million), a derisory sum compared to Russian support for India and one that was reportedly dismissed by Presiden Zia as 'mere lollipops'. Nor is Pakistan without its internal problems. The party of Mr Bhutto, Pakistan's former President, executed by the Zia Government, remains strong and his sons are reported to have recently visited Kabul, Damascus and Moscow in search of Soviet support and to be strongly opposed to Zia's policy of supporting the Afghan resistance against Soviet aggression.

With the establishment in recent years by the Soviet Union of puppet regimes in Ethiopia, South Yemen and Afghanistan, the encirclement of the oil-rich areas of the Middle East is now complete. The Soviets today control access to the Red Sea and the Suez Canal from bases they are currently constructing in the Dalak Islands off the Ethiopian coast, and following their occupation of Afghanistan are now within 400 miles of the strategically vital Straits of Hormuz through which all the oil of Iran and Arabia must pass to reach the West. Soviet plans for the destabilisation of the Gulf region are progressing apace with the outbreak of war between Iraq and Iran, a conflict in which the Soviets have been backing both sides, assisting Iran through Syria and Libya, while supplying arms to Iraq direct. Meanwhile, Iran itself is in an advanced state of disingtegration and in desperate need of ammunition and spare parts for its mostly British and American military equipment – certainly one of the factors instrumental in securing the ultimate release of the US Embassy hostages held captive by the Iranian government for 444 days. A prime Soviet objective in the occupation of Afghanistan was undoubtedly to acquire a far longer common border with Iran so as to secure the subversion of the Baluchi tribes who straddle the borders between Afghanistan and Iran. Through them the Soviets no doubt hope to be able to accelerate the establishment of a Marxist government in Tehran, from which, in due course, the overthrow of the pro-Western governments of Saudi Arabia, Kuwait and the Gulf Emirates may be encompassed. Only decisive leadership by the United States, fully supported by its allies in Europe, can now fend off the accomplishment of one of the Soviet Union's most cherished designs – the subversion and domination of the sources of the Western world's oil supplies. Before leaving office as President, Mr Carter, belatedly facing up to reality, set about laying the groundwork for a redress of the balance by building a US base on the Indian Ocean atoll of Diego Garcia, 2,000 miles from the Straits of Hormuz and accepting the invitation of the governments of Somalia and Kenya (both intensely anxious about Soviet expansionism in the area) to establish US base facilities in Berbera – formerly a Soviet base until they were ejected by the Somalis in 1977 – and Mombasa. Steps were also put in hand for the creation of a US Rapid Deployment Force in case direct intervention to safeguard vital Western interests in the Middle East should be required. All will depend on President Reagan's follow-through. At the moment of writing the fate of Arabia and the Gulf, and with them the fortunes of the West, hang in the balance.

Chapter Twelve

AFRICA INVADED

'Beware the plundering tiger with its deadly cubs now coming in through the backdoor!' With these poignant words of warning President Kenneth Kaunda of Zambia sought to alert his countrymen and the peoples of Africa in a radio broadcast on 28 January 1976 to a sinister new development for the future of the African continent. Kaunda saw more clearly than most Western leaders the mortal threat posed by Soviet adventurism and the Russians' Cuban ally to the independence and stability of the nations of Africa. His words were in stark contrast to those of Mr Andrew Young, the Carter administration's representative at the United Nations, who went so far as to welcome the Cuban intervention with the fatuous pronouncement that 'The Cubans are a stabilising influence in Angola.' The fact that such statements were tolerated by President Carter was evidence of the weakness and erratic nature of the new American administration, charged with responsibility for guiding the destiny of the Western world for the next four years.

However, even the most eager apologists for the Soviet Union found it difficult to explain how Cuba, a tiny sugar and tobacco republic of the Caribbean, next to bankrupt and possessed of only limited military resources, was able to find the sea transport, the military airlift, not to mention the logistic and financial support, necessary to invade the African continent with a force initially numbering 18,000 men equipped with MiG fighter-bombers and T-54 tanks, a figure that was to grow rapidly to more than 50,000. There could never be any question but that the Cubans came in the role of Soviet surrogates, at Soviet instigation and with Soviet support to advance the cause of Soviet imperialism in Africa.

Frustrated in their Middle East designs by the resolve shown by the United States in safeguarding her own interests in that area – principally the State of Israel and Saudi oil – and flushed with the success of Soviet policy in South-East Asia in consequence of the failure of that resolve in Vietnam, Soviet strategists had turned their attentions in the mid-seventies to the continent of Africa. The Russians were astute in their selection of targets. Traditionally cautious – hence the use of Cuban rather than Soviet troops in Angola – they are prone to lean heavily upon half-open doors. The combination of the opportunities presented by the political situation in Africa south of the Zambezi, the disarray of the West European allies and the determination of the United States, in the wake of the Vietnam debacle, to avoid all overseas involvement, conspired to present the Kremlin with a temptation they would need to have been human to resist.

Much play has been made by the political enemies of the West of the 'destabilisation' policy alleged to have been pursued by the United States towards the government of President Allende of Chile. However, whatever outside involvement there may have been in the case of that Latin American republic, it is as nothing when set beside the ruthless and unremitting efforts of the Soviet Union over a generation to destabilise the newly independent Third World countries of Africa, Asia and the Middle East, whose independence has been assaulted at every turn by the Soviets pouring in arms, cash and military support, and exploiting every possible area of conflict. Not even the most fervent protagonists of Soviet expansionism have ventured to accuse the Soviet Union of involving itself in Africa out of love for the African peoples or from any desire to secure and uphold their right of self-determination under independent governments.

The strategic importance of southern Africa was brought into sharp focus by the Portuguese revolution of 25 April 1974 and its aftermath. The revolution stemmed directly from the failure of the Portuguese Government to defeat the forces of terrorism in its African colonies of Angola, Mozambique and Guinea/Bissau which the Soviet Union had supported, trained and armed over nearly two decades. Though the Soviet aim of incorporating mainland Portugal, a NATO ally of the West, within the Soviet bloc was defeated at the eleventh hour by the resolve of the Portuguese people – above all, of the Portuguese peasantry who fought the Communists in the streets and burned to the ground dozens of Communist Party headquarters – on the continent of Africa, Soviet strategy achieved marked successes.

In a short space of time the Soviet Union succeeded in subverting all three of Portugal's African overseas territories, replacing Portuguese influence with their own by the installation of Marxist governments linked to Moscow. Through their intervention with some 18,000 Cuban troops at a decisive stage in the power struggle taking place in Angola, the Soviet Union was able to establish, as it did also in Mozambique, land bases from which to launch and support a terrorist war against Zimbabwe (Rhodesia as it was at the time). In the process and a key part of their design, they acquired important air and naval bases from which, at a future date, to threaten the West's vital sea-lanes round South Africa's Cape of Good Hope, which carry the bulk of Europe's and America's imported oil supplies.

Viewed from the Kremlin their direct intervention in the internal affairs of African states had the great merit of presenting the West with a 'no-win' situation. Soviet strategists based their plans on the assumption that there would be no effective, coordinated Western counter to the Soviet thrust which would be allowed to gather momentum until it engulfed not merely Zimbabwe and Namibia but eventually the Republic of South Africa in a long drawn-out terrorist war. In this war the Africans and the West would be the principal losers while the Russians would emerge as the victors, establishing

Marxist puppet governments closely linked to Moscow, as they succeeded in doing in Angola and Mozambique.

In the event that Western governments did take positive steps to frustrate the Soviet design, there was the likelihood they would do so in such an unsubtle way – aligning themselves exclusively with white-supremacist regimes – that within months they would be forced ignominiously to back down by outraged electorates in Western Europe and the United States. Either outcome would be equally satisfactory from the Soviet viewpoint.

There was a third possibility but it was one that the Kremlin analysts evidently felt they could ignore as it would have required a resolve, a finesse and a ruthlessness that was to be wholly lacking in the conduct of Western policy throughout the seventies. Such a policy would have involved the forging of a multi-racial alliance of black and white states in central and southern Africa, prepared to stand together to resist Soviet expansionism and enjoying the strong support of the United States and the nations of Western Europe. That there was a sound basis for such a policy was vividly demonstrated by the fact that at an emergency summit meeting of the Organisation of African Unity held 10–13 January 1976 in Ethiopia no fewer than twenty-two of the forty-four nations that voted condemned the Soviet and Cuban intervention in Angola that had put in power the Marxist MPLA.

The man who came closest to achieving a serious coordinated Western strategy to stem the advance of the new Soviet imperialism was Dr Henry Kissinger. His policy involved economic and military support (though not to the extent of a commitment of US manpower, beyond specialist training teams) to the governments of Zambia and Zaïre while leaning on the Rhodesian Premier, Mr Ian Smith, to achieve a swift transition to responsible majority rule, and on the South Africans to bring about major advances in the economic and political status of the ethnic populations of South Africa.

Encouraged by indications of a positive American policy to resist Soviet expansionism in Africa, President Kaunda made his courageous denunciation of Soviet/Cuban aggression against Africa, and the South Africans struck north into Angola in September 1975 with a view to driving out the Cubans. Regretably, Kissinger was overruled by the United States Congress which, in the wake of Vietnam, was determined to avoid all new commitments overseas. The consequence was the abandonment in mid-stream of South Africa's anti-Cuban venture. Nor has President Kaunda ventured any further public criticism of the Soviets with whom he has had no choice but to mend his fences.

Just as in the Middle East the ultimate goal of Soviet policy was to gain control of the oil of Arabia and the Persian Gulf so, in the case of Africa, the Kremlin's principal objective was the other great treasure-house upon which the Western industrial nations depend for their prosperity: the mineral resources of central and southern Africa. Here, according to President Siad Barre the initial targets of the Soviet 'Master Plan' were Zaïre and Zambia, both fabulously rich in copper and other strategic minerals. Angola and Mozambique, with their newly installed Marxist governments, would provide bases for their subversion together with Tanzania, whose President Nyerere was described by the Soviets as a fully consenting partner in the Soviet plan 'though occasionally we get him to make neutral-sounding statements to reassure the West'. Having subverted two independent African governments it was their aim to encompass the overthrow of white supremacy in southern Africa.

The importance of South Africa rests not only in its dominating strategic position on the vital shipping-lanes but in the fact that the Western industrialised nations, including the United States, but more especially Western Europe and Japan, remain heavily dependent on the importation of precious metals and strategic minerals for the maintenance of their industrial production and defence potential. South Africa, ranking fifth among the world's mineral producers after the United States, USSR, Canada and China, and accounting for nearly one-third (31 per cent) of the Western world's mineral production, is Western Europe's largest single supplier.

While published figures of national reserves are inevitably incomplete and must be treated with caution, according to these in 1975 South Africa had the world's largest reserves of

Table 3   *Percentages of world reserves (and uses) of selected minerals in the USSR and Africa south of the equator*

	Rep. of S. Africa	Others in Africa south of equator	USSR	Combined USSR and Africa south of equator
1 Platinum group (electrical, glass, chemical, dental, jewellery, automotive and fuel cell industries)	86%	–	13%	99%
2 Manganese ore (steel alloys, batteries, uranium-extraction)	48%	5%	45%	98%
3 Vanadium (alloy for special steels)	64%	–	33%	97%
4 Chrome ore (essential to production of high-grade stainless-steel, and important in weapons-production)	83%	12%	1%	96%
5 Industrial diamonds (used in manufacture of abrasives, industrial dyes, drilling bits and gems)	7%	76%	4%	87%
6 Gold (monetary, jewellery)	49%	1%	19%	69%

	Rep. of S. Africa	Others in Africa south of equator	USSR	Combined USSR and Africa south of equator
7 Fluorspar (steel industry, aluminium, aerosols, uranium-production)	46%	–	4%	50%
8 Asbestos (fire-proofing and construction)	10%	15%	25%	50%
9 Iron ore (iron and steel industries)	4%	–	42%	46%
10 Uranium (nuclear power, nuclear weapons)	17%	10%	13%	40%
11 Titanium (high temperature resistant alloys, especially important for aircraft, jet engine, missile and space uses)	5%	–	16%	21%
12 Nickel (monetary, stainless-steel and nickel alloys)	10%	–	7%	17%
13 Zinc (galvanising iron, alloys, especially brass)	9%	–	8%	17%
14 Lead (roofing, piping, batteries, bullets and coffins)	4%	–	13%	17%

Source: South Africa's Strategic Minerals, W.C.J. van Rensburg and D.A. Pretorius, Valiant Publishers, Johannesburg 1975.

platinum group metals (86 per cent), Chrome ore (83 per cent), vanadium (64 per cent), gold (49 per cent), manganese ore (48 per cent), and fluorspar (46 per cent). She ranked second, after Zaïre, in industrial diamonds (7 per cent) and third, after Canada and the USSR, in nickel (10 per cent). More importantly, though holding only the fourth richest reserves of uranium (17 per cent), in consequence of the fact that the United States and the USSR use most of their own production to meet their own needs, South Africa is expected in the early 1980s to displace Canada as the world's principal exporter of this increasingly vital strategic material and energy source.

While South Africa is by far the richest mineral producer on the African continent, Africa as a whole, south of the equator, is a vast treasure-house containing in Zambia, Zaïre, Zimbabwe and South Africa, four of the five principal mineral-producing countries of Africa, and accounting in 1973 for 87 percent of the value of the continent's total metal production.

In the event that Africa south of the equator were to fall into the orbit of influence of the Soviet Union (already the most self-sufficient industrial nation in mineral resources and second-ranking in world production) the Soviet Union would have achieved a position of total dominance in regard to many strategic minerals vital to the West. It would control the lion's share of world reserves of platinum group metals (99 per cent), manganese ore (98 percent), vanadium (97 per cent), chrome ore (96 per cent), industrial diamonds (87 per cent), gold (69 per cent), fluorspar (50 per cent) and asbestos (50 per cent), as illustrated by Table 3.

With some 59·8 per cent of South Africa's mineral exports, excluding gold, going to Western Europe, including 18·2 per cent to West Germany and 16·6 per cent to the UK, and a further 20·8 percent to North America and 15.6 per cent to Asia, principally Japan, the dependence of these countries on the availability of South Africa's minerals is very high indeed (South African Department of Customs and Excise, *Monthly Abstract of Trade Statistics*, 1979). The impact that would be made on the economies of the Western industrialised nations by any restriction, let alone interruption, of these supplies could be analogous to the energy crisis that resulted from the temporary interruption of oil supplies following the 1973 Middle East war, which triggered an eighteen fold increase in the price of oil between 1970 and 1980 from $1.80 per barrel to $32 (OPEC price for Saudi 'marker' crude) and continues to have dramatic adverse economic and political consequences throughout the Western world and is the direct cause of the world slump at the time of writing. According the report of a Congressional Sub-committee headed by Congressman James D. Santini (*Sub-Sahara Africa: Its Role in Critical Mineral Needs of the Western World*, 1980), the United States is now 'dependent on foreign sources in excess of 50 per cent for 24 of the 32 minerals essential to its national economy'. The report points out that the United States depends on imports from South Africa for a high percentage of her total consumption: manganese (85 per cent), platinum (75 per cent), chrome (44 per cent), gold (36 per cent) and vanadium (20 per cent).

While the efficient production of energy from wind, sun and tides remains as a challenge for the future, the depletion of oil and coal reserves over the coming decades will ensure that nuclear power assumes an ever greater importance as a source of energy. In consequence demand for uranium, already in short supply, is almost certain to increase. If the Soviet Union were able to gain control over 40 per cent of this energy source, as well as coming close to achieving a world monopoly in minerals required for making high-grade alloys essential for aircraft, jet-engine and weapons production, she would have gained a vital strategic leverage over the West in the political, economic and military fields.

Phase two of the Soviet 'Master Plan', looking to the longer term, aims at the achievement by the Soviet Union of physical control (political and military) of the actual sources of the West's mineral and oil supplies. Were this once to be achieved, the Soviets would have manoeuvred themselves into a position where, without so much as a shot fired or the least act of piracy on the high seas, they could, by controlling the rate at which supplies would be made available to the West, be in a position to dictate whether Western economies grow fast, slowly or not at all, or, indeed, are plunged into violent recession and collapse. The dramatic rise in the price of oil over the past decade – causing grave damage to Western economies and in turn triggering extreme domestic political pressures in many countries – may serve as a foretaste of what might be expected in the event that the Soviets were ever allowed to gain physical control of the West's strategic minerals and vital energy sources. It is no wonder they see their African policy as sapping the other defences of capitalism.

The collapse of white-dominated governments in Angola, Mozambique and Rhodesia and their replacement by Marxist regimes in all three countries has left South Africa in a dangerously exposed position along the full extent of her lengthy land border to the north, which stretches from the Atlantic to the Indian oceans. Now, without any friendly buffer-states as neighbours, the Republic is itself in the front line. The governments of both Angola and Mozambique are close allies of the Soviet Union and have long been in receipt of a large volume of Soviet military hardware (though not yet on the scale of the countries of the Middle East) and of aid in the form of large numbers of Soviet-bloc technicians and 'military advisers', which in the case of Angola has included some 18,000 Cubans. For the past five years these surrogate forces have been pinned down by the anti-Communist forces of Jonas Savimbi's UNITA and Holden Roberto's FNLA guerrillas who have been fighting a fierce jungle war to rid their country of the Moscow-sponsored invaders. During this period the Cuban forces have suffered several thousand casualties, though there is no evidence that this has dampened the enthusiasm of the Cuban leader, Fidel Castro, for making himself and his people the willing tool of the Soviet Union in its policies for the forcible exportation of Communism to the Third World. Zimbabwe on the other hand, although ruled by the government of Prime Minister Robert Mugabe's Marxist ZANU-PF party, following its landslide victory in the pre-independence elections of February 1980, has thus far succeeded in keeping the Russians at arms' length, as the latter made the mistake of backing with weapons, cash and training the ZIPRA forces of the defeated candidate Mr Joshua Nkomo who, by coincidence, happened also to be the preferred candidate of the British Foreign Office.

At the time of writing the fate of Namibia, formerly German

South-West Africa, mandated after the First World War to South Africa by the League of Nations, hangs in the balance. This vast territory with its tiny population of barely one million is made up very largely of the barren wastelands of the Kalahari desert but contains important deposits of minerals, principally uranium and industrial diamonds. The South African Government has expressed its willingness to surrender its mandate, paving the way for Namibian independence, but has insisted that this be done on the basis of free and fair elections in which the internal parties are fully represented. The Soviet bloc and its Afro–Asian allies, on the other hand, have demanded that the Communist South-West Africa People's Organisation (SWAPO), which financed and armed by the Soviet Union has for years been conducting a terrorist war within the country, be recognised as the independence government. In January 1981 a conference, convened in Geneva to resolve the matter, ended in deadlock principally due to the unwillingness of the South Africans to accept that the pre-independence elections in Namibia be supervised by the United Nations, the great majority of whose members are dictatorships with no experience of elections, except of the rigged variety in which the voter may choose, if at all, only between the candidates of a single government party.

Nor is pressure on South Africa resulting from the political changes among her immediate neighbours solely external in character but it is having important ramifications for the internal situation within the Republic as well. The speed and dramatic success that has attended the struggle of black nationalist forces, most notably in Zimbabwe, can only have served to strengthen the ground-swell of discontent among blacks in the Republic and to heighten their determination to secure major changes in South Africa. They cannot have failed to note that barely five years after Rhodesia's Prime Minister Ian Smith had declared that there would not be a black government in Rhodesia 'for a thousand years', his place had been taken by his arch-enemy Mugabe and Rhodesia transformed into independent Zimbabwe. With the example of Zimbabwe as encouragement to the black nationalist cause in South Africa, and with three independent Marxist states, all of them sympathetic to that cause, as neighbours, it cannot be doubted that the heat is about to be turned on in South Africa.

The collapse of white rule in Rhodesia came quickly in the end. The turning-point was on 24 September 1976 when Ian Smith in a dramatic and historic statement to the people of Rhodesia announced his acceptance of the Anglo–American 'package-deal' put to him by Dr Kissinger on behalf of the British and American governments, having previously consulted the leaders of the other so-called 'front-line' African states. The key clauses of the agreement were as follows:

1   Rhodesia agrees to majority rule within two years.
2   Representatives of the Rhodesian Government will meet immediately at a mutually agreed place with African leaders to organise an interim government, to function until majority rule is implemented.
3   The interim government should consist of a Council of State, half of whose members will be black and half white.
4   The United Kingdom will enact enabling legislation for the process of majority rule.
5   Upon the establishment of the interim government, sanctions will be lifted and all acts of war, including guerrilla warfare will cease.
6   Substantial economic support will be made available by the international community to provide assurance to Rhodesians about the economic future of the country.

Ian Smith was persuaded of the sincerity of Dr Kissinger and accepted the undertakings given on behalf of the British and American governments that 'upon the establishment of the interim government' sanctions on Rhodesia would be lifted, economic aid made available and, unbelievably, that 'guerrilla warfare' would cease, though how Britain and America planned to honour this latter provision when they were not in a position to exercise any authority or control over the forces of Mugabe and Nkomo is difficult to know. The decision of Ian Smith and his colleagues in the Rhodesian cabinet to accept at face value the assurances given by Britain and America and to announce that they, in return, agreed to majority rule within two years was an act of faith in Britain and America and one that required considerable courage. It is sad to record that, no sooner had Ian Smith announced his acceptance of the terms, launching Rhodesia on the path towards majority rule and independence, than the Socialist government in Britain and the incoming Carter administration in the United States, at the instigation of the Foreign Office and the State Department, both of whom had long treated Smith and his colleagues as pariahs, disavowed the agreement. In Britain Foreign Office officials and Ministers sought to deny that there had ever been any agreement and proceeded to dismiss the terms conveyed by Dr Kissinger as no more than 'a basis for negotiation' – a shameful betrayal of a people who, for their size of population, had flocked in greater numbers than any other to fight for Britain in her hour of need, as fighter-pilots in the Battle of Britain or as Desert Rats in the North African campaign against Rommel.

Smith and his colleagues had, quite simply, been double-crossed and, although spokesmen for the Foreign Office sought to cast doubts upon Smith's honour and integrity, it was their own that was in question. Dr Kissinger has confirmed that, in the light of his own experience of negotiating with him, he had the highest regard for the Rhodesian leader's personal integrity and was most disturbed that the undertakings he conveyed were repudiated by his own government and the British. Even when the Conservative Government of Mrs Thatcher took office in May 1979, British Ministers continued to take refuge behind the Foreign Office contention that the agreement of 24 September 1976 had never been. In the wake of the undertakings given by Mrs Thatcher, under pressure from Lord Carrington and the Foreign Office, at the Commonwealth Prime Ministers' Conference in Lusaka, talks took place in Lancaster House in London to make provision for majority-rule elections and subsequent independence. Significantly the British Government insisted on the right of the terrorist leaders living outside Rhodesia to participate in the election and on the ditching of Bishop Muzorewa who had, shortly before the

British elections earlier that year, been elected as Prime Minister in Rhodesia's interim government. The combination of Muzorewa's humiliation at the hands of the British and the widespread intimidation of voters especially in the tribal trustlands where the majority of Africans still lived and where they were at the mercy of thousands of heavily armed 'election agents', many of whom did not report to the guerrilla assembly points supervised by the British Army, contributed to Mugabe winning by a landslide.

Since coming to power Robert Mugabe, who in his years of exile was supported principally by the Chinese not the Russians, has sought to follow the path of magnanimity in victory and to reconcile the divisions not only between black and white but between the two rival terrorist movements representing the two main tribal groupings – the Mashona majority and the war-like Matabele – though there is evidence that he is having less success in the latter respect. The danger of Zimbabwe sliding into civil war remains. At the same time Mugabe has never concealed his goal of establishing a Marxist state ruled ultimately by a single party – his own. Though a trade mission still operates in Pretoria, Zimbabwe's ambassador to South Africa was withdrawn soon after independence and, more recently, its independent white-run newspapers have been taken over by the government, a predilection for control of the press by government that Mr Mugabe evidently shares with neighbouring South Africa, which has also taken to closing down independent newspapers that do not toe the government line.

With South Africa the last remaining outpost of white supremacy on the African continent it cannot be doubted that the Soviet Union, through its Eastern-bloc allies and the surrogates it controls in the Third World, will seek to ensure that, as the decade progresses, South Africa itself is transformed into a battleground. The Kremlin knows all too well the extent to which the apartheid policies of the South African Government are deeply offensive to many throughout the Western democracies and, indeed, even among a minority of whites in South Africa. Nothing is likely to divide Western nations more than a major Soviet-backed thrust against South

Africa. There is no denying the South African Government's claim that, overall, the black population of the Republic is more prosperous, better housed, better educated and enjoys better health care than the average African anywhere else on the continent. The fact that tens of thousands of Africans from the independent coutries of southern Africa, principally Malawi, Mozambique and Lesotho, flock each year to the Republic to work in the mines is evidence that the regime is not quite so oppressive as many Africans and, more especially, many in the West seek to allege.

But the human misery and degradation inherent in South Africa's policies of 'separate development' cannot be denied. It would be a hard person indeed who did not feel a sense of outrage at the spectacle that takes place almost daily in the Bantu Courts in Johannesburg, as I have had occasion to witness in the company of Mrs Helen Suzman, a Progressive Party Member of the South African Parliament, who has in recent years acted as an outspoken and effective one-man-band opposition to South Africa's Nationalist government. The courts start their work early in the morning. The prisoners, men and women – all of them black – have been rounded up by the police in the previous twenty-four hours and held overnight in wire cages that are packed to overflowing. They are called in turn before the magistrate. Justice is summary.

Almost invariably the accused have been arrested and charged under South Africa's notorious Pass Laws, which (as in the Soviet Union) make it an offence for an individual to travel within his own country without a Pass Book containing permission from the authorities authorising him to visit or reside elsewhere in the country than his own home. Men and women of every age were brought before the court at intervals of approximately one minute during which they were asked why they had contravened the law; after their reply, which had to be brief, sentence was pronounced. Each sought to invent some plausible excuse as to why they were in Johannesburg without permission, instead of in their black homelands, pleading that they had come on a mission of mercy to visit a sick relation or claiming to have come to bury a close member of their family. Almost without exception their stories were not accepted and one by one they were knocked down with jails sentences of ten days here, three weeks there. The truth was that, in the overwhelming majority of cases, they were being sentenced for no other offence than the fact that, unable to find work in their tribal homelands where, for the most part, the land is poor and there is little chance of employment, they had come to the big city to look for work.

Although much of the petty apartheid has been done away with in recent years, the substance of it remains. In spite of the great strength of the South African armed forces which, in a conventional war, would be more than a match for all the countries of black Africa combined, and regardless of the harsh tactics of the South African police, not least it black members, this is a system that cannot long endure. Nor does the recent modification, involving the establishment of Bantustans or African tribal 'homelands' comprising 13 per cent of the land mass of South Africa – usually the less fertile areas and, invariably, the ones without mineral wealth – offer any solution, given the fact that the non-white communities constitute over 80 per cent of the population.

But nothing is to be achieved by making of South Africa a pariah. The nations of the West have a duty not merely to their fellow Europeans but as much to the African and mixed-race communities of South Africa to see that the Republic is led forward on the path of evolution towards justice and harmony rather than plunges (as the Soviet Union, its allies and its fellow-travellers in the West evidently wish) into the large-scale bloodshed of a racial war in which, inevitably, the black population would suffer most of all. The tensions that could be aroused in the United States and Britain – where as a result of a quarter of a century of immigration that continues to this day the coloured birthrate now approaches 10 per cent – by nightly television reporting of whites and blacks killing each other in an all-out racial war do not bear thinking of. The Western nations have a self-interest and an obligation, while recognising both the inhumanity of the system and the genuine fears of the whites, outnumbered as they are by a factor of four to one, to take the South Africans firmly by the forearm and lead them forward towards greater economic and political freedom for the blacks, while at the same time assuring them of support against Soviet-inspired terrorist or military attack from outside. The achievement of such a policy would require a high degree of statesmanship, courage and humanity – qualities not pre-eminent among the leaders of Western nations in recent years – but there remains the chance that South Africa even now could be saved from tragedy. It is urgent that the West starts playing a constructive role to this end.

Chapter Thirteen

CHINA: THE WAKING GIANT

The fiercest critics recent years of Soviet global expansionism have not been the Western democracies, but the Communist Chinese. For their part the democracies have voiced only muffled criticism of the Brezhnev clique's repression of the Soviet people and their foreign adventurism of recent years. As in the 1930s, so today, it is 'not done' to denounce totalitarian dictators for, as used to be said, 'it might make Herr Hitler angry' and then there would be no telling what he might not do. But the Chinese have had no such compunction and have repeatedly denounced the Soviet leadership in terms of such vehemence as to make the speech of Mrs Thatcher, which earned her from the Russians the tag of the 'Iron Maiden', appear like a eulogy at President Brezhnev's funeral.

It was many years before the true significance of the rift between China and the Soviet Union, which began in April 1960 and erupted openly at a special international conference of Communist parties in November, came to be recognised in the West. Indeed it was not until 1971 and the visit of President Richard Nixon to China in what was undoubtedly one of the most significant policy initiatives of his tenure at the White House that the United States established diplomatic relations with Peking.

The passion of the Chinese leaders' distrust and hatred of their opposite numbers in the Kremlin can be explained only in terms of the intensive strife and bloodshed in the Christendom of medieval times. At heart the differences between China and Russia are ideological, inspired by conflicting nationalism. Both Communist giants believe with a fervour that leaves non-believers bemused that *theirs* is the only true path of Marxist/ Leninist rectitude. In the Middle Ages it was rare for Christians to kill infidels for their non-belief – the Crusades were conceived above all to secure the Holy Places of the Bible for Christendom not to slaughter Muslims. But in the case of Christians of another persuasion it was a different matter. Heresy was the supreme crime and, supposedly, a mortal sin. Edward Gibbon in his *Decline and Fall of the Roman Empire* provides a colourful illustration of the point in his passage about the profligate Pope John XXIII: 'The most scandalous charges were suppressed; the Vicar of Christ was only accused of piracy, murder, rape, sodomy and incest . . . ' (Edward Gibbon, Chapter 70,). The most scandalous charges related to doctrinal deviations branded as heresy.

The ideological differences between Russia and China have, if anything, intensified over the twenty-year period that has intervened, with rivalries elsewhere in the world leading even to physical conflict in South-East Asia between China and the Soviet Union's ally North Vietnam and to a major Soviet military build-up along the disputed Sino–Soviet border.

A favourite justification for the Soviet Union's strategic and conventional build-up advanced by apologists for the Soviet cause, and indeed by the Russians themselves, rests on the supposed threat from China and all too many in the West have accepted this at face value. However the truth is that in brute military power the Soviet Union is to China as 100 is to 1. Even in conventional strength the Chinese advantage in numbers, if advantage it be, is far outweighed by the weight of modern and sophisticated weaponry available to the Soviet forces. Though China became a nuclear power with the explosion of its first atomic bomb on 16 October 1964, even today its nuclear potential remains strictly limited with, according to the International Institute for Strategic Studies' *Military Balance*

1980–1 only four inter-continental ballistic missiles with a range of up to 3,800 nautical miles, and some 85 IRBM's and 50 MRBM's with ranges of up to 1,600 miles and 1,100 miles respectively. In relation to the Soviet strategic inventory this is a puny capability; however, bearing in mind the previously backward state of Chinese technology and the fact that since 1960 they have had no outside help whatsoever with arms development, it is remarkable that a developing nation such as China, despite its long history and great civilisation, should have made the strides it has in developing its own rockets, missiles and nuclear warheads. Inevitably it is disconcerting for the Russians to consider the potent military power into which China almost certainly will develop in the future, but the reality is that China, in the present stage of its development, presents no military threat to the Soviet Union.

If evidence were needed of the defensive nature of the Chinese military deployment facing the Soviet Union it may be found in the fact that China's land-based missiles – with the possible exception of their handful of newly deployed ICBMs – are located in such a way that, in the event that they were fired, they would fall almost exclusively on *Chinese* soil. It may be that France's Pluton surface-to-suface missiles have such limited range that, from their present positions close to the Franco–German border, they would, if launched fall on friendly West German territory, but no other country in the world, apart from China, has plans to drop strategic nuclear weapons on its *own* territory. This policy goes to the very heart of the Chinese fear, indeed conviction, that the Soviet Union intends to attack them. They know that they do not have the military strength to hold their ground in the face of such an attack and their avowed intention – confirmed by the siting of their missiles – is to retreat, as the Russians themselves did in the face of Hitler's onslaught in 1941–2, sucking the invader into the Chinese heartland where they would then come under Chinese nuclear bombardment and have to face constant skirmishing and relentless attacks on their supply lines designed eventually to wear them down and force them to retreat. Should it be true that China harbours aggressive designs against the Soviet Union, it is scarcely to be credited that all its military doctrine and the disposition of its strategic capability would be so totally geared to a strategy of defence.

An extension of the Soviets' 'Fear of China' alibi is the argument that the Soviet Union finds itself encircled by aggressive and hostile countries – NATO Europe to the west, China to the east, and ringed all about by US bases in Japan, South Korea, the Indian Ocean, Europe and Alaska. That this view had some validity in the fifties and sixties when the United States, for want of a true inter-continental capability, had deployed its strategic bombers at forward bases from which they could strike the Soviet Union, is undeniable. But today, now that the US capability is based almost exclusively within the continental United States and under the oceans' surface and, above all, that the Soviet Union has overtaken the United States in this field, the argument ceases to have any validity.

The Chinese certainly are very numerous and, as might be expected of a country with a population that exceeds 1,000 million (one-quarter of the human race) they maintain very large conventional forces of some 4.5 million men together with an armed militia of up to 5 million (*Military Balance 1980/81*,IISS). However, not even in the conventional field, in spite of their potentially large numbers, can the Chinese forces remotely be described as presenting a threat to the Soviet Union.

In the course of a visit to China in June 1978, at the invitation of the Chinese Government in my capacity as a defence spokesman for the Conservative Party, I had the opportunity of seeing something of the Chinese army at first hand. From Peking I was taken to visit the Third Garrison Division of the People's Liberation Army at their headquarters some 35 miles to the north-east of Peking. As I watched the Chinese soldiers drilling on their barracks square barely 200 miles from important concentrations of Soviet military power just across the border, I found it strange to reflect that British forces in Germany, more than 7,000 miles away, together with their NATO counterparts, were facing the same potential enemy as the Chinese so keenly fear. The Third Garrison Division had been described to me as a 'mechanised' division; however, the first item on the agenda for my visit was a most impressive display of small-arms handling. A squad of twenty-four men was drawn up on the parade ground in front of me. Each was blindfolded to simulate night-fighting conditions (an aspect of warfare on which the Chinese place great emphasis) and had an assortment of four weapons laid out on the ground in front of him consisting of a rifle, a light machine-gun, a sub-machine-gun and a pistol. At a word of command, each man knelt on the ground and proceeded to strip down each weapon into its basic component parts. As soon as they had finished they stood to attention. The slowest took two minutes and ten seconds to complete the task and, even when it came to reassembling the weapon (still blindfolded), the longest time taken was no more than two minutes thirty seconds.

I had been treated to a remarkable demonstration of Chinese efficiency and expertise in small arms. However, after yet another impressive manifestation of infantry skills, which included an arduous assault course and the scaling, without ladders, of a three-storey building from the outside, I made the mistake of asking if it would be possible to see something of the division's armoured fighting vehicles and tanks since this was, after all, a 'mechanised' division. An awkward silence ensued, then the divisional commander, with obvious embarrassment, explained: 'Unfortunately not possible today – mechanised equipment is in another place. Maybe on future visit . . . . ' It was abundantly clear, despite the unit's designation, that they had no mechanisation whatever beyond a ramshackle collection of ageing trucks, jeeps and buses.

In contrast to the Russian forces that confront them across their lengthy common border, the Chinese army is pitifully equipped with modern weapons of war. With some 11,000 tanks they have barely one-fifth as many as the Russians, including many that are very old indeed and are markedly inferior in capability. Indeed some of their second-category divisions continue to this day to rely in part on horse-drawn transport. Their Soviet counterparts, on the other hand, are bristling with new equipment including the latest T-72 tanks, multiple-rocket launchers, hordes of Hind and Hip helicopter-gunships as well as a vast array of battlefield nuclear missiles.

Ever since the disgrace of Khrushchev, the Soviet military

build-up along the Sino–Soviet border has grown relentlessly both in size and in calibre of equipment. From a force of 20 divisions with 210 fighter-aircraft in 1965, Soviet forces had, by 1980, been increased to 46 divisions with 1,200 fighter-aircraft (DOD, *Annual Report to Congress Fiscal Year 1981*). Not only has this massive build-up been achieved without moving a single division from the NATO front but, as the US Department of Defense *Annual Report* observes, this has come about at a time when: 'Approximately 154,000 men have been added during the past eleven years to the Soviet forces stationed in Eastern Europe, including the 70,000 men and five divisions deployed in Czechoslovakia since 1968.' Referring to the overall growth in Soviet military capability since 1965 the report adds: 'The Soviets have increased the total number of their divisions from 148 to 170 and added about 1,400 aircraft and 31 regiments (squadrons) to their tactical air armies.'

Faced with this tremendous array of military might, it is little wonder that the Chinese have been persuaded that the Soviet Union intends to attack them. Indeed they are convinced that a decision of principle to this effect has already been taken by the Kremlin and that the only question is 'When?'. In addition to the evidence of their own eyes and their experience of the Russians over many years as allies of the Soviet Union, with whom they supposedly still have a Treaty of Friendship, they have convinced themselves of the inevitability of a Soviet attack on ideological grounds. 'The Soviet Union', they aver to every foreign visitor, 'is a social–imperialist power. It is in the nature of all imperialist powers to be aggressive, therefore it is certain they will attack.' So convinced are they of the inevitability of such an attack that, under Peking and their other principal cities, they have built a vast and elaborate network of tunnels and bunkers which my hosts were most eager to show me.

I was taken to a busy street near the heart of Peking and led on foot through the bustling crowds to a haberdashery store jammed with people buying materials and tunics. My guide was recognised by the person running the shop and I was invited to step behind the counter. The crowd stood back and, at the press of a button, the whole counter and floor moved away to reveal a wide stone staircase descending underground.

I was taken down several flights of steps where the air was dank and cool to a veritable rabbit warren of tunnels. At one point the tunnel opened up into a vast underground hall. My guide had explained that it was estimated that at any given moment during the day there could be as many as 10,000 people going about their business in the busy street only 300 yards long above the ground, but that within six minutes of an air-raid siren being sounded the street would be empty and everyone safely underground.

Beneath this small street alone was a network of more that 3,000 yards of tunnels with some 90 concealed access points. There were two levels to the network at depths of 25 feet and 50 feet respectively. Underground there was a militia command post and armoury, kitchens, hospitals, even factories where essential war production could be continued and workers and machinery protected. There were large reserves of food and water and the whole complex was served by its own underground generator, to provide electricity and to operate the air-filtration system. I was led into a large underground chamber set out with trestle tables and benches. My guide declared with evident pride: 'This hall is feeding centre. Accommodate 1,000 people and, very convenient, immediately under Peking Duck Restaurant!' Another typical example of Chinese forethought and planning was the siting of an underground hospital directly beneath a pharmacy.

Peking's network of underground tunnels has been built not solely, or even principally, as shelters. Their function is twofold. First and foremost, they are 'evacuation' tunnels that would enable the civilian population to flee the city, making their way under cover to the suburbs and outlying areas of the city, more than 10 miles and at least three hours' walk away. Undoubtedly Peking's recently constructed underground railway network also has a part to play in this evacuation plan and those foreign visitors who have seen it have remarked on the fact that the platforms are some five times the width the the London Tube or the New York Subway. However a second, and in Chinese eyes, even more important function of the tunnels is to provide a base from which to wage war against an invader. 'These are fighting tunnels!', exclaimed my guide. 'We will defeat the Russians this way, as we defeated the Japanese before.' He went on to explain that the People's Liberation Army and militia would come out of the tunnels at night to attack the Russian forces or, should they venture down into the tunnel complex, would engage them in hand-to-hand fighting underground.

When, later in the day, I visited the American Embassy to see the US Ambassador Mr Leonard Woodcock, something of a rarity in diplomatic circles as a trade unionist and a former President of the United Auto Workers' Union, I happened to mention, as his wife was serving tea, my visit to part of the Chinese tunnel network. Mrs Woodcock was intrigued, 'It wasn't by chance the one under the clothing store?' she enquired. 'And beneath the Peking Duck Restaurant?' I riposted. 'That's the one!' she exclaimed. Although it would seem that foreign visitors to Peking are taken to see *the* tunnel beneath the same crowded little street, there is no reason to doubt that such complexes are reproduced time and again below other areas of the city and, indeed, in most of the main centres of population throughout China. It is impossible to know how effective they might be in the event of a major nuclear attack, although recent tests in the United States have suggested that proper underground protection might be expected to reduce fatalities by 75–90 per cent by comparison with the toll on a wholly unprotected population.

But however effective the tunnels might be in terms of physical protection, their importance was at least as great from a psychological point of view, in the eyes of the Chinese leadership. What better way to explain to the Chinese masses that their erstwhile Communist ally was now their mortal enemy, than to tell them that a nuclear attack by Russia on China was virtually certain, if not imminent, and that they had better get down a hole and dig? This was in fact confirmed to me by Premier Chou En-lai on the occasion of my first visit to the People's Republic in 1971 when in the early hours of one morning my wife and I had a two-hour meeting with him in the Great Hall of the People. As one whose earliest childhood memories were of underground shelters beneath the streets of London during the Blitz, I professed myself sceptical that shelters could be of much value in an age when bombs had become so many times more powerful. 'Perhaps you are right,' pondered the Chinese leader, 'But what is important is that our people should be reorientated towards the new direction of threat.' Chou En-lai went on to explain that the rift between China and the Soviet Union that had come about in the early sixties had been caused by the unwillingness of the Soviet leadership to treat China as an equal partner and, specifically, by their sudden decision to end Russian assistance to China in nuclear weapons development. He expressed the view that the withdrawal of several thousand Soviet technicians working in China's key industries had, in the long term, been beneficial and that China had grown substantially in economic and industrial self-sufficiency since that date as a result.

'We now have,' observed Chou En-lai, 'more than a million Soviet troops, armed with nuclear weapons along our borders, including a third of a million in the Mongolian Republic, who are there under a 'Treaty of Friendship' with the Soviet Union.' He paused, then added sardonically, 'We too have a Treaty of Friendship with the Soviet Union!' The Chinese leader made clear that China took the strongest exception to what he described as the 'unequal' Treaties of Friendship that the Soviet Union had signed with Egypt, India and Iraq with a view to dominating them economically, politically and militarily. He stressed that a major point of difference with the Kremlin arose over the Sino–Soviet border where the Russians in the inter-war years had annexed vast tracks of land the Chinese regarded as theirs and showed not the least willingness to return it. Expatiating on China's relationship with the rest of the world at a time when, in the early seventies, China was just beginning to break out of its isolationist attitude, the Chinese Premier observed: 'You are quite right to be concerned at what I believe is called in the Western world – indeed the Kremlin itself is not above using the phrase – 'The Yellow Peril – after all we do form nearly one-quarter of the world's population. But China will never be a superpower.' By this he presumably intended to convey that he believed China would never behave as a superpower, adding: 'The Chinese people have been insulted and oppressed for centuries. We are not now the people to bully others. The central fact of which you should take note is that no one helped the Chinese people make their revolution – just as no one helped the British people make theirs over a period of several hundred years, or the Americans at the time of their Revolutionary War. Peoples must liberate themselves. We can supply only the ideology.'

In spite of the late Premier's assurances, it is by no means impossible to envisage a situation in which under different circumstances China might become an aggressive power. All that can be said is that, in the present state of its development, this is not now the case. The Chinese in spite of their numbers, have today only a limited military capability, and for the time being, have more than enough in the way of industrial, technological and population problems to keep them occupied for a very long time. With far greater justification than the Russians, the Chinese may indeed claim to feel encircled, threatened as they are by a hostile and, militarily, far stronger neighbour along its northern and western borders, which has established satellite governments along China's southern borders in Vietnam, Laos, Cambodia and Afghanistan and continues to cultivate an anti-China axis with the government of India.

In recent years the suggestion has on occasion been advanced in the West that from a Western point of view nothing could be more satisfactory than if the two great Communist giants were to go to war with each other. Such ideas are foolish and reckless for, apart from the suffering that would be brought to the civilian populations of Russia and China, the truth is that any conflict of such dimensions in the nuclear age would, inevitably, run the risk of dragging the whole world into the conflict. At the very least, people throughout the world would suffer grievously, above all in the long term, from a drastically increased radioactivity in the atmosphere which would pollute and render unusable water and food resources in many parts of the world and might even render whole regions infertile. On the contrary, the West has an interest in cultivating its relations with the People's Republic with a view to invoking its aid in the maintenance of peace and stability in a precarious world and in helping to convince the collective dictatorship in the Kremlin that the whole world will stand against them should they recklessly embark upon military adventures.

China is today making giant strides to bring her people forward but has a desperate need for modern technology, nowhere more so than in the military field, to update and strengthen its military forces. Unofficially China today is one of the staunchest members of NATO, believing very strongly in the importance of the Western alliance and in the desirability of US troops remaining in Europe. In a similar way many Western nations look upon China as as indispensable partner that is at present diverting no less than one-third of the Soviet Union's stupendous military power from the NATO front in Central Europe. In considering sales of modern military equipment and technology, the West would do well to adopt a policy of selling to the Chinese 'anything that can't reach us'.

It is difficult for an outsider visiting China today not to feel that he is the witness of a great human enterprise. It is an enterprise that began with the epic of the Long March, in which Mao Tse-tung and his comrades led 90,000 men and their families, taking with them their livestock, their possessions and even machine-tools. In the space of a year they covered more than 6,000 miles, scaling ravines, crossing snow-covered mountain ranges, fighting skirmishes every two of three days and a battle every fortnight. Only one in ten of the original marchers survived to reach their destination in the mountain fastnesses of Yunan. It would be foolish to demean their achievements, or to assume that the aspirations of the Chinese people are necessarily in conflict with the interests of the peoples of the Western world.

Part V

TOWARDS THE CATACLYSM

Chapter Fourteen

DETERRENCE AND SUBVERSION

The Conservative Government that took office in May 1979 under the leadership of Mrs Margaret Thatcher, following a landslide victory in the general election, found itself confronted by the urgent need to decide the future of Britain's independent nuclear deterrent. Although Britain's force of Polaris submarines, the mainstay of Britain's strategic capability ever since the Royal Navy had taken over the role from the RAF's V-bomber force a decade before, still had another ten to fifteen years of service life, it was estimated that by the early to mid-nineties the hull-life of the four submarines would have expired due to corrosion and metal fatigue. In view of the long lead-time required to develop, construct and bring into service a replacement force in a field of such technological sophistication requiring the mobilisation of vast resources, both financial and human, only an urgent and positive decision could ensure the maintenance of Britain's strategic capability into the future without interruption.

In July 1980 the British Government announced that, having considered the available options and thanks to the full-hearted cooperation of the American Government, it had decided to replace Polaris with a new generation of submarine armed with United States' Trident I missile. As in the case of the Polaris, while the missiles themselves would be bought off the shelf from the United States, both the submarines and the nuclear warheads would be built by Britain. The estimated cost of the programme over fifteen years was put at £5,000 million ($11 billion) which, at an annual rate, represents less than half the loss of the nationalised British Steel Corporation for 1980/1. Expressed in such terms Trident may be seen as a relatively modest insurance premium to pay for a system more certain than any other to safeguard, to the year 2020 or beyond, the peace and freedom that, in spite of past experiences, the British people take so much for granted. Alternative systems such as the cruise missile or even a European equivalent of the Soviets' SS-20 mobile IRBM which might have been built jointly by Britain, France and Germany were considered but, at an early stage, excluded due to their vulnerability to pre-emptive attack and, in the case of the cruise missile, its slowness and the less assured penetrability of the warhead to its target. Compared to anything that could be purchased in the conventional field the cost-effectiveness of Trident, at a price less than Britain's Tornado strike/interceptor aircraft programme, is undisputed. For the same cost Britain could add and maintain one new armoured division, but this is unlikely to be a deterrent to war in the minds of the men in the Kremlin who have no fewer than forty-six armoured divisions at their command.

It was inevitable that the British Government's decision to opt for a new generation of strategic deterrent, coupled with the announcement of its willingness to accept on British soil a force of 160 US Tomahawk ground-launched cruise missiles, should provoke a re-run of the anti-nuclear protests of the fifties and sixties giving a new lease of life to an otherwise moribund Campaign for Nuclear Disarmament. While a handful of idealists within CND may be anxious to see multilateral disarmament that includes the Soviet Union, the main thrust of the organisation, heavily infiltrated by the whole gamut of Communist, Trotskyite and International Socialist activists, is to achieve (in line as it happens with the Kremlin's own policy) the *unilateral* disarmament of Britain, her withdrawal from the NATO alliance and the removal of US bases from British soil.

It is evident that in its deliberations on the question of a

Top: Tomahawk Cruise Missile
Bottom: Transporter/Launcher for Tomahawk

Trident I missile

Polaris replacement the British Cabinet did not give a moment's consideration to the possibility of abandoning the British deterrent altogether. If the reasons for Britain not going naked in the world were felt to be compelling by the Labour Government of Prime Minister Clement Attlee in the period 1945–51, at the time when the United States held the monopoly of strategic nuclear power, they are undoubtedly many times more so in an era in which the Soviet Union has achieved nuclear superiority and has unashamedly embarked on the path of aggression. Nor is it the Soviet Union alone that poses a threat in this field. Many other countries, despite the Non-Proliferation Treaty, are hard at work developing bombs of their own. Already in the 1960s China and India had joined the nuclear 'club' and it is likely, although they have always resolutely refused to give confirmation of the fact, that in the 1970s they were joined by both Israel and South Africa. In the course of the eighties Pakistan and Iraq as well as, possibly, South Korea, Taiwan and Brazil are likely to become nuclear powers. Even the fanatical President of Libya, Colonel Gaddafi, has plans for acquiring a nuclear capability by providing part of the finance for Pakistan's nuclear programme. Even if the Soviet threat were to disappear tomorrow, it is difficult to imagine a British Government abandoning its own capability if, by so doing, it were to place the British people at the mercy of a man such as Gaddafi who has shown himself to be capable of any action, having before now ordered submarines of the Libyan navy to attempt to torpedo the Cunard liner *QE2* as it passed through Mediterranean waters carrying Jewish families on a cruise to the Holy Land.

Although the British submarines will carry only sixteen Trident I missiles, unlike their American counterparts which will have twenty-four, the Trident is a far more potent and sophisticated system than the one it replaces. The 4,000-nautical-mile range of the Trident missiles, compared to the 2,500-nautical-miles of Polaris, increases by a factor of ten the ocean space in which the new submarines may hide while all the time keeping the industrial heartland of the Soviet Union within their target range. Each missile will carry eight multiple independently targetable warheads (MIRVs), compared to only three, which cannot be independently targeted, in the case of Polaris. While the Conservative Government's initial order is for no more than four submarines, the option of a fifth remains open. The argument in favour of a fleet of five is strong, for as experience with the Polaris fleet has shown, it is impossible with only a four-submarine fleet to guarantee more than a single submarine 'on-station' at any given moment. Although the Royal Navy manages to keep two submarines on patrol for at least eight months of the year, there is a clear danger that the ability to guarantee no more than a single submarine at all times risks being seen as inadequate in the face of the continuing escalation of Soviet nuclear weapons targeted on Britain and other Western European countries, especially bearing in mind the possibility of a breakthrough in underwater detection technology which might make a single submarine intensely vulnerable. A fifth submarine at an estimated cost of £600 million ($1·3 billion), a 12 per cent addition to the overall purchase price would virtually double Britain's capability.

The British Government's decision in favour of Trident is a sound one, both from an economic standpoint thanks to the generosity of the United States, which is bearing the lion's share of the development costs, as well as from a technological standpoint given that it is less vulnerable, more powerful and more certain to penetrate any Soviet defences – barring a breakthrough in laser or beam-technology weapons – than comparable systems such as, for instance, the cruise missile. However one factor may have escaped the Conservative Government's consideration when opting for Trident in July 1980: before the force can become operational in the mid-nineties, the programme will have to survive at least two, possible three, general elections with a Labour Party, unless it disintegrates, committed to scrapping it, if not to please Moscow, at least on grounds of supposed 'social priority' in public expenditure. Thus, in the event of a Labour government winning a general election in 1984 or 1988, there could be a serious danger that Trident would be abandoned in mid-stream and Britain find herself, in the last resort, defenceless. It was Dr Kissinger who, at a conference in Brussels in September

1979 to discuss 'Nato: The Next Thirty Years', warned the nations of Europe not to base all their plans for the future on an assumed willingness of the American people to commit Hara-kiri on their behalf to save Western Europe from occupation.

Throughout the seventies, in addition to the Polaris force, Britain kept in service some fifty-six Vulcan bombers which, in a period of tension, could be placed on three-minutes' Quick Reaction Alert (QRA), more than sufficient time for them to get airborne and on their way towards Moscow with their deadly load. There are few sights more impressive than to see, as I had the privilege of doing in 1978 while a defence spokesman for the Conservative Party, these gaunt grey beasts with an awesome beauty to their delta-shaped wings, scrambling for take-off. For several hours at a stretch the crews can wait in their cockpits, with the aircraft fuelled, armed and lined up by the side of the runway ready to roll but with their engines cold. At the word of command – 'SCRAMBLE-SCRAMBLE-SCRAMBLE' – over the radio, backed up by a cluster of green Verey shells fired from the control tower, the engines of the giant bombers roar to life and the jet effluxes ignite. Already within twenty-five seconds the first lumbering giant has entered the runway, closely followed by the others. On the day I saw them at RAF Waddington, one of the Lincolnshire V-bomber bases, four Vulcans careered down the runway simultaneously and, within eighty-five seconds of the command to 'SCRAMBLE', all four were airborne and, potentially, on their way to their targets in the Soviet Union. Because it has to be assumed that there would be no more than three to five minutes' warning, the Air Officer Commanding has the authority to 'launch under warning' in the event of a Soviet missile attack confirmed by two of the Ballistic Missile Early Warning Systems (BMEWS) stations at either Clear, Alaska, Thule, Greenland, or Fylingdales in Yorkshire. It would be impossible to wait for political authorisation to scramble the aircraft without risking their destruction on the ground. From the moment of launch the British Prime Minister would have little more than thirty minutes to confirm the order before the pilots would descend to no more than 200 feet above ground level to commence their penetration run through the elaborate and dense Soviet air-defence screens. In the event of no positive confirmation being received the aircraft would return to base or to a diversionary field.

There is no doubt that throughout the seventies the Vulcans provided an important enhancement to the capability of Britain's strategic submarines. However, by the early eighties, their ability to penetrate Soviet air defences had declined substantially while, at the same time, the vulnerability of their own bases had markedly increased and the Labour Government before leaving office in May 1979 took the decision to scrap the Vulcans by 1983. Not only did the incoming Conservative Government confirm this decision but, as part of a £200 million ($450 million) package of defence cuts announced in January 1981, it was announced that at least one of the Vulcan squadrons was to be disbanded by the end of that year. Bearing in mind that the Trident missiles will not be operational until the mid-nineties and that, meanwhile, the Soviet threat has escalated sharply over the past decade, Britain's decision to scrap entirely her theatre-nuclear capability can only be judged imprudent in the extreme. Even the United States has concluded, in the case of her B-52 bombers, which at twenty years of age are exactly the same vintage as the RAF's Vulcans, that she cannot afford to dispose of such valuable assets. Instead she has decided to extend their fatigue life to the nineties and is in the process of providing a dramatic enhancement to their capability by equipping them as cruise-missile carriers, in which role they would no longer have to penetrate the Soviet air defences but could launch their missiles from a stand-off position. The case is very strong indeed for Britain to do likewise and not to scrap the Vulcans before bringing into service a replacement system. Britain's Ministry of Defence has plans for equipping the V-bomber force with some 500 air-launched cruise missiles, which could have been in service with the Royal Air Force by the time of the 1984 general election at a cost of £450 million ($960 million) at 1980 prices, barely 15 per cent of the £3 billion ($6·4 billion) squandered that same year in subsidies to Britain's nationalised industries.

Whatever may have been the differences between Britain's two major parties, Conservative and Labour, over the postwar years – and they have been bitter and deep above all on economic and industrial policy – both parties have been united in upholding Britain's commitment to the NATO alliance and in their belief in the necessity for Britain to maintain an independent deterrent. Indeed it was the first postwar Labour Prime Minister, Clement Attlee, who, behind the backs of most of his Cabinet colleagues, was responsible for launching Britain's nuclear weapons programme, which led to the successful testing of an atomic bomb in 1952 and to the entry into service in 1955 of the RAF's V-bomber force which for some fifteen years was to be the mainstay of Britain's deterrent. Following the cancellation in 1962 of the Skybolt air-launched stand-off missile, which Britain had hoped to buy from the United States to improve the capability of her V-bombers, Prime Minister Harold Macmillan and President John F. Kennedy in 1963 concluded the Nassau Agreement by the terms of which Britain was permitted to purchase Polaris submarine-launched ballistic missiles from the United States. The agreement provided not only for the submarines and their nuclear reactors to be built in British shipyards but, in conformity with the US Congress' McMahon Act, which bans the transfer of nuclear weapons to any country, for Britain to develop and build her own nuclear warheads. The Labour Government of 1964–1970 under the leadership of Prime Minister Harold Wilson fully endorsed these plans and carried them forward to fruition, although in a moment of economy the fifth Polaris vessel originally planned, which would have enabled Britain to keep two submarines permanently on patrol, was cancelled leaving a force of only four.

From the moment that Britain's Polaris submarines – each carrying sixteen nuclear missiles – entered service in 1969, the Royal Navy took over from the RAF prime responsibilty for Britain's strategic deterrent. It is a testimony to the skill and expertise of the men of the Royal Navy, and their civilian backup at the Rosyth Dockyard on the Firth of Forth and at Faslane on the Clyde, that they have ever since maintained the Polaris patrol without interruption in spite of the small size of the force.

In 1973 the Conservative Government of Prime Minister

Edward Heath embarked on a £1,000 million ($2·5 billion) programme, codenamed Chevaline, to safeguard the penetrability of Polaris in the face of improved Soviet anti-ballistic missiles (ABM) defences around Moscow by equipping each missile with three multiple re-entry vehicles (MRV) or warheads. The project was carried forward by Harold Wilson, Denis Healey and Roy Jenkins when the Labour Government was returned to office in 1974 and, more recently, by James Callaghan who succeeded Wilson as Prime Minister in 1977. It is interesting to note that, like Clement Attlee before them, both these Labour Prime Ministers went ahead with the project behind the backs of most of their Cabinet colleagues, several of whom were extreme left-wingers, publicly opposed to continuing Britain's role as a military nuclear power.

This bipartisan approach to Britain's nuclear deterrent, which has endured for thirty-five years, is now in danger of being ended. There is nothing new about left-wingers in the Parliamentary Labour Party, but until recently they have never been anything more than a voluble but small minority and steps were always taken to ensure that they had no access to any secrets nor any say on sensitive defence matters. Hitherto the only opportunities they had of exercising decisive influence in the defence field came at moments of crisis for a Labour government. A prime example of the exercise of this power came in the wake of the economic crisis that followed the devaluation of sterling in November 1967. The Harold Wilson Government, which had only a threadbare majority in the House of Commons and knew a general election could not long be postponed, had, in February 1965, abolished medical prescription charges at a cost of £24 million ($55 million) and had made the provision of free medicine for all a major plank in their 1966 election campaign. One of the conditions laid down by the International Monetary Fund and the international banks for the vast loans required for the support of sterling was that the British Government should put its economic house in order including, as a litmus test of the Government's good faith, the re-imposition of prescription charges so recently abolished. At a meeting with some of his belligerent left-wingers Harold

Wilson apologised for what had befallen and expressed the hope that his colleagues would not take too hard this major about-turn of policy. No doubt to his surprise, they took it like lambs. But they made one condition: all British forces were to be withdrawn from the East of Suez, including 23,000 from Aden and the Persian Gulf and a further 50,000 from Singapore and Malaysia. Thus was won a key policy aim of the Kremlin. A White Paper was published in 1968 setting 1971 as the date by which withdrawal from all these areas would be completed at a saving of less than £80 million ($175 million) a year.

The announcement took Britain's allies and friends by surprise. US Defense Secretary Robert McNamara had, on more than one occasion in the course of several meetings I had with him over the years, stressed the importance of Britain's contribution to the Western alliance by her continuing presence, albeit in small numbers, in the areas of vital strategic interest to NATO. 'Don't worry', he declared, 'if Britain's Rhine Army is a few thousand men under strength. That's not important – *we* are in Europe. We are not in Aden or the Gulf and, if you were once to leave, it would be impossible for the United States to take your place.' In Iran and the sheikhdoms of the Gulf, since consolidated into the United Arab Emirates, there was astonishment, even disbelief, as I found when I visited the area in the summer of 1969. The then Iranian Premier, Amir Abbas Hoveida, since murdered by the lackeys of Ayatollah Khomeini, told me:

> We had for some time been left in a state of uncertainty about Britain's plans regarding its presence in the Gulf. However, at last, a British Foreign Office Minister, Mr Goronwy Roberts, came out to Tehran and sitting in the same seat that you are now occupying, told me: 'Prime Minister, the British Government has finally made up its mind – it is our intention to maintain our forces in the area for the time being.' Would you believe it? Just six weeks later, the same fellow was back, sitting in the same chair and, full of apologies and embarrassment, told me: 'I am very sorry, Prime Minister, it has now been decided that British forces will *not* be staying after all.'

The British decision to pull out from East of Suez has proved costly for the interests of the West and the consequence has been to undermine the stability of the entire Gulf area and the Horn of Africa and to precipitate conditions that were to lead to an unprecedented increase in oil prices, plunging the entire Western world into a slump unequalled since the thirties. When in 1962 I had first visited Aden, a former coaling-station on the trade-route to India and the Far East, set at the southern extremity of the Arabian peninsula, there were Hunter jets on the airfield at RAF Khormaksar, while Colonel Colin ('Mad Mitch') Mitchell and his gallant Argyll and Sutherland Highlanders were routing the terrorists in the nearby Crater district. On the occasion of my next visit in 1978, just ten years after the Labour Government's fateful decision – looking down from 30,000 feet aboard an executive jet bound for Somalia – I saw the same airfield littered with MiG fighters and Soviet Antonov transports. By then it had become the Soviets' principal resupply base for the major military operations it was conducting in the Horn of Africa using its Warsaw Pact allies and an army of Cuban surrogates to impose the rule of their local puppet in Ethiopia, Mengistu Haile Mariam who had been placed in power following a coup in which Emperor Haile Selassie was overthrown and, subsequently, murdered. Aden, having been a base from which British air and naval forces safeguarded and upheld the right of innocent passage of ships and, expecially, oil tankers with their vital cargoes passing through the southern approaches of the Red Sea bound for the Suez Canal, had become instead a base from which Western and neutral trade on the high seas might, at some future point, be interdicted at the whim of the Kremlin.

However, throughout this period following the disastrous British decision to pull out from East of Suez, Communist and Marxist infiltration into Britain's Labour Party had progressed at such a pace that, by 1980, the left-wingers were no longer the minority, or, to use a parallel with the Russian Revolution, the Mensheviks of Labour Party politics – they had become the Bolsheviks, the majority. The wholly undemocratic structure of the Labour Party, dominated as it is by the trade union movement, enables union leaders through the 'block vote' mechanism to buy votes by the millions, depending on the size of their financial contributions to the party and to cast them on behalf of their members half of whom do not vote Socialist anyway. Ninety per cent of the votes at the Labour Party's Annual Conference are controlled in this way and union leaders – some not even members of the Labour Party but from the totalitarian Left like the President of the Scottish Mineworkers' Union, Mick McGahey, who also happens to be the Chairman of the Communist Party of Great Britain – have a decisive say in the election of the Party's National Executive Committee, charged with the responsibility for policy-making. Thus the party has moved relentlessly from the middle ground of British politics towards the extreme Left.

More insidious still have been the changes that have been taking place at the party's grass roots in the 635 parliamentry constituencies. Relying on the apathy of traditional labour voters, barely 1 or 2 per cent of whom take an active part in their party's affairs – indeed according to Sir Harold Wilson, as he has since become, a 'thriving' constituency Labour Party might have 'as many as 50 paid-up members' – powerful undemocratic elements including Marxists, Trotskyites and full-blooded Communists have been able to infiltrate and take over many constituency associations. By their assiduity and militancy, they have driven out moderate Labour Party stalwarts and gained control. It is this tiny group of activists that has responsibility for the selection of candidates for Parliament, and, especially since the 1979 general election, the Labour Party Members of Parliament have, increasingly, come to reflect the political extremism of the constituency selectors. In a move designed to speed this process left-wingers in the party have long been pressing for (and at the beginning of 1981 succeeded in securing) a change in the rules that will require every Labour MP to pass a process of reselection by their local Labour party, prior to a general election, a move calculated to make the Parliamentary Party even more extreme.

Ever since the 1920s leading members of the Labour Party recognised the threat posed to democratic Socialism by Communist infiltration and the Party had rules, under Clause II of the party's constitution, to guard against it by issuing each year a list of proscribed organisations, membership of which was held to disqualify an individual from party membership. The practice was discontinued in 1973, with disastrous results. Unfortunately it is not Labour Party members alone who are apathetic, but the electorate as a whole. The power of the established party machines, both Labour and Conservative, is such that in 90 per cent of constituencies, regardless of the choice of candidate, the party that has traditionally held a seat may be confident of securing its candidate's election to Parliament. I learnt this early on when in 1967 at the age of twenty-six, I fought my first parliamentary election, a by-election in the Gorton Division of Manchester which had been a safe Labour seat for more than thirty years. The previous member, whose death had caused the by-election, had been a Czech by the name of Konni Zilliacus, a full-blooded Communist who, like a growing number today, used the Labour Party as a mere flag of convenience. Thus the housewives of Gorton spoke with feeling when, in their broad Lancashire accents, they warned me: 'You know what they say in Gorton, luv? Put a pig in a red coat up for Labour and he'll still get in!'

The election of Michael Foot, standing unashamedly as the candidate of the Left in the leadership contest of November 1980, following James Callaghan's decision to stand down, is ample evidence of how far the rot has gone within the ranks of even the Parliamentary Labour Party which, by a majority of ten favoured Mr Foot over the right-of-centre Mr Healey. More recently a special Labour Party Conference meeting in January 1981 decided to remove from Labour MPs the right to select the party's leader and to vest it instead in an electoral college in which the constituency parties and trade unions (some of them Communist-led) would control 70 per cent of votes in any election for the leadership of the party and, therefore, potentially, of the British Prime Minister. Unless the Labour moderates have the courage in large numbers to break away and support the new Social Democratic Party in the middle ground of British politics, possibly in conjunction with the Liberal Party, the probability of a Labour government, dominated by the totalitarian Left, coming to power in the years ahead will have to be faced. No longer will it be a case of the extremists of the Left yapping and baying on the leash of a moderate Labour Prime Minister and Cabinet. The Left would be the government. Only time will tell whether Mr Foot, or his putative successor Mr Anthony Wedgwood-Benn, an opportunist demagogue of the far Left, will ever become Prime Minister of Britain or, if they do, whether they will at the end of the day carry out their threats to abandon Britain's nuclear deterrent, expel America from all her British bases, pull out of NATO, scrap the House of Lords and abolish the monarchy, but that, as it stands tody, is their policy. The implementation of such a programme would lead Britain towards a one-party Marxist state with standards of living and of liberty equal to those of the Soviet satellite countries of Eastern Europe.

Never has the divide in British politics been so great nor the stakes so high. Mrs Thatcher and the Conservative Party have a vision of Britain that is strong, free and democratic, playing its full part within the European Community and in NATO, resolutely standing up to Soviet threats and blandishments until such time as a genuine detente may be established based on the rule of law and respect for the rights of others. The 'Bolsheviks' of the Labour Left, on the other hand, see Britain's future outside NATO and the Common Market, disarmed, protecting outdated industries and working methods behind high tariff barriers and import controls, enjoying close 'fraternal' relations with other Marxist states including the Soviet Union, while at home placing increasing restrictions on the rights and liberties of the citizen and burdening him down with confiscatory levels of taxation – to wit, a veritable 'workers' paradise'.

There are those in the ranks of the Tory Party who express delight at the new extremism of the Labour Party, confident that it will ensure a massive Socialist defeat at the next general election. But they would do well to ponder the fact that elections are seldom won by oppositions: they are lost by Governments. The prospects for Britain, in the event that Labour's anti-democratic Left and the fellow-travellers of the Communist cause were to gain the key to No. 10 Downing Street, are horrific, yet there is a serious danger that the British people might not realise what they have done until it was too late. It would require nothing more than for the British electorate, in the midst of an economic crisis, to throw out a Government, as, in common with their American counterparts across the Atlantic, they relish the prospect of doing from time to time, to discover that in the same instant they had turned their back on Britain's centuries' old traditions of liberty and constitutional government.

There are those who could dismiss such thoughts as fanciful and unreal but it is necessary to look no further than Portugal, Britain's oldest ally and a member of NATO, to know how real and mortal the threat can be. In the wake of the Revolution of Flowers on 15 April 1974, which brought to an end forty years of civilian dictatorship in Portual, the bloodless coup was hailed by the overwhelming majority of Portuguese people, as well as by many in the West, as a victory for liberty and democracy. But the high hopes proved elusive and those Portuguese who had supported the revolution, naively believing that things could not be worse, found themselves confronted by a far harsher reality. The civilian dictatorship of Salazar and Caetano had merely been replaced by a military dictatorship, increasingly Communist dominated. The feared PIDE security police of the previous regime was reconstituted as the *Quinta Division* (Fifth Division) under a Communist commander, Rameiro Correia, who was made responsible for the junta's 'agit-prop' propaganda machine for the 'indoctrination of the masses'. Immediately the number of political prisoners increased from fewer than 800 under Caetano to some 3,000 under the military junta. Among the victims of this repression were not only the Portuguese Communist Party's (PCP) political enemies of the Right but also of the Left. Many Trotskyites and no fewer than 45 self-styled Maoists of the Movement for the Reorganisation of the Portuguese Proletariat (MRPP) found themselves put behind bars.

When in July 1975 I went to report the situation for the London *Daily Telegraph* I found the country's media, including the state-controlled television and radio and most of the newspapers, firmly under Communist control. The walls and windows of Lisbon presented an incredible battlefield of slogans and posters in which the hammer and sickle of the Communist Party and its allies outnumbered the publicity of the democratic parties by nearly ten to one. Among the many wall posters (of which 'Morte ao Fascismo' (Death to Fascism) appeared to be the most popular) a slogan by the fringe Anarchist Party, based on the notice familiar to British television viewers when there are transmission difficulties, 'Do not adjust your set . . .', summed up most succinctly the situation with the words: 'We apologise for this democratic interlude – dictatorship will resume shortly.' When I visited Dr Mario Soares, the Socialist Party leader and clear victor, by a margin of nearly two to one, in the recently held elections in which the Communist and other extremist parties had failed miserably, he told me as we spoke in his ministerial office at the Sao Bento Palace with an earnestness tinged with urgency: 'The moment of truth has arrived: democracy is fighting for its life.' In spite of Dr Soares' overwhelming victory, the Communist-dominated military junta clung doggedly to power. The Portuguese Communist Party was directly under the control of Moscow; indeed, under the leadership of Dr Alavaro Cunhal it had the dubious distinction of being, together with the insignificant Communist Party of Luxembourg, the only West European Communist Party to have gone so far as to welcome the Soviet invasion of Czechoslovakia in 1968. In the 1975 election the hand of Moscow had been more than evident with the Communist Party able to field an estimated 2,000 full-time paid employees, while the democratic parties were virtually broke.

The Soviet Union's brazen efforts to subvert a member of the NATO alliance came perilously close to success. If Portugal remains firmly in the democratic camp and a loyal member of NATO today, it is not thanks to America's CIA, which in the wake of the Watergate scandal was well-nigh dismantled, nor to any help she might have expected from her European allies. At the end of the day it was the Portuguese people themselves who, in the nick of time, saved their country from Communism and incorporation within the Warsaw Pact. It was above all the simple Portuguese peasantry who, not prepared to be kicked around by the Marxist youths from the big cities of Lisbon and Oporto, took to the streets and beat the Communists at their own game, in scenes of fierce hand-to-hand fighting in the course of which more than seventy Communist Party offices were burned to the ground. The Portuguese, it must be said, had the good fortune of being as far removed as is physically possible within Europe from the Soviet bloc. Had they shared a common border with a Warsaw Pact country enabling Soviet tanks to intervene, the outcome would inevitably have been different, however valiant the efforts of the Portuguese.

Portugal is today safely back in the Western fold but there is no reason to suppose that the Soviet Union will lightly abandon its relentless effort to subvert each and every one of the NATO allies. The British should be aware not only of this threat but of the fact that they are seen by the men in the Kremlin as the most highly prized of all potential targets. Unlike Portugal, where many years of dictatorship culminating in its army's defeat at the hand of Soviet-backed Marxist terrorists in Africa led directly to a revolution and a pro-Communist coup, Soviet plans for the subversion of Britain, where prospects for a violent revolution must be seen to be remote, almost certainly envisage an interim stage of 'Finlandisation' before the possibility of a Marxist dictatorship in alliance with the Soviet Union could become a reality.

While there is no reason to suspect that Mr Foot, in spite of his firm left-wing and republican views, is anything other than a patriot and a democrat at heart, his plans, if implemented, would bring Britain to a constitutional no-man's-land, midway between parliamentary democracy and totalitarian dictatorship. The abolition of the monarchy and of the House of Lords would strike at the very heart of the British constitution and would destroy Britains's bi-cameral legislature, the bulwark of the British people's liberties over so many centuries. With all checks and balances removed, a House of Commons infested with the enemies of democracy would find it but a small step to repeal the Quinquennial Act – the electorate's one guarantee of its right to re-elect or, as in its wisdom it may decide, to dismiss a government at least once every five years. This would effectively dispose of the need for any future general election and consign to the rubbish dump Britain's parliamentary democracy which has taken so many centuries of struggle to achieve and so much sacrifice to defend. It is small wonder that Radio Moscow should have hailed with ill-concealed delight the election to the leadership of the Labour Party of Michael Foot – long an unashamed Leftist and an ardent advocate of the unilateral nuclear disarmament of Britain – welcoming him as a standard-bearer of the Kremlin's policies for disarming Britain and securing her withdrawal from the NATO alliance.

Moscow's hopes are by no means pinned on Britain alone, but extend to all the countries of Western Europe, each without exception having active Communist parties which, certainly in the case of France and Italy, command a significant share of the vote at election time, and are supported by an army of fellow-travellers in the trade union movements and the Socialist parties. There can be little doubt that, like Hitler before them, the men who hold sway in the Kremlin hope to achieve their goal of world domination without a war and that no one will be more delighted than they if they can secure their objectives peacefully by threat, deceit and subversion. It is all too frequently forgotten that it was not Nazi Germany that declared war on Britain, but the other way around. It was Britain's refusal to accept the arrangements that Herr Hitler had in mind for Europe and all its peoples that led directly to the Second World War. Had Britain proved amenable to negotiation in 1939, or even as late as 1940, there would have been no war. Nor would there have been a liberation for, with Britain suborned, the United States could never have launched the D-Day landings from the far side of the Atlantic without either naval supremacy or friendly air cover. There is no reason to doubt that the Soviets' preferred goal is the the achievement of a 'Finlandised' or neutral Western Europe divorced from the United States so that the nations of Europe may ultimately be brought within the Soviet orbit. High on the list of Soviet priorities is to kill off the programme for the modernisation and replacement of NATO's long-range theatre nuclear forces, which consist at the present time of 56 ageing RAF Vulcan bombers shortly destined, under present plans, for the scrapheap and 156 USAF F-111 bombers. Although these NATO forces are outnumbered by a factor of 3·5:1, the Soviets continue their build-up unabated, bringing into service a new SS-20 missile every five days and a Backfire bomber every ten.

Once they have recovered from the barrage of verbal flak and rhetoric directed against them in the wake of their invasion of Afghanistan, the Kremlin may be relied upon to make a determined drive to relaunch its detente offensive, directing it in particular against the nations of Western Europe in an effort to persuade them to rebuff any attempt that might be made by the US administration of President Reagan to strengthen NATO's grossly inadequate defences, especially in the nuclear field. A foretaste of this stratagem is already evident in the proposal floated by Moscow in the latter part of 1980, and eagerly taken up and promoted by the friends of Moscow in the British and other European parliaments, for a 'nuclear-free-zone' in Europe. The attraction of this proposal is not quite as great as it may at first appear. The effect would be to remove NATO's theatre nuclear forces from Europe and to bring about the nuclear disarmament of Britain and France. Meanwhile, according to Moscow's proposal, the Soviet Union would withdraw its own nuclear forces from Europe. The catch is that, apart from the fact that the main elements of the Soviet's Long-Range Theatre Nuclear Forces (the SS-20 and Backfire) are both mobile and could be back in Eastern Europe or European Russian within a day or two, even if they had been taken back to a point east of the Urals, they would still have ample range to strike any point in Western Europe. Even by the standard of recent years it would require unbelievably facile governments and supremely spineless political leadership for any of the nations of Europe to fall for such an obvious ploy, but the evidence suggests that the Kremlin is gearing up its propaganda machine with that aim in mind.

The NATO powers are today confronted not only by an external threat every bit as grave and infinitely more deadly than that presented by Nazi Germany in the thirties, but, in addition, by a threat of internal subversion of serious proportions. At least Hitler, by comparison with the Kremlin today, never had a fifth column in Britain worth the name. Today this is a threat that can no longer be ignored.

Chapter Fifteen

THE SOVIET EMPIRE QUAKES

Founded on the doctrine of equality and proclaiming its championship of the cause of the people, the Soviet Union has become a gross caricature of Karl Marx's ideals, which successive incumbents of the Kremlin have corrupted and betrayed. Far from being the egalitarian society that Marx had envisioned while writing *Das Capital* in the British Museum in the mid-nineteenth century, the Soviet Union is today the most class-ridden and unequal society of all the advanced nations of the world. The humble worker and his family, together with the great mass of citizens in every walk of Soviet life, far from being uplifted and favoured as the ideologists had promised and the propaganda of the Communist Party to this day proclaims, find themselves the victims of a cruel confidence trick in which they have become but helots living under the most repressive system to be found anywhere on earth.

Compared to his counterparts in Western societies, the average Soviet worker enjoys an abysmally low standard of living and is denied all rights and liberty, both taken so much for granted in the West. For the most part, housing conditions are atrocious with very many Russians living in dingy, dingy, heavily overcrowded apartment blocks in which, as a rule, cooking, bathroom and toilet facilities are shared by several families. The rare Western visitor who contrives, in spite of all the official obstruction that is invariably placed in his way, to see Soviet life at first hand is usually deeply shocked by what he finds. Food is not plentiful and it is not uncommon, where cooking facilities are shared, to see padlocks on cooking pots, reflecting the fact that a member of the family has probably queued for two or three hours in the early morning darkness and cold to obtain a not very special cut of meat which has cost the family a far greater proportion of the breadwinner's wage than would be the case in the West. Foreign tourists are frequently bemused to see the speed with which a queue of one or two hundred people may suddenly form in a Moscow street, should a street-trader appear on the scene with such luxuries as honey, oranges or lemons.

Consumer goods so common in the West such as cars, deep-freezers, colour television and washing-machines are out of reach for the average Soviet citizen. Even steelworkers and miners, paid substantially above the average, would be lucky to possess one or two such luxuries. Meanwhile the problems involved in obtaining such mundane items as clothes or shoes are enormous. The wonders of the Socialist 'planned economy', together with the bureaucratic incompetence, not to mention the corruption and waste that goes with it, conspire to create acute shortages of many necessities, sometimes not to be found for months on end. A housewife, though she may be ill able to afford it, will buy three or four pairs of the same shoes at a time, sure in the knowledge that she may not be lucky enough to find them again in her size for months to come.

But far more oppressive to the ordinary citizen than these relatively minor (in the Soviet context) inconveniences of life, involving queueing, shortages and the shoddy quality of goods which have become the accepted norms of Soviet life, is the basic denial of all freedom as it is understood in the West. A Soviet citizen is not entitled to a passport or allowed to travel abroad at will. In most cases applications for foreign travel, especially in respect of journeys outside the Soviet bloc states, will be refused. Indeed the applicant will be rigorously cross-examined as to where he obtained the resources to be able to afford such luxuries, and if there is any question of travel to a

Western country he will be grilled as to his motives. Perhaps most surprising of all to a foreign visitor is to learn that the Soviet citizen is not entitled to freedom of travel *even within his own country*. On a par with the indignities and oppression to which blacks are subjected under South Africa's notorious Pass Laws, the Soviet worker and his family are not entitled to travel from, for instance, the city of Omsk to the capital Moscow in order to seek a new job unless their stay is less than three days. Permission and a visa must first be obtained from the authorities and quite frequently would be refused.

Should the worker be so misguided as publicly to voice complaints at his place of work about the system or the political leadership of the Soviet Union, let alone threaten to go on strike to obtain better wages and conditions or to secure the redress of some grievance, he may expect within hours to receive a tap on his shoulder or a visit to his home late at night and an invitation from a pair of grey-suited gentlemen to accompany them in their car. On arrival at their destination, usually a nondescript and anonymous office building, the worker will first be questioned at great length, becoming increasingly anxious as the hours go by, knowing that his wife and family will also be worried, having no idea where he has been taken or why, let alone when they will see him again. Then, as if by accident and often without any overt, merely a heavily implied, threat, his interrogators casually let slip what has been the fate of those before him who have insisted on falling foul of the authorities. The possibilities are manifold, depending on the gravity of the offence. At the bottom end of the scale he might merely lose his job, which, in a society where there is no entitlement to social security, will cause his family to suffer extreme hardship. He might be exiled in his own country, as indeed has happened to the distinguished Academician Dr Andrei Sakharov, to remote areas or to a township in the waste lands of Siberia. In more serious cases it could mean consignment to a forced labour camp where he would endure long hours of heavy outdoor work in extremes of temperature and on a diet insufficient to sustain life for any number of years or, alternatively, a psychiatric establishment where the 'patient' is incarcerated and forcibly administered mind-bending drugs. The chances are that the worker will recognise the error of his ways and will not require a second warning but will be more than relieved to be allowed to step back in line and sink into a conformist anonymity.

If, on the other hand, inspired by a vision of Hell that even Dante or George Orwell was unable to imagine, the citizen succeeds in repressing all instinct of rebellion and, instead, wishes to obtain for himself and his family a somewhat richer life than the grey, downtrodden and servile existence that is the lot of most Russians, he can change all that by becoming a member of *the Party* (naturally there is only one) the Communist Party of the Soviet Union (CPSU). Even that is not as straightforward as is may sound. It is not merely a question of paying a few roubles to obtain a party card, as one might pay 50 pence to join the Conservative or Labour parties in England or contribute a few tax-deductible dollars in the United States to become a paid-up member of the Democratic or Republican parties; on the contrary, it is regarded as a great privilege to be allowed to join the party in the Soviet Union, for party membership is the key that unlocks the door to a life of privilege and prosperity – no doubt the reason it is so jealously guarded and restricted to so select a number.

No more than 7 per cent of the adult population of the Soviet Union are admitted to membership of the Communist Party. An applicant will have his background investigated in meticulous detail. Enquiries will be made about members of his family, of his performance at his job and whether he has been an active propagandist for the Marxist–Leninist gospel. Even his school background will be investigated and it will be established whether or not he was an active member of Komsomol, the Communist Youth League. Having cleared all these hurdles and been accepted into active membership of the party, the applicant is thereupon admitted to the outer chambers of privilege of Soviet society, the principal manifestation of which he will find in a more rapid promotion in his job than would otherwise have been the case.

The new party member is now on the gravy-train and, if he is lucky as well as successful at pleasing his superiors, he may expect to be headed towards the inner sanctums of preferment and exaltation, where the more senior party officials and *apparatchiks* enjoy a lifestyle wholly divorced from that of the ordinary Soviet citizen. He will draw salary based on differentials many times greater than those prevailing, after tax, in a Western society, say, between an army general and a private, or between a surgeon and a hospital cleaner. In addition he has access to a vast array of 'perks', one of which involves the payment of part of his salary, not in cash but with special 'coupons', which entitle the commissar class to gain admittance not only to the *Beryozkas* or foreign-currency shops which otherwise are reserved for tourists from abroad but to special 'party shops' from which the ordinary citizen is excluded. The windows of these 'shops' are usually painted black on the outside to guard against any envious prying eyes. Their range of goods includes not only luxury items out of reach of the average Soviet citizen such as imported consumer goods, and hi-fi equipment, but even run-of-the-mill products, including the staples of diet, at a fraction of their usual cost. An example of this sticks in my memory from a visit I made to the Soviet Union in May 1974 when a 2-kilogramme pack of sugar for which the average citizen had to pay 90 kopek was being sold to the privileged classes of the Party for a mere 30 kopek.

But the aura of privilege for the senior party official extends far wider than merely purchasing commodities at specially favourable rates. It provides them with foreign travel, vast expense accounts as well as an income sufficiently large that their wives do not have to go out to work – a rarity in the Soviet Union. There are even privileged schools on the lines of English public schools to which the elite of Soviet society may send their children without fear that they will have to rub elbows with the children of factory workers or garbage collectors. Their lifestyle is such that even the commissar's wife's poodles are taken to the beauty parlour twice a week in Moscow, like any self-respecting New York City poodle. One distinguished foreign visitor, known personally to me, on visiting a Moscow sable and mink factory enquired of the high-ranking official who was escorting her (who, it later transpired, was a senior serving officer of the KGB) what he thought of a particular selection of pelts. His reply says much for the present state of Soviet society: 'They are not bad,' the KGB man mused, fondling the superb sable with his hand. 'But, speaking personally, when I buy for my wife, I *always* buy from Maximillian in New York.'

The Communist Party of the Soviet Union, like an over-sized giant squid, has tentacles that reach out to control every aspect of Russian life, oppressing the Soviet citizen at all stages of his life from his cradle to the grave. The party controls the government, the armed forces and the bureaucracy. The party seeks to dictate every detail of the country's economic life, and the trade unions exist not to represent the interests of the workers against the bosses but, specifically, to control the workers. The party manipulates the press and the media to ensure that nothing can be published or reported except with its approval. It is the party that decides whether an individual may hold a given job, go to university, move to a different part of the country or obtain an exit visa to leave the country for good. It is the party ultimately, not the law or the constitution, that decides whether a citizen is promoted at his work or consigned until his dying days to a labour camp or lunatic asylum. On every hand and at all times the oppressive burden of the party hangs heavily over the citizen's life stifling all initiative, repressing all enterprise and denying all independence or freedom. The party rules by the carrot and stick principle, alternately tempting the citizen with the promise of privileges and threatening him with the prospect of the Gulag.

The fact that when 'elections' are held, which provide no choice of party, frequently not even of candidates, the official candidates are returned with a majority of 99 per cent or more, is evidence to the world less of the popularity of the candidates, as the commissars mistakenly suppose, than of the massive coercion to which the entire population is subjected. If ever free elections were to be held in the Soviet Union, it is doubtful that even 1 per cent of the population would vote for the Communist Party and the Russian leadership. According to Vladimir Bukovsky was for many years the leader of the Soviet human rights movement – 'The only Liberation Movement in the world', as he put it to a meeting in Brighton of Amnesty International; 'that does not ask for money, or for arms – only for your moral support', adding: 'If you cannot give that, there is nothing to discuss.' Bukovsky, who, for his trouble spent twelve years of his life up to the age of thirty-four, in assorted prisons, labour camps and psychiatric hospitals in the Soviet Union, surprised a group of British Members of Parliament, myself included, when he declared in all seriousness to a meeting at the House of Commons: 'What you do not begin to understand about my country is that there are fewer convinced Communists to be found in Russia today than in any country of the Western world. In the Soviet Union everybody, including the party members themselves, knows that the system is rotten to the core. Even the small, highly privileged minority who profit from the set-up are not convinced by it and certainly would not believe it in their hearts.'

It has become fashionable in recent years among certain people in the West, regrettably not least among Americans themselves, to suggest that the United States is ruled through the Pentagon by a sinister body know as the 'Military–Industrial Complex', intent on placing the United States on a militarist path that would lead to war. Such accusations are sheer fantasy in a democracy in which the executive – in the case of the United States, the President – is subject, through the Congress, to the elected representatives of the people, who in turn are answerable to an electorate through free elections held at regular intervals and based on universal suffrage, and which is further subject to the hawk-eyed scrutiny of a free press and under the overall control of a free and independent judiciary charged with safeguarding and upholding the constitution. More seriously they are mischievous falsehoods promoted by the enemies of democracy to conceal the situation that exists in the Soviet Union where the 'Military–Industrial Complex' *is* the government and has none of the constraints inherent in a free society to control it. Brezhnev himself is a Marshal of the Soviet Union and, almost without exception, the Politburo is made up of generals or ex-generals. Between them they control the party (CPSU), industry, the trade unions, the media, the armed forces and the secret police. Indeed it is a deeply disturbing question, which, at the time of writing, it is impossible to answer, whether in the case of the Soviet Union, the situation is not already out of control. In the unlikely event that Mr Brezhnev had a change of heart and were suddenly to decree that the Soviet Union's three tank factories were to close and that, instead of tanks, Soviet workers were to be supplied with Mini Metros to go to work in, it is by no means certain, given the vested interests involved, that he would have the power to do so. It is a situation that calls to mind lines, of which the authorship is unknown to me, used to devastating effect by Churchill in a speech attacking the Chamberlain Government at the time of the Munich surrender:

> Who is in charge of the clattering train?
> The axles creak and the couplings strain,
> The pace is hot and the points are near
> And sleep has deadened the driver's ear.
> The signals flash through the night in vain –
> *Death* is in charge of the clattering train!

If Soviet Communist rule is oppressive and objectionable for the vast majority of Russians, it may be imagined how much more so this is the case with the estimated 150 million non-Russian nationalities ruled by the Soviet Union. Indeed, today, not even half of the Soviet population is Russian. The national minorities, including the Ukrainians and the Georgians, the Cossacks and the Tartars, not to mention nearly 50 million Muslims, to name but a few, have in fact become the majority and they are all fiercely independent people who would seize any opportunity of breaking away from the Soviet yoke. It goes without saying that the same is true, if possible to an even greater degree, of the subject nations of Eastern Europe, now held under Soviet domination for some thirty-five years. The Soviet empire – for empire it is, its many diverse nationalities never having come together in any voluntary association – depends on police-state terror and military power to maintain its rule. A sophisticated and all-pervasive secret police network is used to instal and uphold puppet governments that, in varying degrees, coerce and terrorise the population. Should the situation ever threaten to get out of control the ready response has always been to send in the Russian tanks, as demonstrated so bloodily in Hungary in 1956 and repeated again in Czechoslovakia in 1968.

Those who hold sway in the Kremlin are probably more conscious than any in the West that they owe their position and maintain their control not through their popularity ratings in the opinion polls, let alone by the free assent of those they presume to rule, but by brute force and fear. They must know that the day they lack the courage to enforce Soviet Communist rule at gunpoint, that day will mark the beginnng of the downfall of the Soviet empire and sound the death-knell of the Communist system in Russia. For those in the West – and they are the overwhelming majority – who do not wish to live their lives indefinitely under the shadow of the Balance of Terror and passionately hope for an end to the present insane nuclear arms race, yet are not prepared to surrender and accept the extension of the Soviet empire, together with the horrors of the Gulag, to Western Europe and the United States, the one hope for the future must be that there will be an evolution within the Soviet empire that eventually leads not only to the liberation of the peoples of Eastern Europe but to the establishment of a government in Russia representative of the wishes of its peoples.

However grievous and shaming it may be to those in the West who yearn for the day when the subject peoples of Eastern Europe may, once again, rejoin the ranks of free nations and the peoples of the Soviet Union obtain the right of self-determination, the Western allies have no choice but to recognise the fact that, faced with a heavily adverse balance of military power against them, both in conventional and nuclear terms in Europe, as well as at straegic level, the West is powerless to help but instead is condemned to the role of an anxious spectator to the drama that is unfolding. Any overt Western intervention within what has come to be regarded as the Soviet bloc – even were it to be welcomed, which it certainly would be, by 90 per cent or more of the population – would lead directly to world war, which under the circumstances of today would inevitably mean nuclear world war, a perilously steep and icy slope on which no foothold or braking-point can be foreseen short of the abyss of ultimate catastrophe. Only the subject peoples may free themselves, and if in the West many found it shaming that, as Soviet armoured units towards the end of 1980 moved into position around Poland, Dr Joseph Luns, Secretary-General of NATO, should have declared not once, but twice, that if Soviet tanks were to roll into Poland, NATO would be powerless to do anything about it, he was doing no more than to state the truth. Many Hungarians in 1956 looked to the West, as it turned out in vain, to support them against the Soviet onslaught. If, at a time of overwhelming Western military superiority the West felt incapable of helping the Hungarians then, how much less is it conceivable that it might be able to help the people of Poland when that supremacy has been lost? Dr Luns' words should be seen less as an invitation to the Kremlin to exert its will, than a warning to the Poles to harbour no fanciful illusions that they can look to anyone but themselves for their salvation.

The significance of recent events in Poland rests above all on the irrefutable evidence they provide of the will and determination of mankind to be free. In the West liberty has degenerated into licence and licentiousness, and is unlikely to be valued again at its true worth until it has been lost. Meanwhile, in the Gulag, the spirit of liberty is being reborn. It may seem a contradiction to claim that in the vast archipelago of prisons, asylums and forced labour camps to which hundreds of thousands in the Soviet Union and Eastern Europe are condemned, it is possible for freedom even to exist, let alone be reborn. But for those who have endured and survived that ordeal, freedom is something spiritual, less a state of being than a state of mind. Vladimir Bukovsky on being sentenced by a Soviet court to a lengthy term of imprisionment declared defiantly to the court: 'You cannot take my freedom away, for it is inside me!'

In spite of all the sophisticated apparatus of the modern police state and regardless of the Soviet Union's vast array of tanks, rocket launchers and nuclear missiles, the Polish people without force of arms or the shedding of so much as a drop of blood carried through in the summer and autumn of 1980 a revolution unprecedented in any Communist state. The creation of a free trade union by the Polish workers' leader Mr

Lech Walesa and his colleagues is, of itself, a remarkable development. The fact that within the space of three months their union Solidarity should have gained *more than ten million members* – as many as the British trade union movement achieved in the first fifty years of its existence – represents nothing less than a revolution, especially bearing in mind that the population of Poland is one-third less than that of Britain. The intense spirit of nationalism of the Polish people is vividly demonstrated by the fact that each Sunday there is standing room only for the celebration of Mass in churches throughout Poland and was further evidenced by the countless thousands who turn out to plant small crosses in the woods in commemoration of the 14,500 Polish soldiers butchered in cold blood by the Soviet NKVD in the forests of Katyn in 1940.

By early 1981 condemnation of developments in Poland by the party leaderships and press in the neighbouring satellite countries as well as in the Soviet Union itself was reaching an ugly crescendo while Soviet and Warsaw Pact forces stood mobilised on Poland's borders poised to attack while yet others were taking part in large-scale manoeuvres inside the country. If the Kremlin were to order Soviet tanks to intervene to restore Communist rule, it is difficult to imagine that the Polish people, including the greater part of the Polish army, would not fight. They would stand little chance with only fifteen divisions as against the ninety-eight divisions of the Soviet Red Army deployed west of the Urals. Futhermore the Russians would be strongly supported by most of the other Warsaw Pact countries whose rulers fear the outbreak of the 'Polish disease' among their own populations. That the Polish army and people would give a good account of themselves and inflict severe punishment on the invaders cannot be doubted, but, given the odds stacked so heavily against them, the outcome is also certain. The cost in blood to the Polish people could be terrible. Though that consideration would weigh not at all in the councils of the Kremlin, the Soviet leadership would have to recognise the anger and hostility that would be felt throughout the world, not least among their own citizens and they are evidently giving the Polish Government under the newly appointed Prime Minister, General Jaruzelski, and the Communist Party led by Stanislaw

Kania a chance to restore Socialist 'normality' to the situation. However it remains to be seen whether the Polish Government is able, in the face of strong but peaceful resistance by Solidarity, which, if its members' families be included, is representative of almost the entire Polish nation, to take back the concessions made in the latter half of 1980.

On the other hand, should the day come when the Kremlin lacks the ruthlessness to impose its will by force, crushing dissidents under the tank-track, it will not only be the satellite countries of Eastern Europe that will break away, but the Union of Soviet Socialist Republics that will itself disintegrate. Either way the masters of the Kremlin must know that the writing is on the wall for Soviet Communism – so long as the Western allies do not themselves falter or fail in the face of the Soviet challenge.

Chapter Sixteen

A STRATEGY FOR
FREEDOM

As the storm clouds gather dark and forbidding on the horizon over war-torn Afghanistan, and as nearer home Soviet forces stand poised to strike at Poland, in defence of whose freedom Britain had declared war on Nazi Germany in September 1939, it is urgent that the West takes stock of the situation before its peoples find themselves on a journey from which there will be no return, a journey on which the options available will become increasingly fewer and more narrow, the path ever more precipitous as mankind lurches and slips with faltering step towards a chasm of darkness where even the flickering candle of life itself may be extinguished once and for all. Never before in all the tens of million of years of man's long and arduous journey from the primeval mists of creation to the present day with all the wonders and achievements of modern technology, has he had it in his power to bring the human story with all its glories and miseries, all its triumphs and disasters, to an abrupt and final end. As Churchill so pithily put it on learning of the successful detonation of the first atomic bomb: 'The idiot child has the matches now!'

Faced with the appalling reality of the peril that today besets the world, it is only natural that some should seek to bury their heads in the sand , living for today and content to let the devil take tomorrow. Others, who at least spare a thought for the world's critically dangerous situation, succumb to panic and are prepared to surrender even liberty itself in the hope of appeasing the threat. But there will be yet others, possibly a majority, who once armed with the facts are prepared to face them squarely and unflinchingly and will demand that, instead of drifting rudderless towards the rocks of disaster, a course be struck, and stuck to regardless of the perils to be met upon the way, until a safe haven is reached.

Peace alone is not enough for the democracies to hold as their objective, for the vilest tyrannies can coexist with peace. If man has any purpose in his brief allotted span on earth, it is surely to leave the world a better place than he found it, and if he has a duty it must be to ensure that the forces of evil and tyranny do not triumph. Thus, in the last resort, freedom must take precedence over peace. Those who are prepared to betray freedom in the hope of securing peace run the risk of losing both, while those who make their twin objectives the maintenance of peace and freedom may well attain both blessings. It is difficult for peoples like the Americans, who have never known invasion, or the British, who have not experienced it for nearly a thousand years, to appreciate the full horrors of having one's homeland occupied by a foreign power. The tortures and bestialities of rule by a totalitarian dictatorship are experiences that the British, unique among the major nations of Europe, have, thus far, been privileged to avoid, though many Americans are refugees from such tyrannies.

Nazi Germany alone was responsible in the early 1940s for the systematic mass murder of six million men, women and children of Jewish origin as well as gypsies and others. The record of the Soviet Union in the 1920s and 1930s under Stalin is, if possible, even more bloodstained, with tens of thousands dying before firing squads and in slave labour camps, while further millions were deliberately allowed to starve to death to bring about the enforced collectivisation of farms to conform with the Communist scheme of things. Nor are these events exclusively confined to the realm of history. The eloquent witness of Solzhenitsyn attests to the scale on which the slave labour and concentration camps of the Gulag flourish to this day. The facts are corroborated by countless others who have been fortunate enough to escape the Soviet Union in recent years and who tell of sane men being imprisoned in psychiatric hospitals and forcibly injected with mind-bending and ultimately mind-destroying drugs. There can be no doubt that if for one minute the Western nations were to abandon their freedom, this is the fate that would befall them too; but what is worse, there would then be none left to give hope of ultimate liberation to those who are tormented and held captive in the largest prison the world has ever known.

The election of Ronald Reagan to the presidency of the United States offers the hope of a new beginning in international relations. As early as his inauguration day, a new awe and respect for the United States was evident. There can be little doubt that an important factor in the calculations that prompted the Iranian Government finally to release the US Embassy hostages after their long ordeal was a healthy regard of the new President who, only a fortnight before had had no qualms about branding the Americans' captors as 'criminals and kidnappers'. With Carter not only the Iranians but also the Russians knew where they stood – he could be relied upon to take the course of least resistance wherever the interests of the West were concerned. Former Prime Minister Harold Macmillan described Jimmy Carter in damning terms as 'Without doubt the weakest President of the United States in my lifetime', a judgment evidently shared by the US electorate. Indeed it is quite probable that the Russians might never have invaded Afghanistan had they not already witnessed the supine inaction of the US administration when presented with a direct challenge to its immediate national interests and sovereignty by a third-rate country, in the form of the seizure of its diplomats by Iran just six weeks before.

With President Reagan about to take up the reins of office, Ayatollah Khomeini and his fellow mullahs might well have reflected on the possibility that if six weeks or so after the new President came to office, they were still behaving like the criminals and kidnappers he had so aptly labelled them and were continuing to refuse to release the hostages, was it not possible that the US 82nd Airborne might suddenly drop out of the sky or the US Marines hit the beaches of southern Iran? Evidently they concluded it was time to make their peace with the United States. Certainly the new President in welcoming the hostages back to American soil left no room for doubt as to what his policy would be in the event that anyone else tried to take US citizens hostage when he declared: 'Let terrorists be aware that when the rules of international behaviour are violated, our policy will be one of swift and effective retribution. Let it be understood there are limits to our patience!'

Above all President Reagan has the opportunity of calling the Kremlin's bluff and exposing the Soviet confidence trick, which for nearly a decade has been based on persuading the US administration and its European allies with a policy of bluster and threats that they were powerless to call a halt to Soviet expansionism except at the risk of all-out war. When the Kremlin saw the way in which the Carter administration acquiesced in the establishment of a Soviet combat brigade in Cuba and tolerated Cuban military forces leaving the island by sea and by air – under the very nose of the United States Navy and Air Force off Key West, Florida – so as to invade Africa and recolonise that continent on the Kremlin's behalf, they knew that they would be pushing at an open door whenever they challenged Western interests anywhere else in the world. For the future much will depend on the Kremlin's perception of the new President and his team, which includes, in the capacity of Secretary of State, General Alexander Haig who, in his former incarnation as Supreme Allied Commander Europe (SACEUR), had occasion to know in detail and appreciate in its full dimension the gravity of the Soviet threat. The policies of appeasement pursued for the better part of a decade, initially by Kissinger on behalf of the Nixon administration and, latterly, by the Carter administration, can now be seen to have failed utterly. The more the United States, unknown to most of its citizens, pursued the path of unilateral disarmament (what else can describe a reduction of two-thirds in the size of the US Navy, the demobilisation of more than one million men of the US Army and the scrapping, without obtaining any concession in return, of the B-1 supersonic bomber?), the more the hawks in the Kremlin were encouraged to believe that they could pursue their expansionist goals with impunity and increasing appetite.

There can be no questioning the commitment to peace of men of the calibre of Henry Kissinger and Cyrus Vance but they were babes in arms when it came to dealing with the Russians, and Kissinger, for his part, has had the frankness to admit as much. For all these high-principled men's untiring efforts to secure effective strategic arms-control agreements and to achieve a genuine detente, the harsh truth must be faced that, by the dawn of the eighties, the world had become an infinitely less secure place, aggression and bloodshed more rife and the East–West balance more precarious with the Soviet Union disposing of twice as many nuclear missiles as it had barely a decade before when the detente policy was being launched with such high hopes. The deception of the peoples of the Western democracies by their leaders has been cynical and unforgivable, bringing the world to the point where all-out war has become a serious possibility.

If Mr Reagan and his colleagues have the courage of their convictions and the determination to call a halt to Soviet militarism and expansionism they have the opportunity – one that, if missed, may never return again – of turning the backs of the United States and the Western allies on the policies of appeasement which have been leading the world towards catastrophe in the eighties as surely as those same policies, pursued by equally high-minded, well-intentioned men half a century before, paved the way for the Second World War.

Nothing should have higher priority on Mr Reagan's agenda than to tell the American people, and the world, the truth, putting bluntly before them the full gravity and mortal danger of the Soviet threat. It is a threat that for too long has been played down and deliberately concealed as a matter of policy by political leaders throughout the Western world, determined not to tarnish the graven image of detente, an instrument with which weak politicians on both sides of the Atlantic sought fraudulently to convince their electorates that they, like Mr Neville Chamberlain before them, had achieved, in the immortal words of the British Premier at the time of the Munich surrender barely a year before the outbreak of war,

'Peace in our time.'

Ronald Reagan, in his capacity as President of the United States, is in a unique position of power, not solely in the military sense but, above all, by the fact that he has at his command the key to unlock the door of public knowledge in a way that none other can do. He has it in his authority to disclose, as President Kennedy did before him with devastating effect at the time of the Cuban missile crisis, the irrefutable and awe-inspiring evidence of America's satellite photography. Kennedy had himself been so impressed by the unadorned clarity and precision of the reconnaissance photographs with which he had been briefed by the experts of the Defense Intelligence Agency that, within a hour of his briefing and giving them only the briefest warning of the fact that time had been reserved on all television networks coast-to-coast, he instructed the same experts to give the American people as a whole the same briefing he had been given as President. Intelligence officials were more than a little surprised, even shocked, suddenly to be told to reveal to the whole world information that until a few hours previously had been classified 'TOP SECRET – SENSITIVE'. The televised briefing had a dramatic impact, for the American people, once taken into their President's confidence, were to stand rock-solid behind him throughout the tense and anxious days of the crisis. If, likewise, President Reagan were to take the American public – together with the United States' NATO allies – into his confidence and, in the course of a televised fireside chat of an hour or two, were to put before them the stark and incontrovertible evidence that satellite photography alone can provide of the scale of Soviet preparations for war, which so far exceeds anything being undertaken in the United States, let alone any requirement of self-defence, the effect is likely to be electric. Far from grudging what is currently being spent on defence, the peoples of America and Western Europe, once convinced by the evidence of their own eyes like Thomas, called Didymus, before them who would not believe in Christ's resurrection until he had put his finger in the holes where the nails had been, will demand that their governments act urgently to strengthen the West's defences before it is too late.

In all the democracies pressure continues unremittingly for

ever higher levels of expenditure on social priority programmes in the form of improved retirement pensions, better health care or hand-outs to industry to save job losses at a time of recession. All these benefits are expected, indeed taken for granted, in addition to an insistence on a continuing and rapid increase in personal living standards. Any government that fails to deliver the goods inevitably runs the risk of incurring the displeasure of its electorate and paying the price of that displeasure at the ballot box. Thus it is not surprising that in the same week in January 1981 that the British Government announced a £200 million ($440 million) cut in defence expenditure and with it the axing of several important high technology programmes, it should have announced a further £1,000 million ($2.2 billion) hand-out to the ailing British Leyland car-manufacturing combine. Evidently the threat of job losses in the West Midlands' motor industry presented itself as a more immediate threat to the British Cabinet than the more nebulous military threat from the Soviet Union on which Mrs Thatcher had waxed so eloquent in many of her speeches. These are the choices that confront all democratic governments on a day-to-day basis and the pressures to transfer resources earmarked for defence to other areas of priority are relentless. Thus it is that defence expenditure in both Britain and the United States has been halved as a percentage of overall government expenditure between 1960 and 1980. Only leadership of a most farsighted and tenacious character can be expected to reverse these trends. But to achieve such a reversal of trend requires public understanding, which in turn is dependent on public knowledge. People will never, voluntarily, accept sacrifices, unless they are given clear and compelling reasons why they must. President Reagan alone among the leaders of the Western democracies has it in his power to provide those clear and compelling reasons by spelling out the devastating evidence that the revelation of American satellite photography alone can provide of the gravity and scale of the Soviet threat. There could be no more effective way of mobilizing opinion, not only in America but throughout the NATO alliance, in support of a strengthened allied defence.

Only an urgent programme of rearmament can redress the

balance between East and West if equilibrium is to be restored before the East–West balance of forces tilts decisively beyond control. The appeasement policies of recent years have been propelling the Western democracies towards catastrophe with an ever-growing momentum and it will require all the authority of the President of the United States, backed up by an informed and resolute public opinion, to arrest the decline of the West and to rebuild the crumbling foundations of peace through a policy of strength.

Any US rearmament programme must address itself to three immediate tasks. First and foremost swift action is required to repair the neglect of years by restoring America's conventional forces to health both in capability and, above all, in calibre of manpower, either by the reintroduction of the draft or by paying the going rate for the skills the armed forces require. Secondly a true strategic balance between the United States and the Soviet Union must once again be established in place of the imbalance written into the terms of the Salt II agreement under which the United States accepted a postion of clear inferiority in which the United States strategic forces were vulnerable to a Soviet first strike while having no equivalent capability. A third and equally urgent priority must be to redress the heavy imbalance that exists today in theatre-nuclear weapons in Europe, where the Soviets have established a 3·5:1 advantage which they are adding to daily. The achievement of these goals will, inevitably, require a major increase in resources devoted to defence, an increase that is long overdue.

As former US Defense Secretary Harold Brown made clear in his *Annual Report to Congress (Fiscal year 1981)*, notwithstanding America's already vast outlays on defence, the Soviet Union is currently spending some 50 per cent more in real terms. Yet more disturbing is the fact that in the case of the United States nearly two-thirds of her defence budget is devoted to manpower costs, leaving barely one-third for the provision of hardware, while in the case of the Soviet Union these proportions are reversed. Thus the Soviet Union is today devoting to new weapons procurement resources that represent twice as great a proportion of a budget that is already 50 per cent larger than that of the United States. Bluntly put, *Soviet spending on new weapons has in recent years been close to three times that of the United States.* The volume of production that has been pouring from Soviet tank factories, submarine yards and missile production lines at many times the rate of US production is concrete evidence of this.

Fifteen years of restraint by the United States in strategic missile production, and of actual unilateral disarmament in terms of her conventional capability, have utterly failed to persuade the Kremlin to moderate its insane arms-escalation policies which pose the gravest threat there has ever been to the peace of the world. Radically different policies are now required to convince the Soviet leadership that the United States and her allies are not prepared to be bulldozed into submission by the unrestrained military build-up of the Soviet Union nor to accept a situation in which for the years ahead the maintenance of peace ceases to be assured but becomes nothing more than a dangerous gamble.

Under the Carter administration the situation was fast being reached in which legitimate doubts might have arisen in the Kremlin about the degree of US commitment to the defence of Western Europe. If there was a lack of confidence among many in Europe about the willingness of the United States to unleash part of its strategic capability to save Western Europe from Soviet occupation – given the instant Soviet retribution such action would invite upon a wholly unprotected US population – how much more might not such doubts exist among those wielding supreme authority within the Soviet Union? The fact that defenceless Afghanistan constituted no conceivable threat to the Soviet Union in no way spared that unfortunate land from Soviet designs and ultimate occupation. Were the incumbents of the Kremlin ever to covince themselves that they could similarly invade Western Europe without risking unacceptable damage to Mother Russia, the scene could be set for catastrophe. The fact that the 300,000 US forces committed to NATO would undoubtedly fight and that presidential authorisation would almost certainly be granted for the use of *tactical* nuclear weapons would, of themselves, be no deterrent to Soviet action so long as they fell only on the unfortunate Germans and Poles, for neither of whom have the Russians nurtured any feelings but of hatred and distrust. In such circumstances the chances of miscalculation by those who harbour aggressive designs are bound to escalate.

So much in the field of defence and deterrence comes down to perception – above all the perception of an adversary. For a quarter of a century following the creation of the NATO alliance, the strength of the United States and its commitment to its allies, in the event of an attack on Western Europe, was so strong as to rule it out as a serious possibility. Then there ensued a period under President Carter during which the United States lost the primacy of world military power to the Soviet Union (a process under way since long before Carter was elected to the presidency) and this, combined with the uncertainty that he managed to engender in the fields of foreign policy and defence, led to mistrust among allies and gave encouragement to the hawks in the Kremlin. The political demise of Jimmy Carter and his replacement by Ronald Reagan had, of itself, the effect of changing the perceptions of the allies of the United States and , by the same token, no doubt of her adversaries as well. By his attitude and reputation alone President Reagan is already sensibly changing the assumptions and perceptions on which decisions of war or peace may be arrived at in the Kremlin. Looking towards the longer term, what judgment is finally made of him in the counsels of the Kremlin will depend above all on whether the new President's performance lives up to his promise. But there can be no doubt that so long as the military strength of the United States and its commitment to the defence of Western Europe are seen to remain high and so long as the Europeans themselves take the defence of their homeland seriously, retaining in the case of Britain and France the capacity in the last resort by themselves alone to inflict unacceptable damage upon the Soviet heartland, there need be no fear of Soviet adventures directly aimed at NATO Europe in the years ahead. Only when that commitment is uncertain or that capability unsure does the world move into uncharted waters, where the dangers become unfathomable.

For too long America's NATO allies, including the Europeans and the Canadians, have taken a free ride off the

United States. In the days when America's power went unchallenged and the nations of Europe had only recently been liberated from Nazi occupation there was justification for this. But today, thirty-five years later, when the nations of Western Europe exceed both the United States and the Soviet Union in population and in wealth, it is unforgivable that Europe should still lean so heavily upon the generosity and commitment of the American people for its protection. While the fact should not be overlooked that the United States' European allies provide three-quarters of NATO's military manpower in Europe, Western Europe (as well as Japan) have in recent years come to rely almost totally upon the United States to provide a naval presence in the Indian Ocean and to safeguard the vital oil-supply routes upon which the prosperity and security of Western Europe as well as Japan depend. The same holds true of the European contribution to the nuclear defence of NATO Europe, though in both these fields Britain and France make contributions to the far greater US capability.

Only Britain with an expenditure of 4·9 per cent of GNP comes close to bearing as great a defence burden as the United States, which in 1980 was spending 5·2 per cent. France and West Germany spend 3·9 per cent and 3·3 per cent respectively, while Japan, the second wealthiest nation in the world, devotes only 0·9 per cent to defence. Given the present level of threat this is a scandalous situation which urgently requires to be remedied. Nothing could be more calculated to discourage the American people from making their contribution to allied defence in Europe and the Pacific than for it to be seen that the nations they are seeking to defend pay little or no heed to their own defence.

Allied to a major US rearmament programme, which must be matched by comparable efforts by America's European allies, it is vital that a halt be called to the expansionist policies of the Kremlin in the Third World, not only for the sake of the nations concerned and the safeguarding of the West's vital interests around the world, but in defence of peace. In the thirties Britain and France by their weakness, and the United States by her aloofness, were responsible for grievously misleading Hitler as to their resolve and with disastrous results.

By their policy of appeasement in the face of repeated violation of treaties and acts of aggression by Nazi Germany, the democracies succeeded in convincing Hitler that they were rotten to the core and that there was no point to which he could not push them in pursuit of his wild expansionist dreams. Time and again he put the former allies of the First World War to the test, first with the occupation and fortification of the Rhineland, then the annexation of Austria, followed soon after by the invasion of Czechoslovakia for which the Munich Agreement paved the way. At every turn the democracies were found wanting. Having established such a track record, how could Hitler conceive that Britain, under the leadership of the weak and discredited Neville Chamberlain, would draw the sword and declare war on Nazi Germany in defence of Poland (a nation she was powerless to protect) as the Nazis and the Soviet Red Army fell upon it and devoured it like jackals under the terms of the Nazi–Soviet Pact, secretly concluded by Ribbentrop and Molotov only four months before?

Exactly the same pattern is in danger of being repeated today. In the face of the Soviet-backed intervention with surrogate Cuban forces in Angola, the West made no response. When the Russians repeated the exercise in Ethiopa, again there was no reaction from the West. Meanwhile Vietnam, also financed and equipped by the Soviet Union and acting at its behest, occupied Laos and invaded Cambodia with more than 200,000 troops. Yet again the West stood impotent on the sidelines. Encouraged by this, the Kremlin by the end of 1979 felt that it could with impunity invade and occupy Afghanistan with its own forces, with every confidence that, barring verbal protests, the Western allies would take no action. High on President Reagan's list of priorities must be the breaking of this pattern of expectation by the Kremlin, for nothing could be more dangerous or lead more readily to miscalculation than for the Soviet leaders to become convinced that there is no point to which they cannot push the United States and her allies in the mistaken belief that they will never react in defence of their own interests.

Faced with the Soviet expansionist challenge in the Third World, the West has three options open to it. One is to follow the pattern of recent years and to take no action, allowing the Soviets and their accomplices to take over country after country, laying hands on the vital interests of the West as they do so. At the opposite end of the scale the West could commit its own forces to the defence of Third World countries threatened by the Soviet Union and its allies. But such a policy would risk re-enacting the Vietnam commitment of the sixties with potentially equally disastrous consequences for the morale and resolve of the United States. In between these two extremes there is a third option, which is to back with arms, cash and technical training those who are resisting Soviet aggression and look to the West for support. If the United States and the nations of Western Europe were to adopt the same attitude towards those who are prepared physically to resist Soviet expansionism in Angola, Ethiopia, Cambodia and Afghanistan as President Roosevelt adopted when Churchill made his famous appeal: 'Give *us* the tools and *we* will finish the job!', the tide of Soviet expansionism could be turned and Afghanistan could indeed be made the Soviet Union's Vietnam.

Any programme of allied rearmament should have two clear objectives, for the accumulation of armaments should never be seen as a desirable aim in itself; indeed it requires little imagination or even intelligence to think of a thousand better ways to spend resources other than on weapons of war and mass destruction, all other things being equal – which at present they are not. The prime and overriding objective must be to safeguard world peace at its highest level by re-establishing a balance that is at present continuing to tilt heavily in favour of the Soviet Union with potentially disastrous consequences. In this regard the United States has no choice but to address herself as a matter of high priority to the critical problem of the vulnerability of her Minuteman missiles with the deployment of MX, while in Europe strengthening both her conventional and theatre-nuclear capability.

But, looking further ahead, the ultimate objective, once stability has been restored and the Soviet Union has come to recognise that its interests rest in reaching agreements with the West not in seeking to bury it under its colossal and unrestrained volume of arms production, must be to call a halt to the arms race and to achieve overall arms-control agreement, based on genuine equality, verifiability and a respect for the rights of others, including those of the nations of the Third World so directly threatened today.

It may appear a contradiction to advocate large-scale rearmament as a means of securing disarmament. But the fact is that appeasement and unilateral disarmament – for instance the abandonment of the B-1 bomber in the forlorn hope that the Kremlin might be moved to make a reciprocal gesture – has been proved to have failed utterly as a means of securing any restraint in the Soviet Union's unremitting nuclear and conventional military build-up. The West cannot afford to continue any further down that path, therefore it has become essential for the alternative to be tried. If the American President were once to make clear to the Soviet leadership that the United States was willing to take whatever steps might be required not to be outpaced by the Soviet build-up and to resist Soviet aggression, there could be no more certain way of killing stone-dead the militarism and expansionism of the Soviet Union which presents such a deadly threat to the stability and peace of the world today, and of turning the world back onto the path of peace and hope.

Seldom in history has the future of mankind depended to so great an extent on one nation or the judgement of a single man as it does on the United States and its President today. Ronald Reagan on his inauguration as the fortieth President of the United States offered this pledge:

> To the enemies of Freedom, to those who are potential adversaries, they will be reminded that peace is the highest aspiration of the American people. We will negotiate for it. Sacrifice for it. We will not surrender it, now or ever . . . .
>
> To those neighbours and allies who share an ideal of freedom, we will strengthen our historic ties and assure them of our support and firm commitment. We will match loyalty with loyalty . . . .
>
> We are too great a nation to limit ourselves to small dreams.

The future of the world rests today upon a knife-edge. The die has yet to be cast that will decide whether the concluding years of the 20th century are to be ones of World Peace or of World War. At the present time it would appear, in the words of the Duke of Wellington following the Battle of Waterloo, to be 'A damn close-run thing'. The extra effort – and sacrifice that is required of the peoples of the Western democracies to make their futures secure is not great. There is no requirement for the NATO Allies as a whole nor for the United States alone, to seek to match the Soviet Union in military output, tank for tank or missile for missile. The principal requirement to ensure the maintenance of peace and freedom on which the whole future of the world depends, is to do enough to deter any threat by making unmistakably clear to any would-be aggressor-nation that the cost to their own country would be far greater than any prize they could possibly hope to achieve through war. The cost of detering war in the nuclear age – however great it may appear – is but a trifle compared to the cost of a failure to deter war. Up to the time of writing there is no evidence that the Western democracies are willing to make even the modest sacrifices required to safeguard the future.

INDEX

ABM treaty, 54-55
Afghanistan, 76, 99, 107, 138, 147, 162-172, 199, 236, 238, 244, 247, 248
Africa, 55, 56, 137, 144-147, 173-189
Aggressor Squadron, 109
AIM9-L Sidewinder air-to-air missiles, 108
Air-launched cruise missiles (ALCM), 80, 84
Airlift, Soviet capability, 137
Algeria, 143
Allende, President, 174
Amin, Hafitsullah, 162, 163
Angola, 107, 138, 173-177, 182, 247, 248
Anti-ballistic-missile (ABM) systems, 50
Apartheid, 187, 188
Argentina, 165
Armed forces, mobilisation capability in U.S. *v.* Soviet Union, 62-64
Artillery, Soviet *v.* NATO capability, 96
AS-4 Kitchen air-launched cruise missiles, 92
Attlee, Clement, 23, 207, 211
Australia, 33, 106
Austria, 100
Azhari, Rexa, 151

B-1 bombers, 50-51, 79, 249
B-47 bombers, 91
B-52 bombers, 80, 84, 210
Backfire bombers, 51, 90-92, 94-96, 126, 127, 131, 222
Badger bombers, 96, 103
Bakhtiar, Sharpoor, 154
Ballistic-missile submarines, Soviet *v.* U.S., 124, 126
Barber, Stephen, 43
Barre, Siad, 144-146, 149, 177

Battle of the Atlantic, 124
Battle of Britain, 102-103
Battlefield nukes, 88
Bay of Pigs, 34
BBC Overseas Services, 152, 153
Beam-technology, 80-82
Bear bombers, 103, 126
Belgium, 25
Berlin blockade, 25, 32
Biological warfare, 66-67
Bison bombers, 103, 126
Blinder bombers, 96, 103
Bloodhound surface-to-air missiles, 110
Blowpipe surface-to-air missiles, 105
Boomers, 135
Brandt, Willy, 164
Brazil, 207
Brezhnev, Leonid, 50, 52, 54, 58, 59, 70, 91-92, 126, 145, 190, 230
Brown, Harold, 78-79, 154, 243
Brussels Treaty, 25, 109
Brzezinski, Zbigniew, 150, 153, 154
Bukovsky, Vladimir, 68, 229-230, 233
Bulgaria, 23
Bunker, Ellsworth, 42

Callaghan, James, 53, 212, 216
Cambodia, 138, 199, 247, 248
Cameron, Neil, 62
Campaign for Nuclear Disarmament (CND), 105, 204
Canada, 33, 106, 165
Carrington, Lord, 113
Carter, Jimmy, 51-53, 78, 79, 81, 82, 92, 95, 126, 149-151, 154-156, 158, 159, 164, 169, 171-173, 185, 238, 239, 244, 245
Castro, Fidel, 182

Challenger tank, 105
Chamberlain, Neville, 117-118, 240, 247
Chamoun, President, 33
Chemical warfare, 65-66
Chevaline, 212
Chieftain tanks, 107
Chile, 174
China, 33, 69, 165, 199-200, 207
Chou En-lai, 197-199
Churchill, Winston, 18, 20, 21, 23, 24,
  28, 30, 49, 84, 118, 166, 231, 236, 248
CIA, 81, 155, 169, 219
Civil defence in Soviet Union, 67-69
Colby, William, 81
Columbia space shuttle, 83
Communist South-West Africa
  People's Organization (SWAPO), 183
Communist Tudeh Party, 150, 151, 155
Concordski, 92
Conference on Security and Coopera-
  tion in Europe (CSCE), 51
Correia, Rameiro, 218
Corvalan, Luis, 68
Cruise-missile submarines, Soviet *v.*
  U.S., 126
  See also names of submarines
Cuba, 34, 173-177, 182, 239, 247
Cuban Missile Crisis, 34-36, 39, 40, 57,
  241
Cunhal, Alvaro, 219
Czechoslovakia, 23, 45, 100, 137, 195,
  219, 232

Daoud, Sadar Mohammed, 163
De Gaulle, Charles, 129
Declaration on Security and Coopera-
  tion in Europe, 55
Defense Advance Research Projects
  Agency (DARPA), 83
Delta Class III ballistic-missile sub-
  marines, 124, 125
Democratic Convention (Chicago,
  1968), 41-43
D'estaing, Giscard, 158, 160
Detente, 51, 52, 54-56, 58, 59, 70, 87,
  92, 97, 240
  origins, 40, 45
DOSAAF, 62, 64
Draft, military, end of in U.S., 52

East Germany, 23, 62, 99, 100
Echo II class cruise-missile submarines, 126

Egypt, 127, 138-140, 143, 144, 155, 199
Eisenhower, Dwight D., 32, 33, 35
Electronic counter-measures (ECM), 80
Estonia, 23
Ethiopia, 107, 138, 171, 214, 247, 248
European Economic Community,
  165-167

F-111 fighter bombers, 91, 92, 94, 96,
  105, 109, 222
Fencers, 103
Fitters, 103
Flexible response doctrine, 65, 88, 101
Floggers, 103
Foot, Michael, 216, 217, 220, 221
France, 25, 149, 157-161, 221, 245, 246
  naval capability, 129

Gaddafi, President, 158, 207
Gaddafi bomb, 158
Gailani, Hassan, 170
Ghandi, Indira, 171
Gorshkov, Sergei, 123, 124, 126-128, 130
Great Britain, 102-120, 203-218, 220-
  223, 245, 246
  aircraft compared to Soviet Union,
    103-105
  attraction as Soviet target, 105-106
  chemical warfare and, 66
  defence expenditures, 113-115, 117-119
  Iran and, 148, 149
  nuclear deterrent strategy, 203-218
  response to Soviet invasion of
    Afghanistan, 165
  role in NATO, 106
Gromyko, Andrei, 55-56
Guinea/Bissau, 175
Gulf Emirates, 172

Haig, Alexander, 113, 239
Harriman, Averell, 50
Hawk anti-air missile, 107, 108
Healey, Denis, 212, 216
Heath, Edward, 54, 212
Heuyser, Robert, 154
Hiroshima, 29, 30
Hitler, Adolph, 59, 60, 70, 85, 102, 117,
  118, 221, 246, 247
HMS *Ark Royal*, 129
HMS *Illustrious*, 129
HMS *Invincible*, 129
Holy Loch, 105

Hong Kong, 165
Hoveida, Amir Abbas, 213
Human rights, 51-52, 54
Hungary, 23, 33, 137, 232, 233
Hussein, Sadam, 157, 159

India, 106, 159, 170-177, 199, 207
Iran, 52, 148-157, 171-172, 213, 238
Iraq, 140, 143, 157-160, 171, 172, 199, 207
Isolationism, 85
Israel, 139, 140, 143, 157-160, 165, 174, 207
Italy, 221
   naval capability, 129

Japan, 29-30, 165, 177, 180, 246
   naval capability, 129
Jaruzelski, General, 234
Jenkins, Roy, 212
Johnson, Lyndon B., 50
Jupiter missile, 91

Kania, Stanislaw, 234-235
Karmal, Babrak, 162-163, 169
Kaunda, Kenneth, 173, 176, 177
Keegan, George J., 69, 80, 81
Kennedy, John F., 32, 34-36, 39, 58, 64, 74, 88, 211, 241
Kent State University, 41-42
Kenya, 165, 172
Kerala Massacre, 167-168
Khomeini, Ayatollah, 152-155, 213, 238
Khrushchev, Nikita, 35, 40, 57-58
Kiev-class carriers, 126-128
Kissinger, Henry, 44, 49-50, 52, 54, 78, 176, 177, 184, 185, 208-209, 239, 240
Korean War, 32-33
Kosygin, Alexei, 50, 58
Kuwait, 172

Lakenheath, 105, 109
Lance tactical missiles, 96
Land Dart air defense missile, 110
Land-based ballistic missiles, 80
   Soviet *v.* U.S., 74-76
   See also names of missiles
Laos, 138, 247
Lasers, 80, 82, 83
Latvia, 23
Lebanon, 33
Lesotho, 187

Libya, 140, 145, 158, 172, 207
Lightning interceptors, 104, 108
Lithuania, 23
Lublin Committee, 19, 20
Luns, Joseph, 233
Luxembourg, 25

McGahey, Mick, 215
McMahon Act, 211
Macmillan, Harold, 20, 39, 211, 238
McNamara, Robert, 88-89, 213
Malawi, 187
Mariam, Mengistu Haile, 214
Meshad, Yahia el, 159
Middle East, 137-140, 143, 144, 146, 157-160, 171, 172, 174
Military reconnaissance satellites, 53, 54, 76, 81-82
Military warning time for mobilisation, 99, 100
Mineral resources in Africa and the Soviet Union, 177-181
Minuteman III land-based ICBM, 74, 75, 80, 248
Mobilisation, warning time for, 99, 100
Mozambique, 138, 175-177, 182, 187
MIRVs (multiple independently targetable re-entry vehicles), 73, 74, 79
Mugabe, Robert, 182-184, 186
Mussolini, Benito, 65
Mutual Balanced Force Reduction (MBFR) talks, 45, 52, 97, 99
Muzorewa, Bishop, 185-186
MVD security troops, 62
MX mobile missile system, 75, 76, 79, 248

NATO, 23, 25, 45, 46, 51, 52, 54, 60-62, 166, 167, 221, 222, 242, 244-246, 250
   armed forces compared to Soviet, 64, 65
   chemical warfare, and, 66
   flexible response doctrine, 88
   importance of Great Britain to, 106
   military capability compared to Soviet, 87-101
   naval capability, 128-132, 135, 136
   response to Soviet invasion of Afghanistan, 164, 165
   trip-wire *v.* flexible response doctrine, 65, 87-88
Nagasaki, 30
Namibia, 175, 182-183
Nassau Agreement, 211

Nasser, Colonel, 33, 139, 140
National Islamic Front of Afghanistan (NIFA), 170
Nazis, 19, 20, 59, 60, 106, 117, 237, 247
Netherlands, 25
naval capability, 129
New Zealand, 33, 106
Nimeiry, President, 145
Nimrod anti-submarine aircraft, 106
Nixon, Richard, 43, 54, 73, 74, 190, 239
Nkomo, Joshua, 182, 184
North Yemen, 148
Nott, John, 108
Novosibirsk (Soviet Union), 66-67
Nuclear-Biological-Chemical (NBC) suits, 66
Nuclear Intelligence Panel (CIA), 81
Nuclear Test Ban Treaty, 36
Nyerere, President, 177

Ohio class ballistic-missile submarines, 124
Oil, 146-148, 161, 174, 181
Olympic Games, 1980, boycott of, 165
Operation Sea Lion, 102

Pahlavi, Reza Shah (Shah of Iran), 148-155, 157
Pakistan, 158, 165, 170, 171, 207
Palestine Liberation Organisation (PLO), 155
Paraguay, 165
Park, Marshal, 118
Particle-beam technology, 80-82
Pentagon, 79
People's Republic of China
See China
Pershing I tactical missiles, 96
Pershing II short-range ballistic missiles (SRBM), 94, 95
Phantoms, 104
Poland, 19, 20, 23, 100, 233-236, 247
Polaris submarines, 94, 103, 203, 207, 208, 211, 212
Portugal, 175, 218-220
Poseidon ballistic-missile submarines, 74, 84
Pym, Francis, 108, 113

Quick Reaction Alert (QRA), 209

Rapier surface-to-air missile, 105, 110
Reagan, Ronald, 76, 83, 84, 172, 222, 238-242, 245, 247, 249
Reston, James, 35
Revolution of Flowers, 218
Rhodesia, 106, 175, 182-186
See also Zimbabwe
Roberto, Holden, 182
Romania, 23
Roosevelt, Franklin D., 18, 20-23, 49, 248
Royal Air Force (RAF), 103-109
Royal Navy, 105, 106, 111-112, 123, 128-129, 132, 203, 208, 211

SA-10 surface-to-air missile, 80
Sadat, Anwar, 140, 145-147, 155, 158
Salang Pass, 163, 164
Salt agreement, 27, 45-48, 55, 74-76, 95-96, 124, 243
Satellites, military reconnaissance, 53, 54, 76, 81-82
Saudi Arabia, 148, 165, 172, 174
Savimbi, Jonas, 182
Schlesinger, James, 154
Scotland, 105
Sea Dart anti-air and anti-missile missile, 105
Sea Wolf anit-air and anti-missile missile, 105
Selassie, Haile, 214
Semipalatinsk, 81
Shah of Iran, 148-155, 157
Short-range attack missiles (SRAM), 80
Silo launchers, Soviet *cold-launch* technique, 76
Six Day War, 140
Skybolt air-launched stand-off missile, 211
Skyflash air-to-air missile, 105
Smith, Ian, 176, 183-185
Soares, Mario, 152, 219
Somalia, 127, 144-146, 172
Sosus, 135
South Africa, 106, 175-177, 179-184, 186-189, 207
South Korea, 207
South Yemen, 148, 171
Soviet Air Force, airlift capability, 137
Soviet Army, 19, 20, 24, 57
Soviet Frontal Aviation, 103-105
Soviet Navy, 123-136, 147
Soviet Strategic Rocket Forces, 75, 78

Soviet Union
  aircraft, 61, 103-105
  armed forces manpower, 62-65
  chemical and biological warfare
    and, 66-67
  civil defence, 67-69
  cold-launch silo launchers, 76
  Communist Party in, 227-231
  lack of freedom, 225-227
  land-based ballistic missiles, 74-76
  military reconnaissance satellites, 53
  naval capability, 60-61
  non-Russian populations, 231-235
  nuclear capability compared to
    U.S., 26-28
  standard of living, 224-225
  tank build-up, 59-60

Soviet-Egyptian Treaty, 140, 144
Soviet-Somali Cooperation Agreement,
  144
SS-4 missiles, 91
SS-5 missiles, 91
SS-N-12 missiles, 126
SS-16 missiles, 74-76
SS-17 missiles, 74
SS-18 missiles, 74
SS-19 missiles, 74
SS-20 IRBM, 75-76, 91, 92, 94, 95, 107,
  204, 222
SS-21 missiles, 96
SS-22 missiles, 96
SS-23 missiles, 96
Stalin, Joseph, 18-21, 23, 49, 237
Standing-start capability, 100
Stealth programme, 82
Strategic Air Command, 80
Strategic Arms Limitation Talks
  See Salt agreement
Strategic nuclear weapons, Soviet
  build-up, 61-62
Submarine-launched missiles, 75
Submarines, U.S. *v.* Soviet, 60-61, 124,
  126, 130, 132-135
Sudan, 145
Suez Canal, 33, 138-140, 146, 147, 171,
  213, 214
Sullivan, William, 154
Surface-to-air missile (SAM) systems,
  80
Suzman, Helen, 187
Sweden, 67

Switzerland, 67
Syria, 140, 143, 172

Tabeyev, Fikryat, 162
Taiwan, 207
Talytsin, Mikolai, 162
Tanks, Soviet and U.S., 59-60, 62, 98*f*
Tanzania, 177
Taraki, Mohammed, 163
Thailand, 165
Thatcher, Margaret, 108, 113, 114, 119,
  120, 164, 185, 190, 203, 217, 242
Third World, Soviet Union and, 137,
  138, 163-164, 174, 182
Thor missile, 91
Thunderbolt II aircraft, 109
Titan land-based missiles, 74, 80
Tomahawk ground-launched cruise
  missiles, 94-95, 204, 205
Tomahawk SLCM, 126
Tornado F-2 aircraft, 105, 109
Tornado GR-1 interdictor-strike
  aircraft, 105
Transporter-erector-launcher, 74, 75
Trident missiles, 84, 124, 129, 203, 204,
  206-208
Trip-wire strategy, 64, 88, 101
Truman, Harry, 23, 24, 28, 32, 33, 36
TU-144 supersonic transport
  (Concordski), 92
Tudeh Party, 150, 151, 155
Turkey, 154, 165
Turner, Stansfield, 154
Typhoon class ballistic missile
  submarines, 124

Underwater detection technology,
  132, 135
United Nations, Korean War and, 32-33
Upper Heyford, 105, 109
Uruguay, 165
United States
  armed forces manpower, 62-64
  defence expenditures, 113-114, 116
  land-based ballistic missiles, 74, 75
  military reconnaissance satellites, 53
  chemical warfare and, 66
  end of military draft, 52
  nuclear capability compared to the
    Soviet Union, 26-28
United States Air Force, 109, 110
United States Navy, 56, 123, 124, 127,
  131-136, 149

Vance, Cyrus, 150, 154, 240
Vietnam, 35-36, 40-44, 107, 138, 174, 199, 247
Vietnam War, 52, 56, 57
Vulcan bombers, 91, 94, 209-211, 221

Walesa, Lech, 234
Warheads, U.S. and Soviet compared, 77t, 78
Warning time for mobilisation, 99, 100
Warsaw, 19-20
Warsaw Pact, 23, 51-54, 87, 91, 96, 97, 99, 100, 109, 128, 166
Wedgwood-Benn, Anthony, 217
West Germany, 100, 114, 165, 180
    naval capability, 129
Westmoreland, William, 42

Wilson, Harold, 114, 119, 152, 212-213, 215
World War I, 64, 65, 85
World War II, 85, 87, 118, 147, 221, 247
Woodcock, Leonard, 197

Yalta agreement, 20
Young, Andrew, 154, 173

Zaire, 176, 177, 180
Zambia, 173, 176, 177, 180
Zia, President, 171
Zilliacus, Konni, 216
Zimbabwe, 175, 180, 182, 183, 186
    See also Rhodesia